The Common Core of European Administrative Laws

Comparative Law in Global Perspective

VOLUME 4

The titles published in this series are listed at *brill.com/clgp*

The Common Core of European Administrative Laws

Retrospective and Prospective

By

Giacinto della Cananea

BRILL | NIJHOFF

LEIDEN | BOSTON

The Common Core of European Administrative Law (CoCEAL). This project has received funding from the European Research Council (ERC) under the Horizon 2020 Research and Innovation Programme "Advanced Grant" Excellent Science (G.A. n.694697)

Library of Congress Cataloging-in-Publication Data

Names: Della Cananea, Giacinto, author.
Title: The common core of European administrative laws: retrospective and prospective / by Giacinto della Cananea.
Description: Leiden; Boston : Brill/Nijhoff, 2023. | Series: Comparative law in global perspective, 2772-5332; 4 | Includes bibliographical references and index. | Summary: "Though European administrative laws have gained global significance in the last few decades, research which provides both theoretical analysis and original empirical research has been scarce. This book offers an important account of the evolution of judicial review and administrative procedure legislation, using a factual analysis to shed light on how the different legal systems react to similar problems"– Provided by publisher.
Identifiers: LCCN 2023025910 (print) | LCCN 2023025911 (ebook) | ISBN 9789004549562 (hardback) | ISBN 9789004549579 (ebook)
Subjects: LCSH: Administrative law–European Union countries. | Administrative procedure–European Union countries. | Judicial review of administrative acts–European Union countries.
Classification: LCC KJE5602 .D45 2023 (print) | LCC KJE5602 (ebook) | DDC 342.4/066–dc23/eng/20230601
LC record available at https://lccn.loc.gov/2023025910
LC ebook record available at https://lccn.loc.gov/2023025911

Typeface for the Latin, Greek, and Cyrillic scripts: "Brill". See and download: brill.com/brill-typeface.

ISSN 2772-5332
ISBN 978-90-04-54956-2 (hardback)
ISBN 978-90-04-54957-9 (e-book)

This book is printed on acid-free paper and produced in a sustainable manner.

Ὣς οἵ γ' ἀμφίεπον τάφον Ἕκτορος ἱπποδάμοιο'

'Thus they busied themselves with the burial of Hector, tamer of horses'.

HOMER, ILIAD, XXIV, 1025–1026

Contents

Preface

This book sprang from a somewhat different intellectual exercise. In 2009, working as member of a newly established transnational group of public lawyers (the Research Network on EU Administrative Law – ReNEUAL), I began to reflect on the different European traditions of public law with a view to ascertaining whether – on the basis of comparative research – there were some best practices that could be used to reinforce the general principles of European Union law. The comparative analysis carried out proved to be a useful tool, and we published the 'model rules' for EU administrative procedure, raising discussion about their reform.

However, the more the group compared the national rules and practices, looking at the various circumstances where its proposals were debated in diverse corners of Europe, the more it became evident that there were sometimes real differences hidden behind a façade of apparent similarities, for example with regard to fairness and openness. Conversely, different legal systems often reached the same results via different ways of engaging with the relationship between norms and exceptions, as formulated by jurists and judges. The duty to give reasons was an instructive example. It thus became evident that some ideas and beliefs about public law – and law itself – such as the existence of a sharp divide between civil law and common law or a single model of administrative courts were not simply unable to make sense of the legal institutions of our time but were also unsound with regard to the past. The birth and development of our public law traditions, the interplay between commonality and diversity, the emergence of shared general principles of administrative law could not be illustrated by those received ideas. I expressed these remarks in an article published in English and German, but I was aware that this first attempt had not dealt with the problem of how we should address some of the basic theoretical questions.

In this respect, the experience gathered through that inspiring transnational group also showed the limits of traditional comparative approaches based on legislative design. The increasing volume of material that emerged from national studies called for a different methodology. I tried to ascertain whether this material could be better understood through a 'factual analysis' based on hypothetical cases, already experienced in the field of private law. Through this methodology, issues that had all too frequently been taken for granted in public law texts (such as whether an individual must be afforded a meaningful opportunity to be heard before an adverse decision is taken by a public authority) must be addressed critically, also in the light of underlying theories. Some adjustments were necessary, however, due to the distinctive features of public law, including the judicial construction of general principles, the legal relevance of government practices, and the impact of new constitutional provisions. Moreover, the previous doubts cast on the reliability of some less recent views on public law reinforced the conviction that only a combination of history and legal comparison could provide the gauge for reflecting on administrative laws in Europe.

The research project that began in 2016 was thus designed to analyze the 'common core' of European administrative laws through both diachronic and synchronic comparisons. Since a large number of experts were involved (almost 120 from thirty-four countries, not only from Europe) in the various lines of research, it may also be said that the new comparative research is a collective enterprise, differing however from the previous one insofar as it seeks to make sense of both shared and distinctive traits.

The financial backing for the entire project provided by the European Research Council must be acknowledged, as must the organizational support from Rome's 'Tor Vergata' University and Bocconi University in Milan. Both universities allowed me to take periods of leave for research and study abroad. The Max Planck Institute for Comparative Public Law and International Law of Heidelberg and the University of Paris II kindly hosted me during those absences, and several universities and research institutions (including the Law School of the 'Pompeu Fabre' University of Barcelona, the University of Cracow, the 'Pazmany' University of Budapest, the Institute of Advanced Legal Studies of London, and the Penn Carey Law School). In addition, the universities of Bologna, Ferrara, Florence, the Milan 'Cattolica', Palermo, the Rome 'La Sapienza', Trento, and Turin in Italy invited me to discuss the research methodology and results.

This book attempts to summarize some of the main results emerging from this comparative research and to construct a theory of the common core that reflects the legal history of Europe, suited to modern administrative States yet open to the influence of two regional organizations that have existed since the 1950's, namely the Council of Europe and the European Community (now the EU). Whatever the success of the enterprise from the reader's perspective, it has been made possible by the contribution of so many persons that it would be hard to mention all of them. Special thanks are owed to Mauro Bussani, my partner in this research, to Jean-Bernard Auby and Paul Craig, whose comments in the early days of the work brought me to the realization that these thoughts, if worth sharing, required a book distinct from the articles and volumes in which the various lines of research had been presented and, last but not least, to Gordon Anthony and Giulia Labriola, who made several comments on the manuscript. I am also indebted to Mads Andenas, Armin von Bogdandy, Allan Brewer-Carias, Roberto Caranta, Bruno De Witte, Luis Maria Dièz-Picazo, Carol Harlow, Stefano Mannoni, Marco Mazzamuto, Neysun Mahboubi, Thomas Perroud, Otto Pfersmann, Alec Stone Sweet, Aldo Travi, Ellen Vos, and Jacques Ziller for their comments, some of which were critical, others encouraging. Martina Conticelli, Angela Ferrari Zumbini, Marta Infantino, and Leonardo Parona have all contributed to diverse aspects of this comparative enquiry. To these and many others, I acknowledge a debt whose importance is not undermined by the fact that, of course, I alone am responsible for all errors or omissions. Adrian Bedford and Paola Monaco revised all the chapters from a linguistic point of view and on the basis of the Brill guidelines, respectively.

Finally, and most importantly, I am indebted to Simonetta, Isabella, Alfonso and Federico for their patience and encouragement during all these years.

Rome, 30 January 2023

CHAPTER 1

The Development of Administrative Law: Fact and Theory

This book concerns administrative law, discussing the results of comparative research focusing on European laws. It has two main themes. The 'major' topic is not so much that there are elements of commonality and diversity between these laws as this is, of course, 'axiomatic'.[1] Rather, it is that their diversity manifests itself within a framework increasingly characterized by the existence of shared and connecting elements, that is a common core,[2] and that these elements do not regard generic ideals that can be shared by almost every legal system, such as the pursuit of justice, but can be defined through canons of administrative conduct that distinguish legal behavior from unlawful conduct. When Schlesinger's research was published in the late 1960's, several reviewers agreed that common core research was a promising prospect.[3] Conversely, a strand of thought in public law continued to deny not just the existence of a common ground, but even the very existence of administrative law in England and the United States. A quick look at the history of ideas may thus be helpful in order to prepare the terrain for reflection. The 'minor' theme, on the other hand, concerns methodology. Arguably, the evolution of European administrative laws can only be properly understood from a perspective that combines history and legal comparison, and the latter would greatly benefit from factual analysis. This first chapter presents a debate between two opposing visions – one suggesting that administrative law never existed and could not exist in the UK or in other common law systems and another arguing that sooner or later it would emerge in all civilized nations. This will be followed by a quick look at two phenomena that have characterized the last century; that is, the birth of the positive State and the de-nationalization of administrative law. The chapter concludes with an illustration of the main features and limitations of the new research.

1 See P Craig, 'Comparative Administrative Law and Political Structure' (2017) 37 Oxford J Leg St 1.

2 RB Schlesinger, 'Introduction' in id (ed), *Formation of Contracts: A Study of the Common Core of Legal Systems* (Oceana 1968) 2.

3 See O Kahn-Freund, 'Review of RB Schlesinger (ed.), Formation of Contracts. A Study of the Common Core of Legal Systems' (1970) 18 AJCL 429.

 | DOI:10.1163/9789004549579_002

1 Two Visions of Administrative Law

It is self-evident that administrative laws in Europe have changed over time and that they have gained importance regardless of the legal system in which they operate.[4] Understanding the causes and nature of this transformation is more difficult, not only because some primary sources (for example, the archives of some judicial institutions) are not easily accessible, but also because there are various opinions about the very nature and purpose of administrative law.

Retrospectively, unlike private law, which has evolved in the Western world during the last two and half millennia, administrative law has a relatively recent history. However, while it is well known that the scientific study of administrative law began in the early decades of the nineteenth century with the first university chairs being set up in France, Italy, and elsewhere,[5] precisely when administrative law – viewed as a branch of law – emerged was, and continues to be, controversial. For nineteenth-century writers such as Gneist and Bryce, administrative law relating to the conduct of State bodies in their handling of public affairs – and its origins – could be traced back to late mediaeval England, if not to the birth of the Holy Roman Empire.[6] Others have emphasized the growth of administrative institutions that took place well before the end of the French *Ancien Régime*. This strand owes much to Tocqueville's thesis that the French political constitution was transformed after 1789, while its administrative constitution remained fundamentally the same.[7] Likewise, Craig has backdated the emergence of administrative law in England to the seventeenth

4 See Craig, 'Comparative Administrative Law and Political Structure' (n 1) 2; S Cassese, 'New paths for administrative law: a manifesto' (2012) 10 Int J Const L 603 (same remark); M Fromont, *Droit administratif des Etats européennes* (PUF 2006) 3 (same remark).

5 Joseph-Marie de Gérando was given the first chair of administrative law in Paris in 1819.

6 R Gneist, *Englische Verwaltungsrecht der Gegenwart* (3rd edn, Springer 1882) § 1.VII; J Bryce, *The Holy Roman Empire* (5th edn, McMillan 1905) 72 (for a description of the 'administrative schemes' of Charles the Great). On the medieval origins of what we call the modern State, see JR Strayer, *On the medieval origins of the modern* (Princeton UP 1970).

7 A de Tocqueville, *L'Ancien régime et la Révolution* (1856), JP Mayer (ed) (Gallimard 1967), where the seventh chapter of the third part has the emblematic title 'How great administrative changes had preceded the political revolution'. Various lawyers followed his thesis: see, for example, R Dareste, *Etudes sur les origines du contentieux administratif en France, IV. Les juridictions administrative depuis 1789* (1857) 3 Rev hist 132; M Hauriou, *Principes de droit public* (Dalloz 1911; 2010) 122; S Cassese, *La construction du droit administratif* (Monthchrestien 2000) 21. Among historians of law, see JL Mestre, *Un droit administratif à la fine l'Ancien Régime: le contentieux des communautés de Provence* (LGDJ 1975) 23.

century.[8] Yet others have viewed administrative law as a product of the French Revolution. This opinion, found in early writers such as de Gérando, as well as by mid-twentieth century scholars such as Rivero, owes much to the thesis that the Revolution changed everything (hence the metaphor of the *table rase*)[9] in two ways: destructively, because most ancient institutions were abolished, and constructively, because a new administrative law was built up and was subject to new judicial institutions, principally the *Conseil d'État*.[10]

This is an important debate, but it cannot be examined here. My intent is simply to observe that in this field of human conduct, as in many others, facts do not speak for themselves: they must be vested with meaning. In our case, we are concerned with legally relevant facts, contextualizing them and seeking to explain their meaning. But interpretations may differ greatly. They do so not only because there exist diverse institutional trajectories, but also because there are different schools of thought. In Europe, the development of the French, Austrian, and German systems of administrative law was firmly rooted in social structure. Not surprisingly, Weber argued that bureaucratic structure was one of the pillars of the modern State and that its highly formalized exercise of power pertained to a specific form of society, which differed from those based either on tradition or on charismatic leadership.[11] But such a framework could not easily be applied to the United States of America, where administration was fragmented and pluralistic. Nor could it be easily applied to the British Empire, which had a vast imperial bureaucracy in India, whereas the growth of administrative institutions at home was regarded with suspicion. The result is that if we look at the relationship between administration and administrative law at the turn of the last century, we can distinguish two opposing visions. In 'continental' countries, there was an increasingly sophisticated 'science' of administrative law, which demonstrated the evolution of national systems of administrative law together with national 'schools', but

8 P Craig, 'The Legitimacy of US Administrative Law and the Foundations of English Administrative Law: Setting the Historical Record Straight', Oxford Legal St. Research Paper No. 44/2016, 3.

9 A Tiers, *Histoire de la Révolution Française* (2nd edn, Furne 1865) and AFA Mignet, *Histoire de la Révolution française depuis 1789 jusque'en 1814* (1825), Engl tr *History of the French Revolution from 1789 to 1814* (Bogue 1846) 397 (emphasizing the novelty of Napoleon's 'system of administration of unparalleled benefit to power').

10 JM de Gérando, *Institutes du droit administratif français* (Nève 1829) 1, 2 (for whom the Revolution determined an '*ordre de chose nouveau*'); J Rivero, *Droit administratif* (Dalloz 1960; 2011) 19.

11 M Weber, *Wirtschaft und Gesellschaft* (1922), Engl transl by R Holton, *Max Weber on Economy and Society* (Routledge 1989).

there was always an underlying assumption that they were an essential element of the State, of every State. On the contrary, in Britain not only the existence of a 'system' of administrative law – but even the existence of *any* type of administrative law – was vehemently denied by those associating themselves with Dicey, the Victorian constitutionalist.

Through an apparent paradox, at the roots of this divergence lies the philosophy of Tocqueville himself. In his study of American democracy, he adopted a contrastive approach to the comparative study of legal institutions, illustrating the differences between the French and the Anglo-American institutions. In a later essay, he argued that what was then called the French model of administrative law would sooner or later be adopted by all civilized nations. This may come as a surprise to some, but critical thinkers are not immune from contradictions.[12] Indeed, emerging facts may lead them to challenge their views. Arguments and theories must, therefore, be analyzed in context.

2 Public Administration without Administrative Law

In his essay on *Democracy in America*, Tocqueville made a comparison between the North American institutions with those of France. He observed that government in America was 'prodigiously decentralized', while in France, centralization had been on the rise since the time of Louis XIV.[13] In America, the ordinary courts heard disputes between individuals and public authorities, whereas in France such cases were handled by special administrative bodies headed by the *Conseil d'État*, which, however, was 'not a judicial body at all, in the ordinary sense of the word, … but an administrative body, whose members were dependent on the King'.[14] This diversity produced another, even more unacceptable, one. In the US and England, government officers were subject to the ordinary law of the land as far as liability was concerned, while a separate legal regime had emerged in France. The *Conseil d'État* was entrusted with the power to authorize legal proceedings against the agents of government before the ordinary courts, which was used as a shield against 'the just complaints of citizens'.[15]

12 M Foucalt, *Naissance de la biopolitique* (Collège de France 1979) 42.

13 A de Tocqueville, *De la démocratie en Amérique* (1831), Engl transl by E Nolla, *Democracy in America* (Liberty Fund 2012) vol I, 145.

14 id, vol I, 177.

15 id, vol I, 177. For further remarks, see D Lochak, *La justice administrative* (2nd edn, Montchrestien 1994) 10.

With his strenuous critique of the arbitrary nature of the French administrative justice system, Tocqueville brought a new perspective to institutions that were all too often taken for granted. At the same time, he contributed to the genesis of the idea that there could be, and were, nations with a public administration that lacked an administrative law, an idea later fuelled by English thinkers. This idea was also influenced by the belief that law was inextricably linked to its social substratum. In *L'esprit des lois* Montesquieu pointed out the infinite diversity of laws and customs and observed that the institutions of government must conform to the spirit of a specific people.[16] His claim that the 'spirit' of a people explains the choice of certain legal institutions is often cited as an acknowledgement of the irreducible differences between countries. Although he observed that such differences often depend on other factors, including climate and geography, this was perhaps the most commonly accepted idea in the nineteenth century. That there is a relationship between law and the spirit of the people was readily absorbed in the German-speaking world. This belief is sometimes associated with the philosophical tradition around Hegel, but it was in the works of lawyers such as Savigny and Puchta that it was explicitly stated. For them, the law was generally seen as a reflection of the spirit of the people from which it springs (*Volksgeist*) and not the will of the legislator.[17] Laws therefore differ from people to people. Their diversity was most evident, *a fortiori*, in the field of public law. For Savigny, this was the consequence of different intellectual traditions. Only private law, based on the Roman legal tradition, was a 'normative science'.[18] Public law, on the contrary, was heavily 'political' and was thus a sort of national *enclave*.

As Watson observed, 'the *Volksgeist*' theory has been amply refuted by numerous jurists, but it lives on and will continue to do so because of its immediate emotional appeal'.[19] Legal nationalism made a strong impact on

16 Montesquieu, *De l'esprit des lois* (1748), ed by V Goldschmit (Flammarion 1979) 40 ('*le gouvernement le plus conforme à la nature est celui dont la disposition particulière se rapporte mieux à la disposition du peuple pour lequel il est établi*'). On Montesquieu's moderate relativism, see C Perelman, *Logique juridique* (Dalloz 1976) § 12.

17 FK Savigny, *Vom Beruf unserer Zeit für Gesetzgebung und Rechtswissenschaft* (Mohr und Simmer 1814) § 2.

18 FK von Savigny, *System des heutigen romischen Rechts* (1840), Engl transl *System of modern Roman law* (Higginbotham 1867) 2 ('private law and not public law belongs to our undertaking'). This opinion had a influence on comparative studies: see, for example, R David, *Les grands systems de droit contemporain* (Dalloz 1966) 82 (affirming, apodictically, that 'le vrai droit demeure le droit privé'; that is, the true law is still private law).

19 A Watson, *Legal Transplants An Approach to Comparative Law* (Scottish Academic Press 1974) 87.

administrative law.[20] In the early 1880s, the German public lawyer von Gneist observed that administrative law was taking shape in Victorian England, and brought ample evidence concerning three new areas; that is, the 'poor laws', health measures, and roads.[21] However, Dicey rejected this view. Central to his argument was the assertion that there was absolutely no kind of administrative law in England. His dislike for the very term 'administrative law' emerged in the opening words of the chapter concerning the 'rule of law compared with *droit administratif*'. His critique was threefold: firstly, it concerned the existence of a set of institutions and rules concerning public bodies distinct from those regulating the conduct of individuals; secondly, it was directed against the creation of special administrative courts as opposed to ordinary courts; lastly, he objected to the 'protection given … to the servants of the State'.[22] For Dicey, these differences reflected a deeper cultural and political divide. It was here that his description of reality metamorphosed into a normative claim, namely that the French system had grown into an instrument of despotism, while in England traditional liberal ideas meant that government power had to be reined in. The English constitutional framework was not, therefore, simply different from those of continental countries; it was superior, because it adhered to the rule of law.[23] His was a defence of the common law tradition,[24] which he deemed could be preserved only thanks the control placed in the hands of the ordinary courts.[25]

Both the descriptive and normative foundations underlying the rejection of administrative law were, however, questionable. Dicey's description did not correspond to the reality of the French institutions. The era of *justice retenue* formally came to an end in 1872 when the *Conseil d'Etat* was granted the power to decide on suits brought by individuals against public

20 See A Plantey, *Prospective de l'Etat* (Editions du CNRS, 1975) 198 (discussing what he called 'nationalisme administratif', that is administrative nationalism) and C Saunders, 'Apples, Oranges and Comparative Administrative Law' (2006) 1 Acta Juridica 423, at 425.

21 Gneist (n 6); his book was translated into Italian in the series of public law created by Brunialti (*L'amministrazione e il diritto amministrativo inglese* (UTET 1896)) and received attention in the Spanish-speaking area.

22 AV Dicey, *Introduction to the Study of the Law of the Constitution* (MacMillan 1885; 10th edn, 1959) 330.

23 P Craig, *Administrative Law* (5th edn, Sweet & Maxwell 2003) 4; M Loughlin, *Public Law and Political Theory* (Clarendon 1992) 46.

24 Dicey, *Introduction to the Study of the Law of the Constitution* (n 22) 339 ('the patriots who resisted the tyranny of the Stuarts were fanatics for the common law').

25 Id, 339.

authorities.[26] The constitutional provision concerning liability, brought into question by Tocqueville, had been modified in 1875. A French colleague and friend of Dicey's, Jèze, was thus ironic in highlighting the inaccuracy of Dicey's description of French administrative law.[27] On the other side of the Atlantic, American scholars Goodnow and Freund also dissented from Dicey's view. Goodnow criticized his claim that administrative law was equally unknown in England and the US.[28] Freund observed that administrative problems in France, England and the US were 'in many respects similar'.[29] Dicey's claim was equally dubious in normative terms. His remark on the rise of collectivism is indicative of his dislike not only of French legal institutions but of the growth of the administrative State. In a later essay, he observed that the period of liberalism in England had been followed by what he called an 'age of collectivism'.[30] However, the belief that there could be an advanced public administration without administrative law proved persistent, as we shall see in Chapter 10.[31]

3 Administrative Law as a Defining Aspect of the New State of the World

We noted earlier that, in his later works, Tocqueville focused his attention on the development of public administrations and administrative law. He did so, in particular, through his opinion regarding Macarel's treatise of administrative law. Macarel, who was both a professor and a member of the *Conseil d'État*, did not simply illustrate government functions in relation to public order, including the administration of the eminent domain, protection from fire

26 See L Neville Brown, J Bell and JM Galabert, *French Administrative Law* (5th edn, OUP 1998) 45–46 (same remark).

27 G Jéze, *Principes généraux du droit administratif* (Giard et Brière 1905) I, 1–2. See also P Leyland and G Anthony, *Textbook of administrative Law* (3rd edn, OUP 2012) 1 (questioning the continuing reference to Dicey as an authority) and W Friedmann, 'French Administrative Law and the Common Law World' (1955) 1 Univ Toronto LJ 145 (criticizing Dicey's 'legend').

28 F Goodnow, *Comparative Administrative Law. An analysis of the administrative systems, national and local, of the United States, England, France and Germany* (Burt Franklyn 1893) 6.

29 E Freund, 'The Law of the Administration in America' (1894) 9 Pol Sc Quart 403, 405.

30 AV Dicey, *Lectures on the Relation Between Law and Public Opinion in England in the 19th Century* (Macmillan 1905) 47.

31 Cassese, *La construction du droit administratif* (n 7) 13; Fromont (n 4) 5.

and flooding, and the construction and maintenance of roads, canals and railways.[32] He argued that the business of government included any issue which, due its nature or subject matter, could have repercussions on all citizens.[33] Hence, public administration was visible 'always and everywhere'.[34]

Tocqueville agreed with the emphasis on changing needs as expressed by social groups.[35] He pointed out that in order to satisfy such needs, new bodies and forms of administrative action were needed. The distance from the previous ones was notable, in the sense that the difference between the powers exercised by public authorities and those of previous ages was one of nature, not degree. A new law had thus emerged: administrative law. It was founded on general principles not laid down by the legislator and therefore not absolute (*'principes généraux et maximes absolues'*). Although these new principles and institutions had emerged in France, they contained seeds that would burgeon elsewhere. Sooner or later, Tocqueville argued, those principles and institutions would be recognized by other European peoples. Interestingly, the underlying reason was neither the originality nor the importance of the French tradition but their conformity with the new state of the world – one that rejected the Marxist vision of socialism[36] but accepted the central role of public functions and services. It was in this sense that administrative law would, by a sort of 'natural diffusion', become a common feature of civilized nations.[37] Administrative law was thus a salient characteristic of the new state of the world.[38]

In the decades to follow, Tocqueville's prediction was confirmed by the prodigious development of administrative institutions in many corners of Europe, a topic we will return to in the next section. Meanwhile, there is another point of general interest deserving of comment, namely the connection between

---

32 M Macarel, *Cours d'administration et de droit administratif* (Plon 1852) 5–7.

33 id, 15.

34 id, 8.

35 A de Tocqueville, *Rapport fait à l'Académie des sciences morales et politiques sur le livre de M. Macarel, intitulé Cours de droit administratif*, in *Œuvres complètes d'Alexis de Tocqueville. Etudes économiques, politiques et littéraires par Alexis de Tocqueville* (Lévy 1866) 63. In the secondary literature, see S Cassese, 'Une des formes de l'Etat nouveau du monde. Reflexions sur le droit administratif français' [1995] Act jur dr adm 167; G Bigot, *Ce droit qu'on dit administratif* (La mémoire du droit 2015) vi.

36 According to the *Manifesto of the Communist Party* (1848), the 'executive of the modern state [wa]s but a committee for managing the common affairs of the whole bourgeoisie'.

37 Tocqueville, *Rapport fait à l'Académie des sciences morales et politiques sur le livre de M. Macarel* (n 35) 71 (*'notre droit administratif deviendra graduellement celui du monde civilisé, … grâce à sa conformité avec la condition des hommes de notre temps'*).

38 Cassese, 'Une des formes de l'Etat nouveau du monde' (n 35) 167.

language and law. Of course, words are the essential tools of the law and, notoriously, a technical term may have no equivalent in another language. Just as often, comparative works point out that language is an obstacle to communication between different peoples, especially in Europe, where many languages from different families are spoken, unlike in Latin America, for example.[39] And it is in this respect that another of Tocqueville's observations should be noted. In addition to emphasizing the driving force of interests, he was among the first, if not *the* first, to underline the change taking place in the language of public law.[40] It was a change that would have a vast influence on Europe as a whole. It has been convincingly argued that one of the more important consequences of the French Revolution was the gradual diffusion of the 'language of rights' across Europe.[41] This line of reasoning provides a key to understanding why – although nineteenth-century law faculties came under the general tendency to 'nationalize' universities as agents of State policy – similar concerns about rights emerged in different contexts. In one form or another, these ideas about public law would fashion the cultural climate in other parts of Europe. Mayer was so convinced of their intrinsic quality that he used French theories as the intellectual infrastructure for building a general theory of administrative law in Germany. In Italy, Orlando found that this general theory constituted a conceptual framework into which scientific theories were required to fit.

4 The Transformation of Administrative Law

This section continues the discussion of the evolution of administrative law from the perspective of its relationship with the growth of government. To stop here would, however, give a misleading picture of contemporary administrative law, since many important government policy decisions are influenced by the rules and decisions that flow from global regulatory regimes, as well as from regional organizations, such as the European Union and the Council of Europe.

Until relatively recently, it was common to think of new government functions and powers being assigned to government departments and agencies in terms of a discontinuity between the nineteenth and twentieth centuries. There was a period, which many called liberal, when theorists believed the State's

39 Fromont (n 4) 1.

40 Tocqueville, *De la démocratie en Amérique* (n 13) 59.

41 E Garcia de Enterria, *La formación del Derecho Público europeo tràs la Revolución Francesa* (3rd edn, Editorial Civitas 2009).

role was to defend the national territory, ensure law and order, and administer justice, while everything else would come about through economic and social forces. However, the situation became more complex, especially in the wake of industrialization and democratization. In Britain, France, Germany, and elsewhere, the industrial revolution led to the considerable expansion of government functions. Between 1830 and 1870, increased regulation was imposed in areas such as factories, railways and telegraphs, housing, and public health.[42] Factories, mines and other places of work came under increasing public scrutiny, especially in the wake of tragedies concerning workers, demanding changes to the law in response to intolerable situations. New technologies, too, required regulation, including international standards, as illustrated by the establishment of the International Telegraph Union (1865), one of the first administrative unions. Housing and public health gained greater importance as a consequence of demographic increase and urbanization. Thus, in the 1860's, Aucoc, a French public lawyer who later became president of the *Société de legislation comparée*, observed that all governments were involved in education, at least at the lower levels, nationalizing new industries such as railways and telegraphs.[43]

Meanwhile, pressure for greater democracy increased. In the first part of the nineteenth century, numerous politicians thought that granting limited political reforms was far preferable to the risk of revolution. This opinion became more widespread after the turmoil of 1848–9 in all corners of Europe, with the exception of Britain and Russia. For example, in France after 1848 the whole adult male population was given the vote,[44] while in Britain the 1884 Representation of the People (Franchise) Act extended the right to vote to almost all male workers. In other countries, where the proportion of electors was lower, what was later called conservative reformism was introduced: Bismarck and other European rulers took unprecedented measures to deliver certain goods and services to the people, often in an attempt to reduce the threat of socialism.[45] In brief, there would be far more government

---

42 See R Gneist, *Das heutige englische Verfassungs und Verwaltungsrecht* (Springer 1857) For a retrospective on English law, see Craig, 'The Legitimacy of US Administrative Law and the Foundations of English Administrative Law' (n 8) (focusing on four fields, that is, health, safety and trade regulation, flood protection, poor relief, and excise).

43 L Aucoc, *Conférences sur l'administration et le droit administratif* (Dunod 1869) 18.

44 JW Garner, 'Electoral Reform in France' (1913) 7 Am Pol Sc Rev 610.

45 For a comparative analysis, see F Bignami, 'Comparative administrative law' in M Bussani and U Mattei (eds), *The Cambridge Companion to Comparative Law* (Cambridge UP 2012) 145. See also, for a historical perspective, G Ritter, *Der Sozialstaat* (De Gruyter 1999).

involvement in society than ever before by the end of the nineteenth century.[46] The years to follow saw greater public access to representative institutions in countries such as Germany and Italy as the right to vote was extended to social groups that had previously been barred from voting. These brought new ideas, and new legislation was adopted as politicians sought to secure votes.

This new legislation required more administration, and in more than one sense. New public bodies were established to discharge new functions, and there was a sharp rise in the number of civil servants. Moreover, there was an increase of what French legal scholarship called *puissance publique*;[47] that is, an 'augmentation of administration's powers'.[48] This change manifested itself both in terms of the administration's ability to impose its will on individuals through adjudication (orders and penalties limiting economic freedom, expropriation and other limitations on private property) and to devise regulations with effects on various groups, if not on society as a whole. These powers were often characterized by a broad margin of discretion, raising concerns about arbitrariness. Many deemed existing legal procedures inadequate to counter misuse and abuse of power. It was not enough to simply introduce administrative mechanisms, including procedures, and judicial safeguards on a larger scale than before: a new law was necessary. Administrative law increasingly filled this gap, and Britain was no exception. Just as in France, Duguit, Jèze, and others argued that administrative law was increasingly about the discharge of functions and services to the citizenry,[49] so Robson promoted a functionalist approach in Britain. In his *Justice and Administrative Law*,[50] not only did he challenge the old dictum that Britain had no administrative law, but he also argued that the time was ripe for developing a rational system of administrative courts.[51] Though his ideas were accepted neither by the majority of scholars nor by politicians, they are representative of a new awareness. Not only had administrative law acquired an intellectual framework, albeit with significant differences within the various legal cultures, but concepts such as 'administrative discretionality', and 'administrative procedure' gained greater acceptance.

A twofold change occurred after 1945, both within and outside national legal systems. What transpired after 1945 is much more than a cradle-to-grave

46 See Goodnow, *Comparative Administrative Law* (n 28) 7 and J Stone, 'The Twentieth Century Administrative Explosion and after' (1964) 52 California L Rev 513.

47 M Hauriou, 'Droit administratif' in *Répertoire Béquet* (Dupont 1897) xiv.

48 Craig, *Administrative Law* (n 23) 58.

49 L Duguit, *Les transformations du droit public* (Armand Colin 1913) IX.

50 W Robson, *Justice and Administrative Law* (Stevens 1928).

51 Loughlin (n 23) 166.

administrative welfare State. In deciding on access to prenatal care, abortion in public hospitals and abortion pills, public administrators affect individual choices concerning births. Other decisions may determine whether and how it is possible to 'rest in peace', for example when cemeteries have to accommodate the building of infrastructures such as highways and railroads.[52] Moreover, modern legal systems recognize interests such as the protection of the environment, bio-diversity, and, more recently food security,[53] which are not a matter for individuals but society as a whole. These interests are extremely important in modern polities. They receive protection from open-textured legislative provisions that require administrative action either in the traditional form of adjudication or in the guise of rulemaking or standard-setting. All these species of power are variably characterized by discretion.[54] If they are all regarded as falling within the scope of administrative law, then the ramifications are significant insofar as a modern comparative research should not focus only on one species or another.

Any comparative research should equally show awareness of the de-nationalization of administrative law that has characterized the last decades. The full ramifications of this process cannot, however, be examined here. The intent of this section is simply to point out the difficulty of reconciling the traditional conception of administrative law as a province of the State and national *enclave* within the new legal scenarios at both regional and global level. Since the early years of the European Communities, they have had their own apparatuses, with powers to regulate and adjudicate in some areas, often with binding effects not only on the member States but also on individual and commercial stakeholders. It is precisely the existence of pervasive and binding administrative powers that has made it necessary to provide legal standards and judicial remedies through the Treaties of Paris (1952) and Rome (1957), in order to limit and structure these powers, making them accountable.[55] Over the years, this had led to a conspicuous body of legal provisions, judicial doctrines, and learned writings; namely European administrative law.[56] This body of law has a twofold impact on national administrative laws. On the one hand,

---

52 J Mashaw, *Due Process in the Administrative State* (Yale UP 1986) 14.

53 RB Stewart, 'Administrative Law in the XXI Century' (2003) 78 NYU L Rev 437, at 450.

54 See DJ Galligan, *Discretionary Powers: A Legal Study of Official Discretion* (OUP 1990).

55 See, among the first commentators, E Stein and P Hay, 'Legal Remedies of Enterprises in the European Economic Community' (1969) 9 AJCL 375.

56 See P Craig, *EU Administrative Law* (2nd edn, Oxford UP 2012); C Harlow, P Leino Sandberg and G della Cananea (eds), *Research Handbook on European Administrative Law* (Edward Elgar 2017); JB Auby and J Dutheil de la Rochère (eds), *Traité de droit administratif européen* (3rd edn, Bruylant 2022).

it regulates the conduct of national authorities when they implement the law of the EU, requesting them to respect a set of general principles, including loyal cooperation and partnership.[57] On the other hand, there is a sort of 'spillover' effect regarding the regulation of problems of administrative law of a purely domestic nature.[58] In this sense, it has become necessary to look at European administration from a comparative perspective.[59]

More recently, there has been a shift of regulatory powers from the States to a variety of regional and global regulatory regimes and authorities whose action can be conceptualized in terms of 'global administrative law'.[60] Through the intermediation of the new regulatory regimes, transnational scenarios have become more frequent, and processes of cross-fertilization and legal transplants have greater relevance and significance.

5 A New Comparative Inquiry

The main characteristics of the new comparative inquiry have already been outlined earlier, so there is no need to rehearse them again.[61] A few words, however, may shed some light on three of its salient features: its purposes, subject, and methodology.

The purposes of the research can be explained by referring not to the traditional distinction between those which place emphasis on satisfying

57 See T Koopmans, 'The Birth of European Law at the Crossroads of Legal Traditions' (1991) 39 AJCL 493 (distinguishing between the principles on the basis of their sources).

58 Craig, *Administrative Law* (n 23) 324. See also M Ruffert, 'The Transformation of Administrative Law as a Transnational Methodological Project' in M Ruffert (ed), *The Transformation of Administrative Law in Europe* (European Law Publishers 2007) 43 (distinguishing three levels of influence; that is, through EU acts, adaptation of national laws, and transfer of legal concepts).

59 See GA Bermann, 'A restatement of European administrative law: problems and prospects' in S Rose-Ackerman and PL Lindseth (eds), *Comparative Administrative Law* (2nd edn, Edward Elgar, 2012) 595.

60 See B Kingsbury, N Krisch and RB Stewart, 'The Emergence of Global Administrative Law' (2005) 68 Law & Contemporary Problems 15; S Cassese, 'Administrative Law Without the State: the Challenge of Global Regulation' (2005) 37 NYU J Int'l L & Pol 663; P Craig, *UK, EU and Global Administrative Law: Foundations and Challenges* (Cambridge UP 2015).

61 G della Cananea and M Bussani, 'The Common Core of European Administrative Laws: A Framework for Analysis' (2017) 23 Maastricht J Eur & Comp L 221. For a similar perspective, see Ruffert, 'The Transformation of Administrative Law as a Transnational Methodological Project' (n 58) 46.

a 'need for knowledge'[62] and those who point out the persistent interest of both foreign law and comparative law in view of the reform of national legal institutions. There are good reasons for examining national legal institutions to define higher standards of administrative conduct, these being preferable to lower standards. There are, however, difficulties with this approach since the descriptive validity of a comparative study aiming to select an 'optimal' set of rules depends, in turn, on the 'correctness' of a number of questionable claims.[63] Space precludes a thorough discussion of this issue here, but suffice it to say that the research presented in this volume has a different goal, namely the advancement of knowledge, though it may well have some practical implications, such as for teaching administrative law.

As regards the subject, two opposing risks had to be avoided: over-and under-inclusiveness.[64] The topic addressed here is administrative procedure. Various reasons underpin this choice. Firstly, as a subject for comparative study, administrative procedure is thought to have both universality, as it is increasingly accepted that administrative procedure is 'a concept at the heart of administrative law',[65] and practical importance. Secondly, focusing on procedure allows us to understand what administrative authorities do and how they do it, including the interaction between the various units of government and citizen participation. Conversely, traditional emphasis on the judicial review of administration is subject to a distorted perspective as it implies a sort of indirect vision of the functioning of public authorities and emphasizes what might be called the negative part of administrative law, based on the remedies available *against* certain administrative acts.[66] The third reason is that several nations have adopted general procedural codes regulating the rights to a hearing across a variety of areas, thus partly modifying the traditional characterization of administrative law as judge made law.

Some methodological choices, too, should be explained. As indicated at the start, underlying the research is the hypothesis that there is a common core between European administrative laws that has evolved over time and that

62 See R Sacco, 'Legal Formants: A Dynamic Approach to Comparative Law (instalment I)' (1991) 39 AJCL 1.

63 O Pfersmann, 'Le droit comparé comme interpretation et comme théorie du droit' (2001) 53 RIDC 275 (critiquing the idea of assembling the best practices).

64 Schlesinger, 'Introduction' (n 2) 3.

65 See RJ Fuchs, 'Concepts and Policies in Anglo-American Administrative Law Theory' (1938) 47 Yale LJ 538; DJ Galligan, *Due Process and Fair Procedures: A Study of Administrative Procedures* (OUP 1997); N Walker, 'Review of Dennis J. Galligan, Due Process and Fair Procedures: A Study of Administrative Procedures' (1999) 62 Modern L Rev 962.

66 Friedmann (n 27) 144.

it relates not only to generic ideals that can be found in every civilized legal system in one way or another, such as justice, but also to some precise requirements of administrative fairness and propriety. These are regarded as empirically testable hypotheses, subject to verification which can be performed in two ways. One is to attempt a historical reconstruction focusing on the validity of empirical evidence in relation to specified hypotheses. Another is to rely on legal comparison, which can be viewed as a 'substitute for the experimental method' used in other scientific domains.[67] Accordingly, two types of comparison will be used: synchronic and diachronic. Conventional as these terms may be, they convey something of the nature of the work to be done, insofar as the former provides a retrospective view, while the latter focuses on the administrative systems of our times.

There are both general and specific reasons for choosing a diachronic comparison. From the general point of view, as Gorla observed rephrasing Maitland's opinion that 'history involves comparison',[68] 'comparison involves history'.[69] It is impossible, therefore, to understand the deeper structures of administrative law with 'only the vaguest idea of how its subject matter has evolved'.[70] History has shown that legal principles and institutions originating in one nation have often been influential elsewhere. During the nineteenth century, French administrative courts and the underlying conception of separation of powers had a great influence in many areas of Europe.[71] During the last century, Austrian ideas about administrative procedure spread to neighboring countries and subsequently elsewhere. A dynamic approach, which takes several decades into account, is thus much to be preferred to a static one, permitting a better understanding of the respective significance of commonality and diversity.[72]

As for synchronic comparison, the growth of administrative procedure legislation suggests that studying it may provide interesting insights. However, this would not suffice to gain an understanding of the interplay between the

---

67 M Shapiro, *Courts. A Comparative and Political Analysis* (University of Chicago Press 1981) vii. For similar remarks, see Kahn-Freund (n 3) 431.

68 FW Maitland, 'Why the History of English Law Was not Written' in R Livingston (ed), *Frederic William Maitland Historian. Selection from his Writings* (Schuyler 1960) 132 (affirming that 'History involves comparison' and that 'an isolated system cannot explain itself'). See also Legendre, 'L'Administration sans Histoire' (1968) 21 La revue administrative 428 (criticizing the 'divorce' between administrative lawyers and historians of law).

69 G Gorla, *Diritto comparato e diritto comune europeo* (Giuffrè 1981) 39.

70 Craig, *Administrative Law* (n 23) 47.

71 See J Rivero, *Cours de droit administratif comparé* (Les cours de droit 1956–57) 27.

72 Cassese, *La construction du droit administratif* (n 7) 19.

commonality and diversity found in European laws. There are, again, both general and specific reasons why it would not do so. The main methodological innovation in Schlesinger's study of the common core is precisely this: rather than seeking to describe national institutions, an attempt was made to understand how, within the legal systems selected, a certain set of problems would be solved. Thus, the problems 'had to be stated in factual terms'.[73] In practice, this meant that, by using the materials concerning some legal systems, Schlesinger formulated hypothetical cases in order to see how they would be solved in each of the legal systems selected. It turned out that these cases were formulated in such a way as to make sense in all such legal systems. The suitability and fruitfulness of this methodology was subsequently confirmed in the framework of the Trento project on the common core of European law.[74]

In the field of administrative law, this type of approach is particularly appealing for two reasons. Firstly, administrative law has emerged and developed with no legislative framework comparable to the solid and wide-ranging architecture provided by civil codes. As a result, its principles are largely jurisprudential, not only in Britain, but also in France and elsewhere. Secondly, in addition to legislation and judicial decisions, governmental practices play an important, sometimes decisive, role.[75] Not surprisingly, as early as in the 1940s, some of the few scholars who devoted their attention to the comparative study of European administrative laws were aware that for a better understanding of their common and distinctive traits it would be much better to build hypothetical cases and confront the solutions that would be given.[76] This innovative suggestion for tackling the problem that concerns us here was not used, however. In the following decade, when a new legal journal, the *International and Comparative Law Quarterly*, launched a comparative research concerning administrative law, it elaborated a well-structured questionnaire, but it was based on legislative design.[77] After Schlesinger's research was published, it was

73 M Rheinstein, 'Review of R. Schlesinger, Formation of Contracts: A Study of the Common Core of Legal Systems' (1969) 36 Univ Chicago L Rev 449.

74 See M Bussani and U Mattei, 'The Common Core Approach to European Private Law' (1997–1998) 3 Colum J Eur L 339.

75 See F Burdeau, *Histoire du droit administratif : de la Révolution au début des années 1970* (PUF 1995) (emphasizing the importance of governmental practice).

76 F Morstein Marx, 'Comparative Administrative Law: a Note on Review of Discretion' (1939) 87 Un Penn L Rev 955.

77 'Questionnaire on Administrative Law' (1953) 2 Int'l & Comp L Q 217. Three reports were published, those regarding Germany, Italy and the Nordic legal systems: see N Herlitz, 'Swedish Administrative Law' (1953) 2 Int'l & Comp L Q 231; O Bachof, 'German Administrative Law with Special reference to the Latest Developments in the System of

found that the same methodology could be applied, among other things, to the control of the legality of administrative decisions.[78] However, there was no systematic use of such methodology. A factual analysis, however, can provide interesting insights.

A final point of general interest concerns the place of theory. Some public lawyers and historians of law engage in an intellectual history of administrative law,[79] with a strong emphasis on individual scholars and networks between them. The comparative inquiry that is presented here examines administrative law, instead. It thus devotes attention to the practical side of the law, including the powers that public authorities exercise and the procedure by which these powers are exercised. This does not imply, however, that legal theory is of scarce significance. To the contrary, it must be taken into due account, because it has greatly contributed to shaping not only the standards that are applicable to a wide range of governmental conduct, but more generally the culture within which these standards are elaborated, balanced and applied.[80]

6 Limits to the Inquiry

Before describing the structure of this essay, we should remark on some limitations to our comparative inquiry. The first, as mentioned previously, is that it focuses on administrative procedure. It cannot be ruled out, therefore, that research focusing – let's say – on local government will provide different results. The second limit concerns the choice of legal systems selected for comparison, while the third regards the factual approach mentioned above; these are two issues requiring discussion.

The choice of the legal systems to be considered is a crucial issue in any comparative research. While the decision to place Europe at the heart of the project was dictated by a variety of reasons including the historical relationships between its legal cultures and the establishment of regional organizations such

Legal Protection' (1953) 2 Int'l & Comp L Q 368; G Miele, 'Italian Administrative Law' (1954) 3 Int'l & Comp L Q 421.

78 Kahn-Freund (n 3) 430.

79 See L Mannori and B Sordi, *Storia del diritto amministrativo* (Laterza 2001). See also A Likhovski, 'The Intellectual History of Law' in MD Dubber and C Tomlins (eds), *The Oxford Handbook of Legal History* (OUP 2018) 151 (discussing various historiographical trends).

80 S Cassese, 'Le amministrazioni pubbliche in Europa. Per uno studio storico-comparato del diritto amministrativo' in *Scritti in onore di Pietro Virga* (Giuffré 1994) 501.

as the Council of Europe and the EU,[81] three further choices must be taken into consideration. The first was to focus not only on the traditional 'major' legal systems – Britain, France, and Germany – but also to include some others, commonly but unjustifiably regarded as 'minor' such as Belgium and Austria.[82] As we shall see in Part 1, both have been involved in the processes of borrowing and legal transplants. The second choice is to consider not only the legal systems that are included within the EU, but also others, in order to ascertain whether similar standards of administrative conduct exist there. As a result, although no research project escapes the limits of budget and workforce, every effort has been made to cover a sufficiently large number of legal systems.

The third choice was to include the EU. On one side of the coin, the EU regulates – through its treaties and other sources – the conduct of public authorities in the member States. On the other is the law that applies to the institutions and agencies of the EU, ie, the European administration in the strict sense. Its existence is a powerful counterweight to the idea that nothing has changed since the advent of the positive State. It sheds doubt on the notion that administrative law is consubstantial with the State and shows the difficulties besetting the traditional idea that administrative law simply reflects national legal traditions. Including the EU is not without its problems, however, given the highly specific nature of European administration, considering that implementation is generally left to national authorities. It may nonetheless be interesting to discover to what extent the defined standards are similar to those followed by domestic legal systems.

The other limitation concerns the level of analysis. Opting for factual analysis raises the question of whether the conclusions can be generalized outside the specific cases examined. This is a something of a challenge. As De Smith put it, 'to prophesy the view that a court will take of the powers or duties of an administrative authority in a particular case must inevitably remain a hazardous undertaking'.[83] Two answers can be suggested. The first is that what is being examined is also administrative procedure legislation. The second is that there

81 See J Rivero, 'Vers un droit commun européen: nouvelles perspectives en droit administratif' in M Cappelletti (ed), *Perspectives for a Common Law of Europe* (Sijthofff 1978) (pointing out the specificity of a common law of Europe in the field of administrative law). But see also B Stirn, *Vers un droit public européen* (Montchestien 2012) 10 (pointing out the institutional differences between the members of the EU).

82 Schlesinger, 'Introduction' (n 2) 2.

83 S De Smith, 'Wrongs and Remedies in Administrative Law' (1952) 15 Modern L Rev 190. See also, in social sciences, AS Gerber, DP Green and EH Kaplan, 'The illusion of learning from observational research' in I Shapiro et al (eds), *Problems and Methods in the Study of Politics* (Cambridge UP 2004) 251.

are certain factors that can increase the added value of a factual analysis. All the hypothetical cases have been constructed referring to some factual circumstances. The underlying idea is that it is only by considering concrete circumstances that one can 'bring to consciousness the assumptions secreted within the structures' of each legal system.[84] Moreover, national experts have not only been asked to indicate the solution more likely to be provided by jurists and judges in their respective legal orders, but they have also been encouraged to reflect on the underlying institutional and cultural reasons, including the role played by legal formants, as theorized by Rodolfo Sacco. Sacco developed the concept of 'legal formants' to describe the many relevant elements in the living law, including legislative and regulatory provisions, judicial decisions, scholarly works and, in our case, government practice.[85] Even when legal requirements cannot be extrapolated from the cases or constitute unsafe guides, discussing background theories can be an aid to understanding how procedural values balance with other values.

7 Structure of the Inquiry

Having clarified the scope and methodology of this inquiry, it will now be easier to describe its structure. First, we present a diachronic comparison, which serves to ensure that the analysis of legal institutions is rooted in a strong historical awareness (Part 1). It includes the establishment of national systems of administrative justice, the judicial construction of the general principles of administrative law in the *Belle Époque*, and the adoption of administrative procedure legislation over the last century.

The synchronic comparison, which is illustrated in Part 2, has two related but distinct purposes. The first is to compare general legislation on administrative procedure in order to ascertain the common and distinctive traits between European legal systems. The second is to discuss the results of our factual analysis with regard to two important forms of administrative action, namely adjudication and rulemaking. The factual analysis is completed by a consideration of the consequences that follow from governmental wrongdoing in terms of liability.

In Part 3, all these findings will be used to test the robustness of our initial hypothesis concerning the possibility of identifying a common core. The

84 Loughlin (n 23) 35.

85 Sacco (n 62) 1.

first step will be to consider its etiology; that is, the causes of what they have in common, as well as the causes of the divergences. The next step will be to examine the development of the common core, what it means, and its nature and extent today.

PART 1

A Diachronic Comparison

CHAPTER 2

Judicial Review of Administration: Institutional Design

This chapter examines the development of administrative laws. It does so with a focus on the history of institutions, the supervisory mechanisms adopted to control administrative power. It does so, however, with an eye on the history of ideas, too. Our analysis begins with the claim that the English and French models of administrative justice must not be regarded only as 'ideal-types' in the Weberian sense but also as prototypes because they were borrowed and adapted in various other parts of Europe. Belgium and Italy provide interesting examples. This is followed by a discussion of how the French prototype was adapted in Austria and Germany with the emergence of another model. Exchanges between legal cultures are also considered. The focus then shifts to how they interact at the supranational level.

1 England and France: Ideal-types and Prototypes

Although judicial mechanisms preceded representative institutions, they gained in importance during the nineteenth century with the advent of new ideas concerning rights, often enshrined in written constitutions in the US, France, and other parts of Europe. By recognizing and protecting certain rights, constitutions envisaged at least some occasions when judicial review was necessary to set aside executive decisions, and in some cases (the US) also to set aside legislation.[86] Subsequently, the demand for justice grew as administrative functions and powers expanded. On the supply side, the gap between the Anglo-American institutions and the French ones widened after 1799.

A brief outline of their distinctive traits may be helpful at this point. French law was based on the distinction between administrative law and private law, viewed as the law governing relations between individuals, in contrast with the

86 R McKay, 'Judicial Review in a Liberal Democracy' (1985), Nomos, vol 25, Liberal Democracy 123.

 | DOI:10.1163/9789004549579_003

principle of the universality of law in England.[87] Unlike in England, the separation of powers in France was meant to prevent ordinary courts from interfering in the exercise of administrative powers. Such powers were under the control of the *Conseil d'État*, institutionally placed within the executive and distinct from the judiciary as its members were not judges but civil servants. In other words, the separation within the executive was functional rather than structural.[88] The *Conseil* also had the power to authorize the ordinary courts to proceed against public officers. Of these three features, the second has been more strongly emphasized in comparative studies, most of which consider England to be characterized by judicial monism and France by dualism.[89]

We should however put things in perspective. There are various reasons for this. Above all, as regards the French *Conseil d'État* the traditional distinction between the two periods of *justice rétenue* and *justice déléguée* has been criticized because, in reality, before that year very rarely did the final decision deviate from the opinions issued by the *Conseil d'État*.[90] Moreover, even before 1872 the *Conseil* had defined procedures and standards for reviewing administrative action, including action against *excès de pouvoir*. It developed them further and thus gradually emerged as a fully-fledged administrative court.[91] Dicey himself recognized this.[92] He also recognized that, when considering how French *droit administratif* had been formed, it was much closer to English law than French civil law as it was a judicial product.[93] Incidentally, in his day, English courts were beginning to develop more specific standards of conduct for public authorities.[94] For some, this was sufficient. For others, creating a more effective system of public law would require a 'new system of courts' similar to those of France.[95]

---

87 Dicey, *Introduction to the Study of the Law of the Constitution* (n 22) 331; G Braibant, La juridiction administrative en droit comparé, 52 Revue adm. 204 (1999); MP Chiti, 'Monism or dualism in administrative law: a true or false dilemma?', Revue admin. (52), 2000, 47.

88 Dicey, *Introduction to the Study of the Law of the Constitution* (n 22) 339; Bigot (n 35) xv.

89 Braibant (n 87) 204.

90 R Bonnard, *Le contrôle juridictionnel de l'administration. Etude de droit administratif comparé* (1934; Dalloz, 2006); Bignami (n 45) 151.

91 Following Shapiro, *Courts. A Comparative and Political Analysis* (n 67) 153, the term 'administrative court' will be used, to ensure consistency and to avoid the confusion which would derive from the word 'administrative tribunal'.

92 Dicey, *Introduction to the Study of the Law of the Constitution* (n 22) Ch 1, 339.

93 id, 373–374 ("droit administrative" is … "judge-made law").

94 M Loughlin, 'Evolution and gestalt of the State in the United Kingdom' in A von Bogdandy, S Cassese and P Huber (eds), *The Max Planck Handbooks in European Public Law*, I, *The Administrative State* (OUP 2017) 481.

95 DB Mitchell, 'The causes and effects of the absence of a system of public law in the United Kingdom' (1965) 13 Public Law 95 at 118.

A better understanding of legal realities also shows the weakness of the conventional view of the English and French systems of administrative justice in an ideal-typical form, in the Weberian sense. In this form, a 'logical construct' is not meant to refer to an ideal in any ethical sense. Rather, it is a heuristic device which serves to help bring order to a variety of given phenomena.[96] An ideal-type gives the 'idea' of a historically given set of phenomena, accentuating one or more characteristics and elements.[97] It is thus constructed to permit us to obtain initial insights into certain phenomena or realities. Weber himself argued that ideal-types should be used in the 'systematic science of law'.[98] Subsequently, several public lawyers have characterized English and French institutions as ideal-types.[99]

There are, however, two problems with this approach. First, precisely because of the decision to stress some elements common to most, but not all, cases, such ideal-types failed to fully take into account certain tensions between the legal realities examined. For this reason, Laferrière, drew a more complex picture of the various systems. He opened his treatise with a comparative analysis and expressed the opinion that the structures of public law were heavily influenced by national traditions.[100] But he observed that, despite opinions to the contrary, setting up administrative courts was not a prerogative unique to France.[101] Indeed, some 'foreign' systems (those of most German states, Portugal and Spain) had the same main structures as French public law, notably separation of powers and a dual jurisdiction over disputes between citizens and the State.[102] He distinguished these systems from other two categories. One was characterized by the absence of dual jurisdiction but at the same time by the enforcement of severe limits to review by ordinary judges (Belgium and Italy). The last group was based on a radically different way to conceive the separation of powers between administrative and judicial bodies (UK and US).[103] Four decades later, another French public lawyer, Bonnard, went one step further.[104] He described the age-old opposition between England and

96 M Weber, *Gesammelte Aufsätze zur Wissenschaftslehre* (1922), English translation by EA Shils and HA Finch, *Methodology of Social Sciences* (Transaction Publishers 1949) 42–43.

97 Weber, *Methodology of Social Sciences* (n 96) 90.

98 id, 43.

99 Cassese, 'New paths for administrative law: a manifesto' (n 4) 10 and 16.

100 E Laferrière, *Traité de la jurisdiction administrative et du recours contentieux* (1st edn 1887, 2nd edn, Berger-Levrault 1896) 25 (une '*grande diversité*', that is a huge diversity).

101 id, x.

102 id, 27.

103 id, 84–87. See also Bonnard (n 90) 219.

104 Bonnard (n 90) 125.

France, but he immediately added that a more articulated analysis was necessary and that it showed that, notwithstanding national differences, a common trend emerged; that is, the creation of administrative courts with general jurisdiction over public law disputes.

The second problem with considering the English and French systems as ideal-types is more profound and requires greater analysis in the rest of this chapter. Essentially, the difficulty is that neither the English nor the French system of administrative justice were, in reality, just an ideal-type. Indeed, the French system of administrative law was seen as a model for other national legal orders. Similarly, the English system, with its emphasis on the role of the ordinary courts, was a source of inspiration. Both must, therefore, be thought of as prototypes.[105]

2 The Reception of the English Prototype: Belgium and Italy

Although Watson observed that the choice of examples is subjective,[106] there are various reasons for starting with Belgium and Italy. Both were new States in the nineteenth century and, consequently, had to choose how to shape their administrative justice systems, and they initially made the same choice, opting for a 'monist' system. Although the ideal-type of judicial monism was England, it was to Belgium especially that Italian reformers looked. There was thus a direct relationship between those two legal systems.[107] But both subsequently reversed their initial choice, albeit at different times and with different institutional ramifications.

For a proper understanding of how judicial institutions developed in Belgium, it is important to consider that it had been under French rule and answerable to the *Conseil d'État* from 1800 to 1815 and then became part of the Netherlands until 1830, under its Council of State. There was no remarkable discontinuity after 1815 as the Crown retained the power to adjudicate

105 See Shapiro, *Courts. A Comparative and Political Analysis* (n 67) 153; G Marcou, 'Une cour administrative suprême: particularité française ou modèle en expansion?' (2008) 123 Pouvoirs 133, at 135. For further discussion of 'prototypical cases', see R Hirschl, 'The Question of Case Selection in Comparative Constitutional Law' (2005) 53 AJCL 125, at 143 (for whom such cases serve as 'representative exemplar of other cases exhibiting similar pertinent characteristics'). But see also A von Bogdandy, 'Comparative Constitutional Law as Social Science? A Hegelian Reaction to Ran Hirschl's Comparative Matters', (2016) 49 Verfassung und Recht in Ubersee 278 (criticizing the use of a social science approach).

106 Watson (n 19) 18.

107 JC Escarras, *Les expériences belge et italienne d'unité de juridiction* (LGDJ 1972).

on disputes affecting territorial bodies and would decide after consulting the Council of State. There was a discontinuity, however, when Belgium declared independence from the Netherlands and was recognized as a separate nation in 1830. It rejected the Council of State as an administrative court.[108] Belgium's Constitution (1831) affirmed the principle that disputes concerning civil and political rights were only to be heard in the ordinary courts, though in the latter case there could be such exceptions as established by law.[109] This decision was reinforced by the prohibition to set up 'extraordinary commissions or tribunals'.[110] Concretely speaking, this meant that there was no administrative tribunal and, above all, no *Conseil d'État*. Ordinary courts had two powers: bringing an objection of unlawfulness, they could disapply administrative acts or measures contested by an individual; they could award damages in cases of wrongdoing arising from public authorities infringing individual rights.[111]

It was a choice for which Dicey found more than mere assonance with the ideas underlying the English Constitution.[112] Others went further, asserting that the Belgian choice was influenced by 'the free institutions of Britain'.[113] This idealized account does not, however, fully consider that the decision was dictated by negative political preferences; that is, a rejection of the previous model of administrative justice imposed by the Dutch. Moreover, ordinary courts were reluctant to affirm the tortious liability of public officials. Until 1920, these courts followed the so-called *imperium* doctrine whereby there could be no liability when public authorities acted within the exercise of their powers.[114]

In other parts of Europe, both intellectuals and political reformers saw the Belgian legal framework as a source of inspiration, and this was true of Italy too. Few years after political unification in 1861, political reformers vehemently criticized the bodies modelled on the French system during the Napoleonic

108 See R Lievens, 'The Conseil d'État in Belgium' (1958) 7 AJCL 572, at 573. On the contrast between the Belgian and Dutch approaches, see Bonnard (n 90) 183. On the similarity between French and Dutch institutions, see Fromont (n 4) 21.

109 Belgian Constitution, Articles 92–93. For further analysis of those provisions, see A Giron, *Le droit administratif de la Belgique* (Bruylant 1881); P Errera, *Traité de droit public belge* (Giard et Brière 1916) 12; D Renders and B Gors, *Le Conseil d'Etat* (3rd edn, Larcier 2020) 5.

110 Belgian Constitution, Article 94.

111 See Renders and Gors (n 109) 5 and Y Marique, 'The Administration and the Judge: Pragmatism in Belgian Case Law (1890–1910)' in G della Cananea and S Mannoni (eds), *Administrative Justice Fin de siècle. Early Judicial Standards of Administrative Conduct in Europe (1890–1910)* (Oxford UP 2020) 73.

112 Dicey, *Introduction to the Study of the Law of the Constitution* (n 22) 205.

113 S Galeotti, *The Judicial Control of Public Authorities in England and in Italy: A Comparative Study* (Stevens 1954) 11.

114 See Lievens (n 108) 574.

period. In the various pre-existing States, they had exercised mixed administrative and judicial functions.[115] They invoked the adoption of 'ordinary and universal jurisdiction', viewed as the only solution compatible with the postulates of liberal constitutionalism. After some years, and following passionate parliamentary debate during which reformers often cited the Belgian system favourably, the Act of 1865 abolished the existing bodies. It almost literally reproduced the words of the Belgian Constitution in entrusting ordinary courts with jurisdiction over disputes concerning civil and political rights.[116] It may be said, therefore, that the nature of the relationship between the two legal systems was not simply one of influence. There is evidence, rather, that the Italian system derived some of its fundamental rules from another one. There was, moreover, a similarity in their underlying assumption that the ordinary courts would guarantee individual interests in the face of undue State interference.

There existed, however, two important exceptions to the jurisdiction of Italian ordinary courts. First, the Council of State (established in 1831) retained its supervision over administrative cases brought before the King in the exercise of 'gracious' royal surveillance over the executive branch. This supervision was very similar to the French one in that the Council of State formally drafted an opinion that was almost always followed by the King. Secondly, the Court of Auditors kept its jurisdiction over the liability of public officials for acts detrimental to the public purse. Ultimately, the 1865 legislation opted for a monist system of judicial administrative review as in England and Belgium, but the jurisdiction of the ordinary courts was 'far from being universal'.[117] This was not, however, the end of the story. It is interesting to see how these political decisions would later be reversed.

3 The Reception of the French Prototype: Italy and Belgium

In Italy, things soon developed very differently from the expectations of the reformers who had worked on updating administrative justice in 1865. The individual interests seeking judicial protection quickly expanded, but the ordinary courts had great difficulties coping with this growing demand for justice.

115 FG Scoca, 'Administrative Justice in Italy: Origins and Evolution' (2009) 2 IJPL 118, at 120; Galeotti (n 113) 11.

116 Bonnard (n 90) 195. See also PB Rava, 'Administrative Courts under Fascism' (1942) 40 Michigan Law Review 654, at 656 (pointing out the 'Belgian pattern').

117 Galeotti (n 113) 243.

Whether this depended on the intrinsic limits of ordinary judicial process or the limited knowledge that ordinary judges had of most new administrative matters or on their bias against the new interests emerging within society is another, and controversial, question.

What is certain is that a movement to improve administrative justice emerged in the early 1880s. At the roots of the movement, which was both cultural and political, lay a strong critique of the legislation adopted in 1865. In a famous speech, Silvio Spaventa argued that an effective system of administrative justice would inevitably require a new system of courts with a separate jurisdiction. He proposed the creation of a separate administrative jurisdiction, similar to that adopted in the Habsburg Empire and several German states.[118] This shows that both the advocates of administrative courts and their opponents looked to foreign models. In 1889, a judicial panel was established within the Council of State on the grounds that it was easier to secure a mixed composition of lawyers and administrators essential to the sound administration of justice. Commentators have agreed that the new administrative court served to alleviate injustices for citizens, whose interests had previously remained unprotected. It thus served 'to restore justice'.[119]

However, the Council of State could only annul unlawful administrative measures but could not award compensation for damages. 'Full' justice was thus unavailable. Moreover, while it enjoyed full functional independence from the executive, insofar as its decisions could not be modified, this was not the case in organizational terms as the executive could appoint new judges. Despite these limits – or because of them – the new institutional design would continue to develop over the decades to follow. Two other panels were created within the Council, and it was entitled to adjudicate disputes concerning not only legitimate interests but also rights *vis-à-vis* public administration services. Subsequently, the Constitution of 1948 confirmed a 'dualistic' system of administrative justice, as well as the exclusive jurisdiction of administrative courts concerning rights, albeit in a limited number of fields.[120] As a result, the jurisdiction of the Italian Administrative Court is similar to the power of annulment of the French *Conseil d'État*.[121]

---

118 S Spaventa, *Giustizia nell'amministrazione* (1880), in id, *Giustizia nell'amministrazione e altri scritti* (Istituto di studi filosofici 2007) 17.

119 Scoca (n 115) 125. See also Rava (n 116) 656 (same thesis).

120 See Miele (n 77) 430 (same thesis).

121 G Treves, 'Judicial Review in Italian Administrative Law' (1953) 26 U Chi L Rev 419, at 432 (for the remark that, comparatively, excess of powers was intended much more broadly than the French concept of *détournement de pouvoir*).

Meanwhile, in 1946, after half a century of political debate, Belgium too took a similar step when the *Conseil d'État* too was granted judicial powers.[122] That this decision was taken in the political system which had been the first to follow the English may come as a surprise. Its supporters stressed the need – again, in functional terms – for greater protection of both individual and collective rights. In the words of learned commentators, administrative action was mostly 'not subject to any judicial control'.[123] Moreover, the beliefs and ideas about judicial review that shaped the approach of ordinary judges led them to exercise undue caution, especially when ordering public authorities to pay damages for infringing the rights of the individual.[124] Others argued that the ordinary courts were not adequately equipped for this task as they lacked expertise or technical knowledge and were not given the training to deal effectively with disputes arising under new social programmes. Another possible explanation is that, after WWII, the old suspicion of the French model of the *Conseil d'État* had diminished.[125] Whatever the soundness of these views, the Belgian example shows that history and national culture are not the only factors to shape modern systems of administrative justice.

4 The Austro-German Prototype

The French model also exerted its influence in the Habsburg Empire. The story of administrative justice in the Empire is seldom told in comparative studies, partly reflecting the idea that it is more important to look at the 'major' legal systems. But this idea is both misleading and reductive because an analysis of the supposedly 'minor' legal systems often provides important insights, as in the Belgian case. Moreover, and more specifically, Austrian legislation gave rise to a new judicial institution, an administrative court, to regulate possibly disproportionate power by public authorities.

In the late eighteenth century, monarchs introduced a number of administrative reforms, also in the light of new theories of government (Cameralism).[126]

122 G Debeyre, *Le Conseil d'État Belge* (Douriez-Bataille 1963).

123 Lievens (n 108) 572.

124 Renders and Gors (n 109) 13.

125 See M Vauthier and P Moreau, 'Etude sur l'influence exercée en Belgique par le Conseil d'Etat de France' in *Le Conseil d'Etat. Livre jubilaire pour commémorer sont cent-cinquantieme anniversaire* (Sirey 1950) 481.

126 See, for further remarks, K Tribe, 'Cameralism and the Science of Government' (1984) 56 J of Modern History 263.

According to these theories, it was always possible in the early nineteenth century to appeal to, and obtain rectification from, a higher level within the administrative hierarchy.[127] However, individuals obtained no judicial protection from administrative arbitrariness. Judicial safeguards were provided by the 1848 Constitution, which was, however, revoked in 1851. This way of handling individual complaints was criticized on the grounds that it failed to ensure the separation of powers as the administration adjudicated its own cases. There was increasing support for creating an administrative justice system that would be separate from both the administration and the ordinary jurisdiction. The *Grundgesetz* (Fundamental Law) adopted in 1867 required the administration to act in accordance with general laws and reshaped the courts.

Few years later (1875), the Court of Administrative Justice (*Verwaltungsgerichtshof – VerwGH*) was created. It had a twofold jurisdiction as it adjudicated on disputes between the Empire and its provinces, as well as on disputes between the individual and the administration once all administrative appeals had been exhausted. In this respect, the Court's jurisdiction concerned public law disputes and was shaped in general terms, as opposed to the limited powers granted to other courts in the German states.[128] Importantly for our purposes here, the Court's grounds for action included unlawfulness and the infringement of 'essential procedural requirements'. On this laconic legislative basis, the Court assessed the legality of the procedures that gave rise to the adoption of administrative decisions and orders. It thus gradually established the basic principles of administrative procedure.[129]

It came to enjoy ever greater prestige. This was evident, for example, in the discussion that preceded the creation of the judicial panel within the Italian Council of State. It was also clear after the dissolution of the Habsburg Empire, when some nations that had been part of it established their own systems of judicial control over administrative action. Both Czechoslovakia and Hungary created administrative tribunals, entirely separate from the ordinary courts. This can be explained by the fact that the judges appointed often came from imperial bodies and enjoyed the prestige of the Administrative Court. The Polish case is even more interesting as it included peoples that had formerly come under the administration of three empires: the Habsburg, the German,

127 H Schambeck, 'The Development of Austrian Administrative Law' (1962) 28 Int Rev Adm Sc 215.

128 Bonnard (n 90) 252.

129 Schambeck (n 127) 219; A Ferrari Zumbini, 'Standards of Judicial Review of Administrative Action (1890–1910) in the Austro-Hungarian Empire' in della Cananea and Mannoni (n 111) 41.

and the Russian. Poland set up a Supreme Administrative Court 'patterned to a great extent after the model of the Austrian' Court.[130]

The evolution of German institutions was partly similar. In the early nineteenth century, some German states established a so-called '*Administrativjustiz*',[131] an instrument for handling complaints within the public administration, which was increasingly criticized for what was perceived as failures of justice. This dissenting movement supported the judicial solution ('*Justizlösung*'). The political events of 1848 also seemed to have moved in that direction. The Constitution of the German Empire of 28 March 1849, adopted in Frankfurt, contained a Charter of Fundamental Rights and provided for their judicial protection. Section 182 provided for the end of the forms of justice in place within the administration and granted courts the power to 'decide in all matters of law'.[132] This provision showed striking similarities with the Belgian Constitution of 1831, though not as literally as in the case of the Italian legislation of 1865. However, the Prussian monarchy refused this constitutional framework, with its strong emphasis on individual rights and the principles of parliamentary democracy.

The debate about administrative justice continued in the years to follow. Two schools of thought emerged; one was favorable to the creation of 'public law courts', with an evident similarity to the English model, while the other school favored the development of mechanisms to eliminate the abuse of discretion but without interfering with administrative action. Although Gneist was an admirer of the English institutions, he was the leading figure of the second school of thought, which gradually came to prevail.[133] The first administrative court, with independent judges, was set up in the Grand-Duchy of Baden in 1863. Other German countries followed, including Essen and Prussia (1875), Württemberg (1877), and Bavaria (1878). The Prussian Court, of which Gneist

130 M Wierzborski and S Mc Caffrey, 'Judicial Control of Administrative Authorities: A New Development in Eastern Europe' (1980) 18 The Int Lawyer 607.

131 M Eichberger, 'Monism or Dualism?' (2000) 53 Revue admin 10, at 11.

132 The original German phrase is as follows: '*über alle Rechtsverletzungen entscheiden die Gerichte*'. For further remarks, see G Nolte, 'General Principles of German and European Administrative Law: A Comparison in Historical Perspective' (1994) 57 Modern L Rev 191, at 199; K Ledford, 'Formalizing the Rule of Law in Prussia: the Supreme Administrative Law Court 1876–1914' (2004) 37 Central Eur History 203, at 210–211.

133 See R Gneist, *Der Rechtsstaat* (Springer 1872) ch. XI. For further remarks, see M Stolleis, 'Judicial Review, Administrative Review, and Constitutional Review in the Weimar Republic' (2003) 16 Ratio Juris 266, at 269 and *Public Law in Germany, 1800–1914* (Berghahn Books 2000) (distinguishing between administrative law and the previous science of the 'policey').

became president, was particularly influential in the development of administrative law, although the other courts had their own case law, and sometimes a more advanced one. Writing at the end of the century, Goodnow concluded that 'administrative courts [...] have, with some modifications, been adopted in the larger part of Germany and are now an essential part of the administrative system' of that country, more or less as in France.[134] The Weimar Constitution (1919) did nothing to change the system. Quite the contrary, Section VII, while reiterating the importance of ordinary courts, established the foundation of both national and regional administrative courts 'as provided by law, for the protection of individuals against ordinances and decrees of the administrative authorities'.[135] After WWII, it was confirmed and strengthened by the Basic Law (1949) and the creation of a Federal Administrative Court few years alter.

In sum, from the outset, the Habsburg Empire had a single administrative court for the whole Empire as opposed to the plurality of courts that characterized Germany until the second half of the twentieth century. That said, in both cases, administrative courts were preferred to ordinary courts. The influence of the French model was undeniable. However, these courts had only judicial functions, being devoid of any advisory role, so a third model emerged.[136] Other countries followed such model, including Sweden, where the Supreme Administrative Court was established in 1909, and Yugoslavia, where a specialist court was created in 1923.[137]

5 French Systematics in Germany

The influence of French administrative law is confirmed by a quick glance at the history of ideas, as openly acknowledged by Mayer, traditionally regarded

134 FJ Goodnow, 'The Executive and the Courts' (1886) 4 Pol Sc Quart 533, at 544. See also JW Garner, 'The Judiciary of the German Empire (I)' (1903) 17 Political Science Quarterly 511.

135 Weimar Constitution, Article 107 (English translation available on the website <www.germanhistorydocs.ghi-dc.org> accessed January 2023). For further analysis, see Eichberger (n 131) 12.

136 See Bignami (n 45) 153 (same remark).

137 On Sweden, see H Ragnelman, 'Administrative Justice in Sweden', in A Piras (ed), *Administrative Law: the Problem of Justice* (Giuffrè, 1991) 277 (for whom it was only after 1971 that the Court regularly cited its precedents) and H Wenander, 'Full Judicial Review or Administrative Discretion? A Swedish Perspective on Deference to the Administration' in G Zhu (ed), *Deference to the Administration in Judicial Review. Comparative Perspectives* (Springer 2019) 407 (explaining the national views about the type and intensity of judicial review). On the specialist court created in Croatia, see D Derda, 'Administrative Law in Croatia' in R Scarciglia (ed), *Administrative Law in the Balkans* (Cedam, 2012) 76.

as the founder of German administrative law.[138] Before examining his argument, two preliminary elements should be mentioned. First, Mayer considered French scholarship to illustrate the necessity of defining more precisely the contours of administrative law. It was to this end that he gave a full account of the French model in his book of 1886.[139] The other important element is context. Mayer taught in Strasbourg, which had been annexed to the German Empire after 1870, for more than twenty years (1882–1903). It is for this reason that, in the preface of his book, he observed that 'our administrative law is in substance still that of France' but then added that French administrative law was of more general interest.[140] He specifically used it as a sort of model for his ambitious project to elaborate a systematic analysis of German administrative law.[141] Borrowing Horatius' well-known metaphor, it might be said *Graecia capta ferum victorem coepit* (that is to say, Greece captured its conquerors).[142]

In his treatise, Mayer claimed that French administrative law was not simply more structured and systematic, but that it could – and had to – be taken as a model.[143] He affirmed that if there was something commendable in it, it was its great respect for the activity of the State, while in Germany it had traditionally been seen as a private person.[144] Another interesting ground was the separation of powers, regarding which he focused on French writers, albeit adopting a somewhat attenuated version of the doctrine.[145] Moreover, he followed the French doctrines of fundamental rights and *res judicata* since German legal culture lacked any corresponding institution.[146] We can, therefore, appreciate not only the nature of Mayer's delimitation of the scope of administrative law, but also his method. His approach was scientific, though it was far removed from rigorous positivism in the sense that he did not see law as a mere *datum*

138 See, among others, E Forsthoff, *Lehrbuch des Verwaltungsrechts* (1958), French translation by M Fromont, *Traité de droit administratif allemand* (Bruylant 1969) vii.

139 O Mayer, *Theorie des Französischen Verwaltungsrechts* (Trübner 1886).

140 id, vi-vii (my translation).

141 See Forsthoff (n 138) vii (for whom Mayer found the source of inspiration in French administrative law); P Gonod, 'The Heritage of Otto Mayer: Actes Administratifs Unilatéraux and Verwaltungsakte in a Franco-German Comparison' in M Ruffert (ed), *The Model Rules on EU Administrative Procedures: Adjudication* (Europa Law Publishing 2006) 17 (same remark).

142 Horatius, *Epistulae*, II, 159.

143 O Mayer, *Deutsches Verwaltungsrecht* (1894), French translation by the author, *Le droit administratif allemand* (Giard et Brière 1903) I, § 1, XIV.

144 Mayer (n 143) viii. For further remarks on this point see, M Kunnecke, *Tradition and Change in Administrative Law: An Anglo-German Comparison* (Springer Verlag 2007) 69.

145 Mayer (n 143) 71–75.

146 id, 93 and 270, respectively.

to be analyzed and classified. He viewed it, instead, as an ordered whole where the order was given by the observer, who explicitly referred to concepts elaborated elsewhere. Mayer therefore referred to French systematics.

If we were to observe only this, however, we would not render him justice. In the opening statement of the preface to the French edition of his treatise, he observed that in the various nations that constituted the 'old European civilization', administrative law was based on certain general principles that were the same everywhere.[147] Among these principles was the separation of powers. Legal mechanisms were required to ensure that public authorities did not infringe the limits stemming from the law. Mayer encapsulated such limits in the concept of '*Rechtsstaat*'.[148] He viewed this type of State as the opposite of the *Polizeistaat*, where the law did not limit the powers of the State. There was still another principle, expressed by the maxim *audi alteram partem*. He began by noting that French law respected this maxim even when the executive power was a judge in its own case, as well as the similarities that existed between French law and that of Bavaria.[149] However, for him, the right to be heard (*droit à l'audition légale, Anspruch auf rechtliches Gehör*) was a common feature of judicial proceedings in the other German countries in accordance with an established maxim of justice, though not a general principle of administrative procedure.

Mayer was fully aware of the many differences between French and German concepts and legal institutions, especially in view of the contrast between the uniform nature of the former and the variegated nature of the latter (administrative law was not unified until the 1960s). However, he pointed out two related but distinct phenomena. One was the influence exerted by French law over German law either indirectly, when it was adapted to the realities of the host State, or directly, when it was simply copied ('*simplement copié*'); the other was the parallelism of ideas and theories ('*parallélisme des idées communes à tous les Pays*').[150] Although this parallelism could have been constructed in a purely functional manner in the light of the new necessities produced by the growth of government, this was not the case. His argument goes much deeper; indeed, it touches on the fundamental point at issue. Mayer argued

147 id, xiii (for the remark that administrative law is based on certain general principles which are the same everywhere).

148 id, 10 and 24. The concept of *Rechtsstaat* had been developed in the earlier works of Robert von Mohl and Rudolf Gneist: for a retrospective, see E Hahn, 'Rudolf Gneist and the Prussian Rechtsstaat: 1862–78' (1977) 49 Journal of Modern History 1361.

149 Mayer (n 143) 69.

150 id, xiv.

that French administrative law was a model, and it was also regarded as such elsewhere, including Italy.

6 German Systematics in Italy

In Italy, the initial similarities to French legal culture were evident in the work of Romagnosi. After teaching private law, he devoted himself to the emergent administrative law. The dominant influence of French public law philosophy can be seen first of all in the systematic approach to the study of administrative institutions. It may also be found in the belief that questions of public interest prevailed over private ones since this reflected to the 'order of things'; it may also be seen in the concern for protection from the excessive exercise of power by public authorities.[151] Well after Romagnosi, Italian lawyers devoted particular attention to the works of Gérando and Macarel.[152]

The 1880s were a time of discontinuity. A new strand of thinking with regard to public law was emerging. It was associated with Orlando and other public lawyers who were either his disciples or close colleagues. Two aspects of his scholarship, in particular, are relevant to our purposes here. The first was the influence of German systematics. After studying law in Italy, Orlando spent a year in Munich, where he became familiar with the works of Gerber and Laband concerning the *Rechtsstaat*. A few years later, he published his 'manifesto' for a new form of public law. He lived at a time of rapid social and political change, when the institutions of the new Italian State were yet to be consolidated. He affirmed that, in this context, the duty of public lawyers was to strengthen these institutions by adopting 'the legal method' and seeking the guidance of first principles.[153] As Orlando put it in very clear terms, this method was inspired by German systematics, which, unlike others, made a clear distinction between the study of law and that of politics and philosophy. His theory of administrative law was also influenced by the ideology of the *Rechtsstaat*. He echoed Mayer's emphasis on the administrative act, viewed as a manifestation of the sovereignty of the State, as well as the need for legal

151 G Romagnosi, *Instituzioni di diritto amministrativo* (1821; Il Mulino 2015).

152 See A Sandulli, 'Administrative Law Scholarship in Italy (1800–2000)' (2010) 60 Riv trim dir pubb 1055.

153 VE Orlando, *I criteri tecnici per la ricostruzione giuridica del diritto pubblico* (1889), in *Diritto pubblico generale* (Giuffrè 1954) 3. On Orlando's role in the formation of a new public law, see S Cassese, *Cultura e politica del diritto amministrativo* (1973), French transl by M Morabito, *Culture et politique du droit administratif* (Dalloz 2008) 25.

boundaries in order to prevent arbitrariness in the logic of the *Rechtsstaat*.[154] It is this combination of method and values that underpins the dominant strand in public law.

The other aspect of his thought that deserves mention is his opinion on commonality and diversity. He argued that doctrinal constructs were largely different, while the general principles were the same everywhere.[155] The same opinion was expressed four decades later by a German *emigré* to the US, Morstein Marx, for whom it was 'proper to speak of Continental administrative law as one system, irrespective of distinguishable shades which mark the individual national setting'.[156] The question we need to address in the next chapter is precisely whether there was simply a diffusion of the French model or a more complex phenomenon. Before so doing, it is helpful to pause a little, in order to point out the role of legal scholarship. For all the importance of judge-made law, scholars such as Hauriou, Duguit, Mayer and Orlando provided a distinctive and authoritative contribution to the development of law in terms of the search for a conceptual unity of administrative law, as well as of the definition of a body of general principles which could be used to control the exercise of governmental powers in order to avoid arbitrariness.[157]

7 Beyond the State: Judicial Remedies in the European Communities

The conjecture that a common core of administrative laws emerged during the last decades of the 19th century from the viewpoint of judicial review of administration can be further tested on another ground; that is, beyond the State. The EC/EU is fertile ground for our analysis, because there was an

154 For example, Gneist's essay had been translated by Artom: *Lo Stato secondo il diritto e la giustizia nell'amministrazione* (UTET 1881). It was to these German theories that also politicians such as Minghetti referred to in their critique of arbitrariness: *I partiti politici e l'ingerenza loro nell'amministrazione* (Zanichelli 1881) 237.

155 VE Orlando, *Principi di diritto amministrativo* (Barbèra 1891) 16.

156 See F Morstein Marx, 'Comparative Administrative Law: The Continental Alternative' (1942) 91 Un Pennsylvania L Rev 118; R Parker, 'Review of Adamovich, Handbuch des österreichischen Verwaltungsrechts (1952)' (1956) 5 AJCL 147 (same remark). But see JM Galabert, 'The Influence of the Conseil d'Etat outside France' (2000) 49 Int'l & Comp L Q 700 (mentioning Belgium, Netherlands, Italy, Greece, Turkey, as well as Egypt, Lebanon and Colombia outside Europe).

157 See C Harlow, 'Changing the Mindset: the Place of Theory in English Administrative Law' (1994) 14 Oxford J L St 419, at 420 (for the remark that England differed from this trend).

administration entrusted with powers directly affecting citizens and firms, but the treaties made no specific provision for administrative law.

The starting point is what is generally regarded as the genetic act of European integration; that is, the speech (drafted by Monnet and other high civil servants) given by the French foreign Minister Schuman on 9 May 1950.[158] Schuman proposed, first, that the High Authority should discharge regulatory policy in two particular, but strategic, areas: coal and steel, and, second, that it would have the power to take 'decisions' which would 'bind France, Germany and other member countries', as well as decisions which would 'be enforceable' within their legal systems, ie, on the bodies operating in them. Third, Schuman envisaged establishing a 'means of appeal against the decisions of the Authority'. There now existed the idea of a counterweight – although not yet of judicial remedies – to hold those regulatory powers to account. Judicial remedies in the strict sense were provided for by the Treaties of Paris (1952) and Rome (1957), which created the ECJ. This topic has generated much comment in scholarly literature, and there are a variety of opinions on the nature of the Court. However, especially among the early commentators, at least three features of the new institution were clear enough.

Firstly, once the drafters of the treaties had taken the unprecedented decision to endow the High Authority with the power to take decisions *vis-à-vis* the States and businesses, they were faced with a 'similar problem' to that typical of national legal systems: how to ensure judicial protection from unlawful acts by public authorities, in this case of a supranational nature.[159] They opted for a fully-fledged court of law, whose mission was to ensure compliance with the law in the interpretation and application of the treaties, namely the ECJ.[160] It had a clear 'vocation to ensure observance of law and justice'.[161] Schwarze, among others, has suggested that the switch from the internal appeals provided by the Schuman Declaration to judicial mechanisms was requested by the German delegation and that Monnet was initially reluctant to accept it.[162] This is an interesting contribution to a debate that normally points out the

158 For further remarks, see JHH Weiler, 'The political and legal culture of European integration: An exploratory essay' (2011) 9 I-CON 678, at 683.

159 See G Bebr, 'Protection of private interests under the European Coal and Steel Community', (1956) 42 Virginia L Rev 879, at 880.

160 Article 29, Treaty of Paris establishing the ECSC; Article 173, Treaty of Rome, establishing the EEC. See Craig (n 60) 319 (observing that the ECJ was "mainly an administrative court").

161 Stein and Hay (n 55) 375. See Craig (n 60) 313.

162 J Schwarze, 'Concept and Perspectives of European Community Law' (1999) 4 Eur Public L 227, at 229.

influence exerted by French ideas, norms and institutions.[163] This influence showed through in two choices made by the drafters of the ECSC Treaty: to institute an auxiliary of the Court, the advocate-general,[164] the equivalent of the *commissaire du gouvernement* with the French *Conseil d'État*, but it did not exist within the other four legal systems with a Council of State and the adoption of a strict separation of powers between administrative and judicial institution, in the sense that the Court could only annul contested decisions without altering their contents.[165]

Secondly, not only did supranational institutions show the influence of national administrative laws, but even the basic principles governing their action were not newly created but 'were largely drawn from the public laws of the member states'.[166] According to Lagrange, a member of the French *Conseil d'État* who took part in the negotiations of the Treaty of Paris and was later one of the first advocates-general, the Treaty included all the actions allowed before the Conseil, particularly those for annulment and liability.[167] More evidently, the Court's grounds for judicial review bore a similarity to those found in French administrative law. There were four, including lack of competence, procedural violations, violation of the Treaty or 'any other rule of law relating to its application', and misuse of power ('*détournement de pouvoir*').[168] Anyone familiar with public law systems will be aware that these grounds for review coincided almost literally with those of the *Conseil d'État*.[169] It was precisely for this reason that some commentators argued that French administrative law could in many instances 'serve as a valuable secondary source of law' in interpreting the provisions of the treaties that drew on established French principles and rules.[170] However, other national laws, notably those of Belgium and Italy, included grounds of review such as lack of jurisdiction, infringement of

163 Bebr (n 159) 881 (for whom the Community structure and its law were 'strongly influenced' by French administrative law).

164 Article 31, ECSC Treaty; Article 173, EEC Treaty.

165 See DG Valentine, 'European Coal and Steel Community' (1955) 18 Modern L Rev 187 (commenting the first two rulings of the ECJ).

166 Bebr (n 159) 881.

167 M Lagrange, 'La Cour de justice des Communautés européennes du Plan Schuman à l'Union européenne' in P-H Teitgen (ed), *Mélanges Fernand Dehousse* (Editions Labor 1979) II, 137. See also T Buergenthal, 'Appeals for annulment by enterprises in the European Coal and Steel Community' (1961) 10 AJCL 227, at 228 (same thesis).

168 Article 33, ECSC Treaty; Article 173, EEC Treaty.

169 Stein and Hay (n 55) 384–385 (adding that similar grounds for appeal can be found in common law countries, for example natural justice and abuse of discretion); Schwarze (n 162) 20.

170 Buergenthal (n 167) 228, fn 7.

the law, and misuse of powers. Moreover, the reference made in Article 33 to the violation of a procedural requirement had some analogies with the Anglo-American concept of due process and fairness[171] and the same can be said of the provision whereby, prior to imposing a sanction, the High Authority had to 'give the interested enterprise an opportunity to present its views'.[172]

Lastly, Article 33 of the ECSC Treaty confirmed the earlier remark regarding the importance of the twin objectives of seeking to ensure regulatory effectiveness and holding power accountable. It established that the Court could not examine the evaluation of the situation resulting from economic facts or circumstances in the light of which the High Authority made its decisions, except when it was alleged to have misused its powers. Although there is no provision in the EEC Treaty with the same content as Article 33, in numerous instances the Court has declared that EC institutions enjoyed wide discretionary powers with regard to both the definition of the goals to be achieved and the choice of the appropriate means.[173]

At this point, a final comment is necessary. As the new administration was entrusted with powers that directly affected business, it looked like an obvious choice to draw inspiration from national administrative laws, and the French one was particularly important. It would not be appropriate, however, to say that there was simply a transposition of French institutions and norms. On the one hand, the administrative laws of the six founders of the Communities (France, Germany, Italy, Belgium, the Netherlands and Luxembourg) largely shared the grounds for appeal.[174] On the other hand, there were additional and innovative elements, for example reference to 'any other rule of law'. The EC thus developed institutionally as an amalgam of national systems. The next step of our analysis is to consider whether a common core emerged at the level of what the French call '*le fonds du droit*'. This matter will be addressed in the next chapter.

171 Stein and Hay (n 55) 383.

172 Article 36 (1), ECSC Treaty. For further remarks, see Bebr (n 159) 896.

173 Stein and Hay (n 55) 393; P Craig, 'Legality, Standing and Substantive Review in Community Law' (1994) 14 Oxford J Leg St 507, at 532; id. (n 60) 351 (describing the Court's 'light touch' on facts and discretion).

174 Bebr (n 159) 881; Lagrange (n 167) 139 (according to whom the French system was, at least in part, '*connu du droit des autres Etats members*'; that is, known by the other legal cultures).

CHAPTER 3

The Judicial Construction of General Principles (1890–1910)

We saw in the previous chapter the frequency and significance of borrowing and transplanting ideas, institutions, and norms among various European legal systems. This chapter discusses the outcome of these judicial mechanisms and decisions by first looking at the meaning and importance of our empirical analysis and then by illustrating the results, including a look at the rise of litigation, focusing on the problems facing courts and the solutions they devised to solve them. Particular attention will be given to the importance of judge-made law and especially to general principles such as legality and procedural fairness. We will argue that the historical evidence highlights the difficulties of the traditional view that there was a fundamental diversity, a divide, among European administrative laws.

1 An Empirical Analysis

There is, of course, more than one way to conduct a diachronic analysis. It is sufficient to glance through the pages of the most representative public lawyers at any given time to grasp the role of general principles. Alternatively, in the light of the existence of legislation introducing adjudicative mechanisms, a careful analysis may provide the basis for comparing their powers and styles of review in a way similar to that adopted by Laferrière in the same period. Lastly, an empirical analysis, based on an examination of judicial decisions, can also be made.

The first approach is especially appealing to those who emphasize the role of scholarship[175] and thus deem that administrative law did not exist before its conceptualization in academic literature.[176] Underlying this approach is an unspoken premise, namely that legal literature reflects the institutions that actually work in other systems. There are at least two difficulties with this

175 For example, Dicey, *Introduction to the Study of the Law of the Constitution* (n 22) 369, cited Leon Aucoc and other French authors, as well as Otto Mayer's treatise on German administrative law.

176 See Mannori and Sordi (n 79).

assumption, however. The first is the risk of failing to admit that things – in our case legal realities – might exist before being conceptualized by scholars.[177] Secondly, their reliability is even more questionable given the difficulty in distinguishing between description and prescription, most notably in Dicey. While it is true that context matters, we must also accept that ideology matters too.

Laferrière's approach sees the expansion of administrative justice in more functional and less ideological terms. And yet, the premise of *legislation comparée* has in itself been challenged by two distinct views, each of which ascribes less importance to legislation. Firstly, a scholar of comparative law has to examine not only legal rules but also the broader context in which they operate[178] as courts have to apply legislation, and the legislative measure ends up turning into something different from the political expectations underlying it. Secondly, until a few decades ago, the role of legislation in administrative law was far less incisive than in other fields, especially in countries with codes of law. Thus, for example, Jennings observed that Belgian jurisprudence had 'by a series of important decisions of the courts since 1920 adopted the main body of French administrative courts relating to *fautes de service*'.[179]

The reasons just mentioned support the third approach. It builds on the insights of leading *fin-de-siècle* authors such as Hauriou, who argued that administrative law was essentially judge-made.[180] However, it is not enough to gather facts: they must be assessed.[181] The next section provides an analysis of judicial decisions, followed by some remarks concerning the interplay between commonality and diversity.

2 Administrative Litigation: Similar Problems

A few preliminary caveats may be appropriate at this point as the data available are both differentiated and fragmented. They are differentiated because, at the beginning of the timeframe of interest to us, just a few dozen disputes were adjudicated in the Habsburg Empire and Italy, in contrast with the hundreds

177 For this remark, see Bigot (n 35) xxv.

178 J Bell, 'Comparing Public Law' in A Harding and E Orocu (eds), *Comparative Law in the 21st Century* (BIICL 2002) 236.

179 I Jennings, 'Administrative Law and Administrative Jurisdiction' (1938) 20 J Comp Leg & Int Law 100.

180 Hauriou, 'Droit administratif' (n 47) 6.

181 P Badura, *Die Methoden der neuren Allgemeines Staatslehre* (Palm and Enke 1959).

of disputes that the French *Conseil d'État* decided each year. Moreover, generalizations are problematic because the data shows state-by-state and year-to-year variations. With these *caveats*, two tendencies emerge: firstly, there was a general increase in litigation concerning public authorities, and, secondly, the work of the courts defined and refined general principles. This phenomenon will be examined in the next section, while the question of litigation will be analyzed here in both quantitative and qualitative terms.[182]

Quantitatively, the trend can be measured according to the increasing number of cases brought before the courts either seeking the annulment of an act or measure adversely affecting individual rights or to sue a government for damages. In the early years of the period examined here (1890), French administrative courts handled hundreds of cases a year,[183] while the other national courts held but a few dozen hearings. However, two decades later, the gap had become ever smaller. For example, of the 300-plus cases adjudicated by the Italian Council of State over these two decades, the majority were brought in the closing years.

In qualitative terms, a growing number of claims were brought against administrative measures limiting civil and economic rights. Everywhere, direct attacks on these restrictive measures came from those subject to police measures meted out on the grounds that they had acted against shared social values or threatened the political order, such as persons considered to be rioters or seditious elements. Likewise, many applicants challenged expropriations and other measures limiting the right to property, such as demolition orders, the imposition of duties on the owners of land bordering rivers, and the transformation of private roads into public ones.[184] Moreover, a new type of claim was brought against the use of government largesse. A leading example of this new trend is the ruling of the French *Conseil d'État* in *Terrier*.[185] After a municipal authority had promised a certain amount of money to cull vipers, the applicant brought evidence of his activity in this sense and sought to obtain the specified amount of money. The local authority refused to comply

182 This paragraph and the following ones draw on della Cananea and Mannoni (n 111).

183 A contemporary observer found that the administrative judge handled '300 cases of correction of excess of power': GJ Rosengarten, 'The French Judicial System' (1909) 57 U Pa L Rev 294.

184 For some remarks about flood protection in France, see Laferrière (n 100) 544. See T Perroud, 'Concluding remarks on the Unity of the Liberal World as Regards State Regulation of Property', in M Conticelli and T Perroud (eds.), *Procedural Requirements for Administrative Limits to Property Rights* (Oxford University Press, 2023) 316 (arguing that the ECHR has been based on existing common principles and has strengthened them).

185 *Conseil d'État*, 6 February 1903, *Terrier c/ Département de Saône-et-Loire.*

with its promise, and the lower court refused to let the applicant challenge its decision. But the *Conseil* recognized that the applicant had rendered a service to the local community, so this entitled him to receive money from the public purse. Lastly, the standards and practices concerning the recruitment of civil servants and their career ladder also changed over time. More and more lawsuits were being brought by persons contesting their exclusion from public employment selection procedures and by employees suing because they had not received a promotion or contesting disciplinary measures. In this regard, all national courts had to decide whether civil servants were entitled to certain rights to a hearing before being dismissed.

In summary, notwithstanding the diversity of the mechanisms available, judicial approaches reflected the emergence of similar problems related to the growth of government, as well as a notable similarity of opinion regarding the idea that provisions concerning access to legal remedies should never be narrowly construed. It remains to be seen whether this similarity also concerned standards of administrative conduct, a theme that will be considered in the next section.

3 Devising Solutions: Legality and Procedural Fairness

Although the courts showed an awareness that the execution of legislation increasingly required ministers and local authorities to be granted discretionary powers in the years of interest here, they also demonstrated a willingness to ensure that those powers were based on concrete foundations and were subject to conditions. The demarcation line between discretion and law was problematic because there were frequent divergences as to where the line should be drawn. It was, moreover, not uncommon for courts to make distinctions based either on facts or functional considerations. While acknowledging this reality, we may nonetheless observe that the demarcation line between discretion and law was facilitated by the idea of the way administrative powers were granted to public authorities.

The demolition of houses in the context of urban regulation is an example in point. A public authority could order the demolition of a house if it was unfit for human habitation or risked causing harm to others, or else if certain procedural requirements had to be met. Courts frequently verified compliance with both conditions. One kind of case was linked to the conceptual justification for judicial intervention, for which two grounds were provided: ensuring scrupulous conformity to the goals and boundaries set out in legislation, and the protection of citizens' rights. The second kind stressed administrative procedure as a means of checking government power in a broader sense. Oversight in this context had traditionally been exercised through a variety of mechanisms ranging from ordinary courts to bodies that were formally part of the executive branch but enjoyed some degree of autonomy. It also started to be become part of administrative procedure itself.

This type of justice is important when addressing the theme of administrative procedure. One starting point is the legislation that created the Administrative Court of the Habsburg Empire. It rested on the then-novel premise that everyone was entitled to challenge a measure taken by government authorities. In the absence of specific procedural requirements laid down in legislation, it was the Court that clarified the meaning of the relatively brief text the provision that referred to the infringement of essential procedural requirements. In so doing, it referred to ideas and beliefs about public law that could be considered to be widely held, particularly with regard to public authorities deciding without hearing those who would be adversely affected by the effects of their decisions. A ruling of 1884 and another of 1894 provide good examples of what was required. In the first case, a road built and managed by private individuals was transformed into a public road. The question at issue was not so much the existence of the authority to transform a road, which was justified either by the power of eminent domain or was laid down in specific regulations. The problem was, rather, how this authority was exercised, because the public body in question had provided these individuals with no opportunity whatsoever to be heard. Interestingly, the Court endorsed their claim that they had a right to be heard on the grounds that this was in the 'nature of things' ('*Natur der Sache*') and annulled the challenged measure.[186] Similarly, the Court observed that public authorities were required to hear interested individuals. It added that this was necessary in order to gather and balance all the relevant facts.[187] On the facts of the case, it would appear that the rules that follow from the nature of the things were infringed because the public authority failed to carry out a thorough fact-finding procedure before reaching a final decision.[188] Alternatively, the Court's policy may be seen to reflect the idea that individuals being heard was a natural consequence of their status within society.

In terms of this rationale of procedural safeguards, a similarity between the rulings of the German and Italian administrative courts emerges. A ruling issued by the Bavarian administrative court is particularly helpful in understanding

186 Judgment of 24 October 1884, No 2263.

187 Judgment of 10 November 1894, No 8150.

188 See H Schaffer, 'Administrative Procedure in Austria. 80 Years of Codified Procedure Law' (2005) 17 Eur Rev Publ L 875 (pointing out the 'creative' jurisprudence of the Court).

the principles of procedural justice. Not only did the Court acknowledge that the applicant was entitled to receive judicial protection *vis-à-vis* a challenged measure on the grounds of procedural irregularity, but it held that the existence of a fundamental procedural flaw affected the legality of the measure even though the applicant had not referred to that specific infringement.[189] It thus appeared to no longer consider itself bound by the old maxim that a court may decide solely on the basis of the arguments (and evidence) presented by the parties and in accordance with the law.

A glance at the case law of the Italian Council of State confirms that administrative courts did not hesitate to be bold. In the early years of the last decade of the century, the application of the *audi alteram partem* principle in the field of public employment was at a low ebb in the case law of Italy's highest civil court, the *Corte di Cassazione*. Either because of its positivist attitude or from a sense of deference towards the political authorities, the Court held that civil servants could be dismissed without notification of the charge against them or an opportunity to be heard unless this was explicitly provided for by sector-specific rules. Conversely, in *Chiantera*, when the former secretary general of a municipality challenged his dismissal on the grounds that he had not been heard, the Council of State provided a concise but illuminating discussion of the principle. It rejected the defendant's positivist argument that administrative procedure was not subject to the more stringent requirements of criminal trials. It argued that hearing the accused person was a 'principle of eternal justice, reflecting the sacred right of defence'.[190]

In a country such as Belgium, where ordinary courts reviewed administrative action, the judge not only followed the same reasoning, but also used almost the same words. The case concerned the dismissal of a doctor who worked in a public institution. When the doctor challenged the dismissal on the ground that he had not had a real opportunity to be heard, the respondent argued that procedural rules had no place in that context. The court did not accept this argument, holding that the right to be heard derived from a 'higher principle of justice', though it rejected the application on the grounds that he had had more than one opportunity to make his case.[191] This confirms that, in the foundational period of administrative law, conceptual doctrines that had characterized earlier eras in other fields of the law demonstrated surprising

189 Judgment of 30 March 1903.

190 Fourth chamber, decision of 29 December 1895, no 423 (my translation), followed by another one in 1896, *Carnevale*.

191 Brussels Tribunal, judgment of 3 December 1973.

vitality[192] and contributed to shaping the justification and content of process rights, in systems with different courts.

It may be interesting to compare these findings with those concerning the two legal systems that have traditionally been viewed as being not simply different but incompatible, namely those of France and England. The French *Conseil d'État* did not explicitly refer to general principles of law. However, it discretely applied them in more varied ways. One of these was to distinguish the *détournement de pouvoir*, ie, the misuse of powers, from the *détournement de procédure*, which occurred when the administration followed a procedure other than that envisaged by existing rules.[193] Another way was to give weight to the circumstance that a specific formality had been disregarded, or a specific process right had been infringed. This is confirmed, *a contrario*, by the *Conseil's* decision in *Winkell*, where it affirmed that a particular civil servant was not entitled to be heard before dismissal[194] on the ground that he had taken part in a strike. *Commissaire du government* Tardieu argued that the legislation of 1905, whereby civil servants were entitled both to be notified and heard, was not applicable in this case. The *Conseil* endorsed this interpretation, and it is evident that it was strongly influenced by the fact that the needs of the State were involved. In his comment on the decision issued by the *Conseil*, Hauriou could not help noting that, if this was not juridically wrong, it was at least unsatisfactory, because it was not explained in terms of law. He went one step further – and it was a remarkable step – when he observed that the *Conseil d' État*, the arbiter of the legality of administrative action, could have simply refrained from applying the 1905 legislation on the ground that it was unconstitutional.[195] This was only because, in its opinion, the higher public interest required that notification and comment requirements not be applied.

On the other side of the Channel, two approaches to cases appear particularly relevant. One line of authority concerns natural justice under the guise of *audi alteram partem*. For example, in *Hopkins*, the Court of Appeal ruled that, even though an individual had erected a building infringing the by-laws

192 In a similar vein, see Craig, *Administrative Law* (n 23) 412.

193 M Hauriou, *La jurisprudence administrative de 1892 à 1929* (Sirey 1929) I, 258 (*'formalités de procédure'*). Interestingly, the Constitution of 1852 contained a renvoi to the rights recognized and protected by the Declaration of 1789: see A Batbie, *Traité théorique et pratique de droit public et administratif* (Cotillon 1862) 286.

194 Conseil d'Etat, 7 August 1909, *Winkell.*

195 M Hauriou, *Révocation de fonctionnaires publics se mettant en grève et communication préalable du dossier, Note sous Conseil d'Etat, Winkell et Rosier* (Sirey 1909).

of the Board of Health, the latter could not exercise its authority to demolish it without providing the owner with an opportunity to be heard.[196] Another series of cases concerned the dismissal of civil servants. In this respect, English courts can rightly be regarded as forerunners with regard to sackings in the light of the *Bagg*'s case of 1615.[197] This case is particularly interesting, firstly, because it provides a justification for procedural limits to power, which goes beyond instrumental rationales such as control over compliance with legislative intent because it is based on a non-instrumental rationale; that is, the idea that removal without hearing is in itself a bad thing.[198] Secondly, this case may be distinguished, in some respects, from later ones in which natural justice was applied only to judicial or quasi-judicial decisions.[199] Within these limits, the *Sharp* decision of the same year may be viewed as indicative of the gradual evolution of natural justice. When the Court affirmed, *per* Lord Halsbury, that the discretion accorded to public authorities had to be exercised 'according to rules of reason and justice, not according to private opinion, … according to law, and not humor', adding that its exercise could not be 'arbitrary, vague and fanciful, but legal and regular', it applied standards that in modern terminology would be called legality, rationality, and procedural propriety and fairness.[200]

Of course, these findings concerning deprivation of office and administrative limitations on the right of property cannot be over-generalized. In other areas, the courts may have given a more limited application to court hearing rights on the grounds that an overriding public interest required it or, more generally, the administrative authority was granted wide discretion. Special considerations could be pertinent, moreover, to particular individuals (for example, police forces) or circumstances (wartime). However, two facts emerge quite clearly. Firstly, courts applied similar concepts and techniques in similar cases with a view to ensuring that procedural justice was done. Secondly, administrative courts gradually ensured adequate protection of the rights of the individual. This improvement regarded, in particular, the French *Conseil d'État*. According to an American observer, Garner, it was 'probably safe to say

196 Court of Appeal, *Hopkins and Another v. Smethwick Local Board of Health* (1890).

197 See Craig (n 60) 35 (for whom the Bagg's case was of seminal significance for process rights); D Oliver, *Common Values and the Public-Private Divide* (Butterworths 2000) 45 (same remark).

198 For this distinction, see P Craig, 'Unilateral Single Case Decisions: A UK Perspective' in Ruffert (n 141) 38.

199 Court of Appeal, *Fisher v Jackson* [1891].

200 Court of Appeal, *Sharp v Wakefield* [1891].

that there is no other country where private rights are better protected against arbitrary and illegal acts of public officers'.[201]

4 Devising Solutions: Government Liability

Government liability in tort is another key test for our hypothesis, being traditionally regarded as one of the causes of the divide between the European systems of public law. Some weaknesses arising from this divide have already been illustrated in the first chapter, but it is time now for a more structured analysis from the historical and comparative perspectives.

Historically, it is important to bear in mind that all mediaeval legal systems shared the idea that the State could not be held liable.[202] The result was immunity, justified on the ground that the State or the Crown was the holder of sovereignty.[203] Thinkers such as Blackstone, who endorsed the maxim '*the King can do no wrong*', deemed that this was in the nature of things.[204] The famous ruling of the French *Tribunal des Conflits* in *Blanco*, that the State was not subject to the rules of the Civil Code governing non-contractual liability, could be – and was – viewed as a confirmation of the old doctrine.[205] This view was not, however, immune from weaknesses, because, it did not (necessarily) follow from the inapplicability of the rules of the Code that government was immune, as Santi Romano observed in relation to Italy.[206]

In approximately the same period, both French and Italian courts finally acknowledged government liability in tort. In France, the *revirement* came from the *Conseil d'État* in *Tommaso Greco* and *Auxerre* in the context of actions brought against the exercise of police powers. The *Conseil* not only rejected the traditional view that immunity was incompatible with State sovereignty, but it also rejected the doctrine that police powers were subject to a particular

201 JW Garner, 'Judicial Control of Administrative and Legislative Acts in France' (1915) 9 Am Pol Sc Rev 637 (for the remark that the decisions of the Conseil were not 'generally' in favour of the administration).

202 L Ehlrich, *Oxford Studies in Social and Legal History*, VI, *Proceedings Against the Crown* (1216–1377) (Clarendon Press 1921) 92.

203 R Bonnard, 'Civil Responsibility Toward Private Persons in French Administrative Law' (1932) 36 Economica 148, where he confirms the conclusions reached in his book *De la responsabilité civile des personnes publiques en Angleterre, aux Etats-Unis et en Allemagne (étude de droit public étranger)* (Giard et Brière 1914).

204 W Blackstone, *Commentaries on the Laws of England* (1765–1770) book I, Chapter 7, 244.

205 *Tribunal des conflits*, 8 February 1873, *Blanco*.

206 S Romano, *Principi di diritto amministrativo* (3rd edn, Società editrice libraria 1912) 62.

regime, coming under the special rules for servants of the State.[207] Once again, it was Hauriou who observed that the underlying reason was the need to avoid a denial of justice, while confirming the discretionary powers attributed to the public authorities in view of an increasing range of collective interests.[208] In the years that followed, the *Conseil d'État* maintained the distinction of legal sources affirmed in *Blanco*, mitigating it by defining and refining government liability in tort in order to ensure that the action of the State was subject to the rules of law.

In contrast with the assertion that French administrative law was a constant source of inspiration for other Continental legal systems, these did not opt for a wholly separate body of law dealing with actions for damages against public authorities, nor did they leave it to the discretion of administrative courts. Neither Belgium nor the Habsburg and German empires took this path. The basic idea was that government liability was to be regulated by the ordinary rules and was thus subject to the provisions of civil codes. The Civil Code of 1900, which introduced the same system of substantive law throughout the whole of Germany, specified it unequivocally. There was, however, an area where French administrative law was particularly influential, ie, the fundamental distinction between two types of administrative acts or measures formulated by the *commissaires du government*. On the one hand were the measures used for administrative activities that differed little from those of private bodies (*actes de gestion*), while on the other, there were measures such as those of taken by the police in the exercise of their public powers (*actes d'autorité*), as in the *Tomaso Greco* case, or the decision to limit free economic initiative by creating a monopoly, as in the *Blanco* case.[209] In France, this distinction served to delimit the boundaries of the jurisdiction of the ordinary and administrative courts, respectively. Elsewhere, it was used as the standard for setting the limits of government liability in tort. For example, Italian courts tended to exclude it when public authorities exercised discretionary powers. This confirms the circulation of legal doctrine, although it does not always assume the same form or effects that it possessed in other contexts.

---

207 *Conseil d' État*, 10 February 1905, *Tommaso Greco*; 17 February 1905, *Auxerre*.

208 M Hauriou, 'La consécration de la responsabilité de l'administration dans les services de la police. Note sous Conseil d'*État*, Section, Tomaso Greco et Auxerre (1905)' [2013] Revue générale du droit *online*.

209 See E Picard and G Bermann, 'Administrative Law' in E Picard and G Bermann (eds), *Introduction to French Law* (Wolters Kluwer 2008) 63 (for whom such a distinction was used to widen the scope of State action and administrative law).

In England we found no such distinction between the various types of administrative action. We found instead evidence of the persistence of a private law approach to liability, in the sense that there was no special legal regime for the servants of the State. At the end of the 19th century, the courts began to restrict the actions brought by individuals against the servants of the Crown. Thus, in *Raleigh,* Judge Romer radically excluded that, when they acted within their competence, they could be held liable for damage that occurred to others.[210] The underlying reason was that the wide application of discretion that exists in administrative law had to be taken into due account. The more restrictive policy seems to have prevailed at a later date.[211] For this reason, some decades later, Davis echoed Dicey's words, raising the issue of whether 'English courts at any time would have held the Prime Minister liable personally on account of the exercise of discretionary power'.[212]

5 The Role of Judge-Made Law and the Place of Legal Theory

Two final comments concerning the importance of judicial standards of administrative conduct and the interplay between common and distinctive traits may be appropriate at this juncture.

A quick comparison with private law is enlightening. Private law was codified in France at the turn of the nineteenth century (1804). This extended to the territories under direct French rule, such as Northern Italy, as well as other countries, eg, Belgium (1804). Other States followed, including Austria (1811), Italy (1865), Spain (1889), and Germany (1900).[213] Hence Roscoe Pound's opinion that the era of codes 'reinforced the idea of law as a body of rules in Europe'. Conversely, in the field of administrative law, there was no comprehensive and systematic body of rules. Accordingly, the 'creative role of the judge' was more important than it was in the field of private law. Not only the standards governing judicial trials but also those concerning administrative procedure were judicial constructs. In brief, administrative law emerged as judge-made law,[214] and general principles – rather than rules – were the building blocks of national legal systems.

210 *Raleigh v Goschen L.R.* (1898).

211 C Harlow, *Understanding Tort Law* (Fontana 1987) 128.

212 KC Davis, 'Administrative Officers' Tort Liability' (1956) 55 Mich L Rev 201, 202.

213 See S Samuel, 'The Codification of Law' (1943) 5 Un Toronto L J 148, at 150 (showing the differences between the French and Austrian civil codes) and R Pound, 'Hierarchy of Sources and Forms in Different Systems of Law' (1933) 7 Tulane L R 475.

214 See JW Garner, 'French Administrative Law' (1924) 33 Yale LJ 637; A Diamant, 'The French Council of State: Comparative Observations on the Problem of Controlling the

Universally, these were evolutionary principles; they were not the product of rational design but of individual decisions. What stands out regarding this type of decision is that the general maxim applied by the court is to be regarded as a broad, and often variable standard, allowing more than one application, depending on the facts and interests of each case. Although respect for precedent was systematized only in the English system, in continental legal systems too, the process of developing these standards began with a first case, followed by later decisions, gradually assuming a definite shape before being applied to further cases, but not without nuances. Such development was unavoidably gradual. Moreover, it was supported by the work of learned lawyers who systematized the principles elaborated by the courts. Mention must be made at least of the works of Hauriou and Tezner in the French and Austrian legal systems, respectively, which were well known to scholars in other national contexts.[215]

Aside from the empirical discovery of widespread judicial lawmaking, the question that arises is how the judicial construction of general principles was justified. Obviously, for the courts, the easiest thing was to say that their function was to discover – and not to make – the law, in order to avoid any accusation of arbitrariness and overreach. However, as noted earlier, they could seldom call upon principles already established by legislation. As a result, they had to choose between the following options. The first, used especially in the English courts, was to refer to the binding authority of longstanding principles, such as the two fundamental maxims of natural justice. Another option was interstitial lawmaking, namely filling the gaps left by statutory or customary law. In the French legal system, as observed by Letourner, this argument was reinforced by the prohibition of allowing denial of justice under the pretext that the law was obscure or that there was no law at all.[216] A third option was to make a reference to the core values of the legal order, such as justice and equity, not to be considered as a term of art in English law but, more broadly, as fairness and impartiality. Interestingly, the principles defined by the French *Conseil d'État* were said by Laferrière to be, in one way or another, 'inherent in

Bureaucracy of the Modern State' (1951) 13 J Pol 583 (same remark). See also M Shapiro, *The Supreme Court and Administrative Agencies* (The Free Press 1968) 106 (same remark about US administrative law).

215 B Schwartz, 'French and Anglo-American Conceptions of Administrative Law' (1952) 6 U Miami L Rev 433, 436. On Hauriou, see P Arrighi, 'Hauriou: un commentateur des arretes du Conseil d'Etat', in *Le Conseil d'Etat. Livre jubilaire* (n 125) 341.

216 Under Article 4 of the French Civil Code, 'a judge who refuses to give judgment on the pretext of the silence, the obscurity or the insufficiency of the law may be prosecuted as guilty of denial of justice' (my translation). See M Letourner and R Drago, 'The Rule of Law as Understood in France', (1958) 7 Am. J. Comp. L. 147.

our public and administrative law'[217] The decisions taken by the Austrian and Italian administrative courts concerning the right to be heard provide an example of this last way to justify the judicial construction of general principles. There was also, however, a reminiscence of the doctrines of natural law. On the other hand, the Austrian Civil Code of 1811 expressly gave judges the power to refer, if necessary, to the principles of natural law. But, as observed earlier, far from being restricted to descriptive analysis of judicial performance, legal scholarship played an important role in defining the general framework within which the courts evaluated the activities of government and administration.

It was within these terms that it was correct to say that judges made law. While new legislation required new administration, it frequently did not provide public officers with adequate standards of conduct. There were, therefore, some areas inadequately regulated by law, if at all. Those gaps and loopholes were filled by a new law, shaped by judges and jurists: administrative law.[218]

6 The Emergence of Common Principles

A further demonstration of the existence of common standards of administrative action would emerge four decades later in the case law of the ECJ, as can briefly be demonstrated from an examination of the *Algera* case.[219]

The dispute arose from an unlawful act issued by the General Secretariat of the Common Assembly of the ECSC. After issuing an act that granted some financial benefits to a group of employees, the administration became aware that the act was based on an erroneous analysis and consequently decided to withdraw it. The employees then challenged the administration's new decision, alleging that it did not have the authority to withdraw the earlier one and that its decision was unreasonable. The first problem was deemed particularly

217 See Laferrière (n 100) xiii and B Jeanneau, *Les principes généraux du droit dans la Jurisprudence administrative* (Sirey 1954), though the author has subsequently noticed the limitations emerging in the case law of administrative courts: 'La théorie des principes généraux du droit à l'épreuve du temps' in *Etudes et documents du Conseil d'Etat* (Conseil d'Etat 1981) 36. See also R Drago, 'The General Principles of Law in the Jurisprudence of the French Conseil d'Etat' (1962) 11 Am Univ L Rev 126. See also J Jowell, 'Courts and the Administration in Britain: Standards, Principles and Rules' (1988) 22 Israel L Rev. 410 (observing that for UK courts the justice of the common law had supplied "the omissions of the legislature").

218 See Mayer (n 143) 65 (for whom private law had 'ceased to be the only possible law').

219 ECJ, judgment of 12 July 1957, Joined cases 7/56, 3/57 to 7/57, *Algera et al. v Common Assembly of the ECSC* (*Algera*).

sensitive by the Court, since neither the Treaty nor the regulation governing staff expressly provided for such authority. Faced with a *lacuna* in the legal system stemming from the Treaty, the Court resolved it in three steps. Firstly, it stated that it was axiomatic that, in order not to deny justice, it was obliged to resolve the problem. It thus acted as if in EEC law there was a norm similar to the prohibition of the denial of justice established by the French Civil Code .[220] Secondly, it affirmed that, in so doing, it would look at 'the rules acknowledged by legislation, learned writing and case law of the member countries',[221] that is, from a comparative perspective.[222] Lastly, after examining national administrative laws, the Court observed that an unlawful measure conferring benefits on individuals could in principle be withdrawn or revoked everywhere, but there were significant differences related to the importance accorded to the passing of time. Therefore, it accepted 'the principle of the revocability of illegal measures at least within a reasonable period of time'. Interestingly, the Court paired an argument based on coherence – namely that if a certain measure is contrary to law, the public authority that issued it has the power (if not the duty) to withdraw it – with a comparative argument. In this respect, it examined all the relevant domestic laws and used an approach that might be said to be based on a sort of minimum common denominator while, in more recent cases, it has been less inclined to do so. Several other examples might be added, including good faith,[223] proportionality, and due process, but that would not add much to the general point that is being made here; that is, as Treaty of Paris laid down a thin legal framework, the Court was left to develop general principles of administrative law.

The Treaty of Rome brought a further impulse in this direction from the perspective of government liability. While the Treaty of Paris followed the French model of liability for *faute de service*, the Treaty of Rome took a different stance. According to Article 215, the non-contractual liability deriving from the damage caused by the institutions and servants of the EC in the performance of their duties would be regulated 'in accordance with the general principles common to the laws of the member states'.[224] Literally, the provision

220 J Schwarze, 'Judicial Review in EC law – Some Reflections on its Origins and the Actual Legal Situation' (2002) 51 Int'l & Comp L Quart 7.

221 ECJ, *Algera*, § III.

222 ECJ, *Algera*, § III (*'une étude de droit comparé'*).

223 See the opinion issued by Advocate-General Roemer on 15 July 1960 in Joined Cases 45 and 59/57, *von Lachmuller et al. v Commission*.

224 A similar provision can now be found in Article 340 TFEU. For further analysis, see W Lorenz, 'General Principles of Law: Their Elaboration in the Court of Justice of the European Communities' (1964) 13 AJCL 24.

referred to the Community. However, it could be interpreted as implying that the six founding States shared a general principle of tort liability. The existence of such a principle was implicit in the substantive decision that not only ruled out immunity but also clarified that the Community, not the employee, should bear the burden for the normal consequences of administrative action. It was implicit, too, in the *renvoi* to the 'general principles common to the laws of the member States'. The general point being made here is, therefore, that the creation of the new institutions rested on the understanding that there was not only diversity but also commonality between national administrative laws, at least at the level of general principles.

CHAPTER 4

Sowing the Future: Austrian Administrative Procedure Legislation

The previous chapters examined the consolidation of administrative laws, with a focus on judicial review. This chapter presents, instead, an account of the change that occurred after 1925; that is, the emergence of general legislation on administrative procedure. This change, as it emerged initially in Austria, affected some of the nations previously included in the Habsburg Empire. What were the main forces underlying this crucial transition, which conditions were fulfilled, what were the stages, and how did it come about? This chapter responds to these questions as follows: it provides an account of Austrian administrative procedure legislation; it argues that the term 'influence' is unsuitable for making sense of the interaction between legal systems in the area conventionally referred to as *Mitteleuropea* and suggests that the concept of 'diffusion' may be more appropriate; finally, it observes that Austrian ideas about administrative procedure also reached countries that did not adopt any form of general legislation.

1 Early Views on the Codification of Administrative Procedure

The idea and suggestion that administrative procedure should be regulated by legislation date back almost two centuries. In Restoration France, de Gérando was already devoting considerable attention to the study of administrative procedure and suggested its codification.[225] Three decades later, Mallein reconsidered the issue and concluded that the disadvantages of codification vastly exceeded its advantages,[226] a conclusion that would remain unchallenged in France for many years. Consequently, despite the influence of French administrative law from the point of view of judicial review, two other European

225 J-M de Gérando, *De la procédure administrative* (Thémis 1822) 4, 57 at 60. For further remarks, see B Seiller, 'L'administrateur éclairé. La procédure administrative non contentieuse selon Gérando' (2013) 33 Revue d'histoire des facultés de droit et de la culture juridique 425, at 428.

226 J Mallein, *Faut-il codifier les lois administratives: examen de la question* (Maisonville et fils 1860).

 | DOI:10.1163/9789004549579_005

countries seized the leadership regarding the regulation of administrative procedure, namely Spain and Austria.

In Spain, legislation was approved by Parliament in the same year as the Civil Code (1889). Though the Act dealt mainly with the judicial review of the administration, it also laid down a few general provisions concerning administrative procedure, particularly on hearing the interested parties and the notification of administrative acts.[227] Its importance cannot, therefore, be neglected, also because it set an important precedent for the administrative procedure legislation adopted in 1958.[228] However, its effectiveness was undermined because each central department developed its own rules of procedure, leading to the emergence of a 'disordered body of rules'.[229]

This explains why the Austrian administrative procedure legislation of 1925 was not the first.[230] However, with some justification, it is usually regarded as the most important of its time for two reasons. On the one hand, it meant that comprehensive administrative procedure legislation was enacted; on the other, this legislation soon exerted an important influence over other European legal systems. These aspects will be considered in the sections that follow.

A brief terminological clarification is called for. The term 'codification' is often used in more than one way. It is sometimes taken to mean a statement of existing practice in a piece of legislation. Another option is the definition of general principles with the approval of parliamentary institutions. This may preserve the flexibility of the law, but it is not regarded as a real form of codification, unlike the complete and systematic statement, in code form, of both general principles and detailed rules. There may be various solutions between the last two options, depending on whether the law is stated from sector-specific rules, practice and judicial decisions, or created.[231]

227 Act of 19 October 1889, known as '*Ley Azcarate*'.

228 G Langrod, 'La codification de la procédure administrative non contentieuse en Espagne' (1959) 12 R Adm 74 (same remark).

229 L Ortega, 'A Comparison with the Spanish Regulation of Administrative Procedures' (2010) 2 IJPL 296, at 297.

230 The opposite view, expressed by R Parker, 'Administrative Procedure in Austria' (1965) 14 AJCL 322 is thus inaccurate.

231 For further analysis, see Fromont (n 4) 11.

2 The Austrian Turn: Background

There is certainly no shortage of studies concerning the Austrian administrative procedure legislation of 1925, mainly – though not only – in academic works written in German.[232] It may be helpful to take stock of the existing literature from four points of view. Firstly, several commentators agree that Austria benefited from the extensive case law of the Administrative Court (*Verwaltungsgerichtshof*) created in 1875. For five decades, the Court's rulings obliged public authorities to respect not only traditional rights, such as property and freedom of trade but also procedural rights. The Court took important steps in this direction. Initially, it judged individual cases without even citing its precedents. It thus acted from a sort of micro perspective. A macro perspective was provided by academic works, particularly those of Tezner.[233] The macro perspective examined more systemic concerns and sought to address them.

Secondly, as is often the case with administrative procedure legislation, including that of the US and Germany,[234] it is the result of a complex and lengthy political process.[235] As early as 1875, when the Court was created, there was some debate as to the principles it had to guarantee, but eventually the very concise formulation that was approved referred to 'essential procedural infringements'. Subsequently, while some observers argued that the Court's case law was not sufficient to ensure adequate protection of individuals' rights, the executive emphasized the need for its action to be 'unhampered by legalistic norms'.[236]

Thirdly, there are some shortcomings in the standard account according to which there was not only a fundamental continuity between the judicial definition of procedural requirements and primary legislation but also a sort of natural progression. There are two aspects to consider. One is that a first attempt to adopt administrative procedure legislation was made in 1911, but it failed.[237] The question that thus arises is what conditions favored the 1925

232 See E Mannlicher, *Die Osterreichische Verwaltungsreform des Jahres 1925* (Springer 1926); G Pastori (ed), *La procedura amministrativa* (Neri Pozza 1964); MR Hernritt, 'La nouvelle procédure administrative autrichienne' in *Annuaire de l'institut international de droit public* (PUF 1932) 251; Schambeck (n 127) 215.

233 F Tezner, *Die rechtsbildende Funktion der österreichischen verwaltungsgerichtlichen Rechtsprechung* (Verlag der Österreich Staatsdruckerei 1925).

234 See W Gellhorn, 'The Administrative Procedure Act: the Beginnings' (1986) 72 Virginia L Rev 219 (discussing the process that led to adoption of the APA).

235 Schambeck (n 127) 219.

236 Parker, 'Administrative Procedure in Austria' (n 230) 324.

237 Schambeck (n 127) 219.

reform. The other aspect concerns legislative intent. According to the standard account, the legislator addressed the question of whether legislation should be required for administrative procedure in the framework of institutional reforms, at the heart of which lay the new Constitution. In other words, the legislative intent was to generalize and thus reinforce the procedural requirements drawn up by the Administrative Court.

However, there is more than one reason for viewing the argument from legislative intent with caution. First, a silent premise underlying the argument is that, in a democracy, parliamentary process operates in such a way that Parliament is either the direct initiator or the controller of all that emerges formally as primary legislation. But the reality is different, as most of what becomes legislation stems from the bills introduced by the executive. It is, however, amended as it goes through the parliamentary stages.

The argument from legislative intent is also weakened in a more specific way. It is predicated upon the assumption that Parliament simply did what it wished to do. For some, it did so principally intending to simplify administrative action, which might have contained public expenditure.[238] This assumption does not, however, fully accord with the facts. What the facts tell us is that the inclusion of administrative procedure legislation within the reforms needed was also influenced by external pressure. It was one of the conditions for delivering the loan requested by Austria.[239] This is a healthy caveat against the belief that there is a necessary correlation between judge-made law and legislation in that the latter codifies the former. As will be observed in the next section, such a belief does not withstand scrutiny. Moreover, to the extent that Austrian administrative procedure legislation was influenced by external pressure, this indicates that we should be willing to consider a broader range of factors, including external pressure for reform.

Thirdly, the argument from legislative intent neglects the importance of context in another respect, namely, its cultural side. As a matter of fact, it does not take into due account the influence of a particularly prestigious school of thought: that of Kelsen. His influence was particularly noticeable in the constitutional requirement that 'the entire public administration shall be based on the law'.[240] It was within this cultural and institutional background, in the

238 Pastori (n 232) 97.

239 A Ferrari Zumbini, 'The Austrian AVG: an Underestimated Archetype with Deep Roots and External Factors' in G della Cananea, A Ferrari Zumbini and O Pfersmann (eds), *The Austrian Codification of Administrative Procedure: Diffusion and Oblivion* (OUP 2023) 195.

240 Article 18 (1) of the Austrian Constitution (in the original text: '*die gesamte staatliche Verwaltung darf nur auf Grund der Gesetze ausgeubt erlassen*').

golden years of Viennese culture, that a friend and disciple of Kelsen, Merkl, formulated a more precise concept of administrative procedure.[241] This was necessary, first, because it was vital to draw up a concept of administration, viewed as a public function similar to the legislative and judicial ones and, secondly, because this was felt to be indispensable in view of the postulates of the Vienna School, and its gradualist conception of law in particular. In his treatise, therefore, Merkl affirmed that an administrative procedure, in the strict sense, only existed if the course of action was not left to the free choice of the public authority but was previously defined by a legal norm setting out both the goal to be achieved and, to a greater or lesser extent, the way in which it was to be achieved.[242] Interestingly, it was only on the last page of that chapter that Merkl mentioned the Austrian Act of 1925, and he did so only to acknowledge that the Act had the merit of clarifying for the first time that public authorities could modify an administrative act. In other words, his concept of administrative procedure was not based on a particular legislative framework. It was, rather, the product of Kelsen's pure theory of law.

3 The Austrian Turn: Principles

The Austrian legislation of 1925 included five statutes: the first clarified that agencies would be subject to other statutes; the second was the Administrative Procedure Act; the third Act regulated criminal administrative procedure; the fourth concerned the execution of administrative decisions, while the fifth established simplification measures.

Of the general principles governing administrative procedure, at least four deserve mention. The first is the prohibition of bias or impartiality. Interestingly, these legislative provisions dealt with both family and political ties and contained a default rule concerning the 'other important reasons that are likely to cast doubt on their impartiality' (§ 7). Needless to say, this was a problem widely felt at the time, given the growing influence exerted by mass parties, as distinct from the political patronage of the relatively small political organisations of the liberal period.

241 A Merkl, *Allgemeines Verwaltungsrecht* (Springer 1927), Spanish translation by JL Monereo Pèrez: *Téoria general del Derecho administrativo* (Editorial Comares 2004). Not only did Merkl dedicate his treatise to Hans Kelsen, but he also explicitly referred to his mentor's work saying that the treatise had the purpose of drawing the consequences of the pure theory of law.

242 Merkl (n 241) 272.

The second principle was the individual's right to be heard before a public authority could take a decision that might adversely affect his or her interests. While this principle was found, at least from the time of the *Belle Époque*, in other legal systems, it was not only clearly stated in the Austrian legislation, but there was also an important distinctive trait, namely that participants' submissions could also be presented orally (§ 13), in which case they could 'be recorded in transcripts so as to convey their essential content' (§ 14) and, therefore, be kept. The generalized solution was more advanced than those of other legal systems at that time and is still so with respect to more recent legislative frameworks, where there is only an exchange of documents between citizens and public authorities. Thirdly, the files kept by the competent administration were accessible to the party concerned ('inspection', in the terminology of §17).

Fourthly, the content and form of the administrative decision were regulated in detail. To adopt Shapiro's subtle distinction,[243] there was not only a giving-reasons requirement in its simplest or purely procedural version, namely the requirement to provide at least some reason for the decision of a public authority exercising its discretionary power. There was also the requirement to provide reasons 'if the position of the party [had not been] fully taken into account or if the objections or applications of the participants [had been] rejected' (§ 58). There was thus a sort of dialogue requirement as the public authority was obliged not only to justify its choices but also to do so in the light of the arguments and evidence produced by the interested party. From the comparative perspective, it is interesting to add that the Austrian legislation neither imposed a procedure for rulemaking nor set out general standards governing it. In this respect, it differed from the US APA (1946), which established notification and comment requirements.

All this helps to explain the opinion that the US APA and the Austrian legislation can be situated at opposite ends of an ideal continuum. In this view, the former is an ideal type of administrative procedure legislation bringing debate and pluralism within the administrative sphere. The latter, instead, is based on the idea that administration, in the operational sense, should not differ substantially from the judicial function. This is evident at the level of general principles, such as neutrality and independence, and in the language of legislation, for example, when it uses the term 'parties', typical of judicial proceedings. Moreover, it clearly emerges in the recognition and protection of the right to be heard, as a protection from any Kafkaesque and dehumanizing

243 M Shapiro, 'The Giving Reasons Requirement' [1992] Un Chicago Legal Forum 175, at 186.

series of events that would give the individual no possibility to interact with those who wield public authority.[244]

In this case, there is, however, an excessive emphasis on the judicial model. Firstly, one commentator has observed that other requirements of natural justice, eg, that the tribunal be unbiased, were 'not so firmly entrenched in Austrian law'.[245] Secondly, the idea that each case must be adjudicated by an independent umpire is clearly appealing, but it should not be forgotten that the Austrian legislation was adopted at a time of fundamental change, ie, from that of a State entrusted mainly, though not only, with the functions concerning the maintenance of social order to one intending to have a decisive influence on the shape of the social order.[246] As a variation of the preceding argument, Austrian reformers were not unaware that a governmental agency also has the task of implementing policies. But, unlike in the US, they were less concerned with rulemaking, among other things because essential public services were delivered by public bodies[247] and retained the traditional idea that the administration *par excellence* is one which takes the form of individual decisions, which confirms that context matters, on both the institutional and cultural levels. However, as will be seen in the next sections, what characterizes it, together with the intrinsic quality of Austrian administrative procedure legislation, is its diffusion across Central and Eastern Europe.

4 An Area of Agreement between Legal Systems

The research findings show three points of general interest. The first is that there was indeed a spread of Austrian ideas and norms, but it was uneven. It was more robust in some nations that adopted some kind of administrative procedure legislation, namely Lichtenstein, Czechoslovakia, Poland, and Yugoslavia.[248] It was much weaker in other neighbouring countries, such as

244 Franz Kafka's *Der Process* was written between 1914 and 1915, but was published posthumously, in 1925.

245 Parker, 'Administrative Procedure in Austria' (n 230) 327.

246 Bachof (n 77) 368.

247 Parker, 'Administrative Procedure in Austria' (n 230) 325 (suggesting that the American problem of rate-making procedure was not as important in Europe because most public utilities were owned by the State).

248 See the national reports in della Cananea, Ferrari Zumbini and Pfersmann (n 239). These findings are confirmed by other recent studies, including B Bugaric, 'Post-Communist Slovenia: between European Ideals and East European Realities' (2016) 22 Eur Pub L 25 (2016) (affirming that the Yugoslav APA 'was categorically modelled upon' the Austrian APA) and J Stasa and M Tomasek, 'Codification of Administrative Procedure' (2012) 2 TLQ

Hungary and Italy, where no general legislation was adopted, although the Austrian codification generated interest among public lawyers. There was less interest, culturally and politically, in still other legal systems, those of France and Germany.

Secondly, that area of agreement between Austria and its neighbours was even more interesting than had been thought, from two points of view. The concept of 'administrative procedure' was regarded as distinct from the innumerable forms of administrative proceeding provided for, governed either by sector-specific rules or by practice and custom. Moreover, an area of agreement can be identified not only in terms of generic values and ideals such as justice and good governance but in terms of principles and standards. Two examples, concerning the right to be heard and the duty to give reasons, look particularly interesting. The individual's right to be heard was recognized and protected by all the other legal systems that adopted general administrative procedure legislation. There were, however, some nuances. For example, in Liechtenstein, not only were individuals entitled to make their case but each party had the right to 'express its views on all relevant facts and circumstances', including those 'brought forward by other parties' and experts.[249] The Yugoslav APA required parties to be 'duly heard'.[250] The Austrian solution concerning reasons was followed too, but to a lesser extent. Whereas in Lichtenstein the administration was required 'to justify the decision taken in a convincing manner',[251] Polish legislation established a more limited requirement to give reasons only in the event of an adverse decision, and that of Yugoslavia required the decision-maker to give a statement of reasons concerning the 'decisive' aspects but made an exception if the party's request was fully met.[252] While all this confirms that there was an area of agreement in terms of principles, it also shows that there were different aspects within such an agreement; these concerned both the contents of the procedural requirements and their limitations.

The third point of general interest concerns the relationship between general administrative procedure legislation on the one hand and sector-specific rules and case law on the other. This relationship has seldom been considered in previous comparative studies, but it is both interesting and important to understand whether, and to what extent, procedural protection has changed.

---

59 (affirming that the Czech Republic's regulation of administrative procedure 'stems directly' from the Austrian tradition).

249 Article 64 (3), Liechtenstein LVG.

250 Article 76, Yugoslav LGAP.

251 Article 83, Liechtenstein LVG.

252 Article 109, Yugoslav LGAP.

For this purpose, four issues have been selected, the first of which concerns the internal functioning of public authorities, especially disciplinary measures against civil servants; the other regards some important 'external' decisions, including authorizations and licences, expropriation, and urban planning.

Although these issues obviously do not provide an exhaustive picture of the whole field of administrative procedure, they furnish some elements of comparison. The dismissal of a civil servant provides a good test for understanding the extent to which the power of the State is limited. Interestingly, in all the legal systems that formed part of the cluster, the State had discretionary power to dismiss its servants, but this power had to be exercised within the strictures of administrative procedure. Moreover, the procedural requirements illustrated above, the right to be heard, and the giving-reasons requirement had to be respected. As regards the opening of a pharmacy, it was subject to administrative authorization, and the power to issue was discretionary, sometimes including an assessment of technical expertise, and sometimes 'good reputation and trustworthiness', too. However, this authority had to be exercised in a regular administrative procedure, in the course of which the applicant had the right to an oral hearing and then, in the event of an adverse decision, judicial remedies could be used in the courts. Expropriation is important, too because the right to property was protected by Western constitutions and civil codes. However, they allowed private property to be seized, provided it was in the public interest and that compensation was paid. There was nothing akin to any procedural protection equivalent to the 'due process clause' in the US Constitution. Some protection was provided by sector-specific rules and case law. For example, if building a railway line required the expropriation of both land and houses owned by an individual, a particular procedure – sometimes a legislative one – had to be followed, in the course of which the person concerned could intervene and receive legal assistance. Lastly, urban planning became an increasingly important manifestation of administrative power. Amid various differences concerning the nature of authority and its allocation, before 1945 a certain procedure had to be followed everywhere, in the course of which neighbours had to be informed; and in some cases, appeals could be brought before higher administrative authorities.

5 A Case of Diffusion

The discussion thus far has shown that Austrian administrative procedure legislation has been very influential. However, the concept of 'influence' is not satisfactory. Some use it at the macro-level, for example, in studies concerning the influence exerted by French administrative or judicial institutions in other legal systems.[253] Others use it at micro-level, for example, concerning the influence of the proportionality principle within the legal systems of the EU member States.[254] It is, therefore, used in different ways and contexts. Wieacker's analysis of the assimilation of Roman law in the field of private law in Germany confirms this criticism. He observed that 'the simplest concepts, such as 'influence' or 'impact', are harmless but rather meaningless'[255] and elaborated the contours of 'reception'. Nevertheless, this concept, too, is used in more than one way: generically, with regard to various uses of foreign law in various contexts, and specifically, in relation to the dissemination of Roman law in Germany and other parts of Europe at the time of *jus commune*.[256]

The concept of 'diffusion' conveys the impression of the spread of something across space.[257] While academic studies initially focused essentially on private law, there is also recent scholarship concerning borrowing and transplants in constitutional law.[258] The concept of 'diffusion' looks promising because we can rely on it to accomplish two goals. One concerns this particular case, and we may be able to identify the characteristics that made Austrian administrative procedure legislation significant for other legal systems. More generally, pinpointing the factors that led to the diffusion of such legislation could help better understand other cases involving similar legislative frameworks, including Spanish administrative procedure legislation in Latin America, which will be examined in the following chapter.

As regards *Mitteleuropa*, three elements are worth mentioning. First, this case involves a plurality of legal systems, unlike many others where there is a bilateral relationship between a donor country and a recipient one. A group of legal systems responded to like conditions in a similar way, adopting basically

253 See, for example, Galabert (n 156) 700.

254 See M Cohn, 'Legal Transplant Chronicles: The Evolution of Unreasonableness and Proportionality Review of the Administration in the United Kingdom' (2010) 58 AJCL 583 (offering an interpretation which highlights exchanges within Commonwealth countries).

255 F Wieacker, 'The Importance of Roman Law for Western Civilization and Western Legal Thought' (1981) 4 B C Int'l & Comp L Rev 257 at 270. See also CS Lobingier, 'The Reception of Roman Law in Germany' (1916) 14 Mich L Rev 562.

256 W Wiegand, 'The Reception of American Law in Europe' (1991) 39 AJCL 229.

257 W Twining, 'Social Science and the Diffusion of Law' (2005) 32 J of Law & Soc 205; id, 'Diffusion of Law: A Global Perspective' (2006) 1 JCL 237; S Farran and C Rautenbach, 'Introduction', in S Farran, J Gallen, J Hendry and C Rautenbach (eds), *The Diffusion of Law. The Movement of Laws and Norms Around the World* (Routledge 2016) 2.

258 See, for example, N Tebbe and RL Tsai, 'Constitutional Borrowing' (2010) 108 Mich L Rev 459.

similar principles and institutions. Nevertheless, they did so asymmetrically as the principles and institutions elaborated in Austria were taken as a model by the other legal systems, with a view to modernizing their administrative institutions. Finally, they did so without any sort of formal coordination.

Another element concerns the paths to reform. They were less indirect than we observed in our previous enquiry into the judicial formulation of general principles of administrative law from 1890 to 1910. For example, the English model of judicial review of administration was appreciated by both German and Italian liberals, also with a nod to the Belgian institutions. Conversely, in this case, there was a direct one-way transfer from Austria to its neighbours.[259] However, there was not so much a 'transposition' of Austrian law. Instead, its ideas and principles were developed within the other legal systems. This probably explains both the success of the attempts to innovate domestic legislation and its durability.[260]

There is still another important element that concerns the instruments used by reformers: formal instruments were used to adopt administrative procedure legislation everywhere. The predominant choice in both Poland and Yugoslavia, like Liechtenstein, was to act through parliamentary legislation, while Czechoslovakia proceeded by way of executive regulation. But there was always a formal adoption of the framework governing administrative procedure. However, the success of the Austrian model largely depended on the fact that it was not perceived as foreign law,[261] despite the dissolution of the Habsburg Empire. It was supported by jurists and judges who had worked within the Habsburg institutions and shared the same legal and linguistic culture. Legally, the primary justification for the requirements of procedure was the ideal of *Rechtsstaat* and its corollaries: that uncertainty about the procedure to be followed and disregard for the pre-established order make errors more likely, the outcome of administrative action less (or not at all) predictable and, last but not least, can undermine public confidence in the fairness and propriety of the decision-making process. Linguistically, German was the *lingua franca* of all those lawyers and judges. The process whereby ideas and

259 This expression is borrowed from Twining (n 257) 205.

260 For further analysis on this point, see D Berkowitz, K Pistor and JF Richard, 'The Transplant Effect' (2003) 51 AJCL 163, at 167 (suggesting that 'countries that have developed their formal legal order internally have a comparative advantage in developing effective legal institutions over countries on which' such institutions were imposed externally).

261 For example, the Austrian law on administrative procedure was translated and published in the Polish Official Journal. See also CT Reid, 'The Approach to Administrative Law in Poland and the United Kingdom' (1988) 36 Int'l & Comp L Q 817 (for whom the Polish law was 'closely modelled on the Austrian Code of 1925').

legal institutions spread beyond Austria through this group of nations was thus qualified by the existence of *vicinitas* and *affinitas* (vicinity or proximity and affinity) to borrow the concepts used by Gorla,[262] reinforcing those ties. As a specialist of the Habsburg Empire, Evans, observed at the end of his book on the making of the commonwealth that what had once been united could not be entirely dissolved.[263] Hence the remark that this commonwealth was a laboratory for multinational coexistence and should, therefore, be reconsidered not only because of the authoritarian and communist regimes that replaced it.[264]

6 The Wider Reach of Austrian Ideas

Thus far, we have considered the area of agreement that emerged between some legal systems. However, the area of disagreement is also significant because the negative results, which do not support the initial hypothesis and in some sense disprove it, limit and qualify the relevance and significance of the positive results.

To begin with, not all the peoples formerly included in the Habsburg Empire adopted general administrative procedural legislation. A case in point is Hungary, which only adopted such legislation after the failed attempt to eliminate Soviet rule in 1956. Notwithstanding the commonality of principles and practices with Austria under the previous legal system, both Hungarian politicians and public lawyers were against the adoption of general administrative procedure legislation. Nor was legislation of this type adopted by the major European administrative systems. Included among these is not only the UK, but also the principal administrative systems of Continental Europe in the first half of the twentieth century: those of France, Germany, and Italy. They provide a contrast to the *Mitteleuropean* countries because they did not follow Austria in adopting administrative procedure legislation during the timeframe of interest here. And the contrast is interesting for two reasons: their private law was codified at that time, and they adopted general administrative procedure legislation at a later stage.

262 Gorla (n 69) 639.

263 RJW Evans, *The Making of the Habsburg Monarchy 1550–1700. An Interpretation* (Clarendon Press 1979).

264 See Bugaric (n 248) 25 (observing that Slovenia did not completely replace the Austrian law after 1919).

It would thus appear that there was broad disagreement between the legal systems compared. However, we should ask ourselves whether there is a risk of superficiality in confining legal comparison to the level of 'positive law'.[265] Some commentators have observed that the area of disagreement among the legal systems of Europe is probably considerably narrowed if one takes into consideration not only legislative provisions but also other sources, including the general principles defined and refined by the courts, and government guidance to public authorities and administrative customs.[266] This observation aligns with our findings in the previous chapter that the supposed contrast between the UK and France was much less significant than had been believed. In all those legal systems, the general principles including legality, due process of law, and publicity served to prevent misuse and abuse of power by public authorities. It cannot be ruled out *a priori*, therefore, that the law on administrative procedure that can be found in the countries that have opted for one type of general legislation or another may not be very different from the law that exists in the absence of such legislation. This task will be accomplished on the basis of a 'factual analysis', as will be explained later.

Meanwhile, the importance of the Austrian tradition can be better understood from a dynamic perspective. During the previous century, it was the administrative act (*décision administrative*, *Verwaltungsakt*),[267] that held centre stage because it was the ordinating concept with a view to judicial protection in some respects, reflecting the vision of the contract that, according to a strand of thought in private law, prescinded from previous activities and operations. On the contrary, in the Austrian legislation of 1925 administrative procedure – as opposed to the administrative act or determination – had a fundamental importance. What emerged was a process-oriented vision of administration in the functional sense. Thus, a public authority could not take a decision – for example, as to whether a company should be awarded a license or should be ordered to cease a conduct regarded as not fairly competitive – without respecting certain procedural requirements. The influence of this view

265 For this caveat, see Schlesinger, 'Introduction' (n 2) 42.

266 JB Auby, 'Introduction' in JB Auby (ed), *Codification of Administrative Procedure* (Bruylant 2014) 27 ('living without an APA'); P Craig, 'Perspectives on Process: Common Law, Statutory and Political' (2010) 55 PL 27.

267 See M Hauriou, *Précis de droit administrative* (Larose & Forcel 1893) II (focusing on the '*acte d'administration*') and Mayer (n 143) (focusing on the *Verwaltungsakt*). See also S Rose Ackerman 'American Administrative Law under Siege: Is Germany a Model?' (1994) 107 Harvard L Rev 1279, at 1289 (for the remark that the German APA "does not apply to the formulation of legal regulations and administrative guidelines").

of administrative law was wide-ranging. Although expressed in highly sophisticated terms by Merkl, the Austrian tradition owed much to the previous fifty years of judicial development, to the work of academics such as Bernatzik and Tezner. Sandulli, the public lawyer who wrote the first monograph on administrative procedure in Italy, expressly recognized the importance of those works, for example.[268] Some years later, Langrod did not hesitate to admit that in the French and German legal cultures there was no such thing as a precise concept of administrative procedure.[269] More recently, Weil has pointed out that the French legal literature was 'uninterested in how the administrative decisions are taken … when one speaks of 'administrative procedure', … what is meant … is the procedure in the courts'.[270] Subsequently, administrative procedure has become increasingly important in public law.[271]

A doctrinal change thus occurred that was similar to what Shapiro highlighted with regard to the US. He observed that Gellhorn regarded as ideological (in a negative sense) Pound's charges that those who supported the adoption of the APA sought to regulate the practices of agencies 'rather than to subject those practices to the rules of traditional private law'.[272] Other writers, such as Landis, called for a greater focus on the administrative process.[273] As a consequence, a new 'model of administrative law as administrative process' emerged,[274] and the legal relevance of requiring that

268 AM Sandulli, *Il procedimento amministrativo* (Giuffrè 1940) 2.

269 G Langrod, 'Administrative Legal Procedure and Administrative Law' (1956) 22 Int J Adm Sc 5–94; id, *La doctrine allemande et la procédure administrative non contentieuse* (IIAS 1961) 7.

270 See P Weil, 'The Strength and Weakness of French Administrative Law' (1965) 23 Cambridge L J 243.

271 J Barnes, 'Towards a Contemporary Understanding of Administrative Procedure' in Z Kmieciak (ed), *Contemporary Concepts of Administrative Procedure. Between Legalism and Pragmatism* (Wolters Kluwer 2023) 23.

272 See R Pound, 'The Challenge of the Administrative Process' (1944) 30 ABA J 121 (criticizing the 'bad adjustment between law and administration') and CH Koch, 'James Landis: The Administrative Process' (1996) 48 Adm L Rev 419 (noting that Pound considered the growing administrative machinery as 'marxist'). See also JM Beermann, 'Common Law and Statute Law in Administrative Law' (2011) 63 Admin L Rev 2 (for the remark that the law of administrative procedure is heavily influenced by legislation) and AE Bonfield, 'The Federal APA and State Administrative Law' (1986), 72 Virginia L Rev (on the APAs adopted by US States).

273 JM Landis, 'The Administrative Process: The Third Decade' (1960) 13 Admin L Rev 17 (for the remark that the administrative process rarely received attention from students of administrative law).

274 Mashaw (n 52) 26.

administration – functionally intended – shall be conducted according to established and published procedures was gradually recognized. The importance of administrative procedure as the ordinating concept will have to be tested in two ways: with regard to legislation and through a factual analysis.

CHAPTER 5

The Development of Administrative Procedure Legislation

The previous two chapters have examined the development of judicial mechanisms in Europe and the judicial construction of some common standards of administrative conduct. The Austrian codification of administrative procedure in 1925 gave rise to a gradual change in the relationship between legislation and judge-made law. After 1945, the appeal of administrative procedure legislation grew and became so great that we find it increasingly widespread among various legal systems. It is appropriate, thus, to take stock of the various waves of legislation. This is followed by a closer look at three areas. One is, again, *Mitteleuropa*, which deserves further analysis in the light of the advent of socialist governments. Another is Spain, whose legislation also exerted a vast influence on Latin America. Scandinavia is the third area of interest. The chapter closes with an examination of the relationship between the types of State and administrative procedure legislation.

1 Moving towards Administrative Procedure Legislation

After WW II, as the functions and powers discharged by public authorities expanded and administrative action became more diverse, there was increasing awareness that it needed better regulation. This gave rise to political debates which lasted several years, sometimes decades, in countries such as Belgium and Germany.[275] Even where such debates had no immediate impact on the development of legislation on administrative procedure, they showed wider acceptance of the desirability of a general and comprehensive legislative framework. A 'movement towards administrative procedure legislation' thus emerged.[276]

The process of statutory law change is interesting to chart: three main phases can be discerned. The first regards a group of European countries that followed

275 See G Langrod, 'Le projet-modèle du code de procedure administrative non contentieuse en Allemagne occidentale' (1964) 17 Revue administrative 508.

276 This phrase is borrowed from B Schwartz, 'The Model State Administrative Procedure' (1958) 33 Wash L Rev & St B J 1 (pointing out the spread of state legislation in the US).

the Austrian model during the 1950s and the early 1960s.[277] Like Austria, they adopted general legislation on administrative procedure, but they were not liberal democracies. For example, Spain adopted its new legislation under the authoritarian regime of Francisco Franco. In Central and Eastern Europe, the legal systems that either kept their legislation or adopted it were under Soviet rule. The relationship between this type of legislation and the nature of government is, thus, more complex than it might appear at first sight and needs to be explored. The second wave affected Northern Europe. Norway was the first country to adopt administrative procedure legislation in 1967. Others countries followed some years later, including Sweden (1971), Germany (1976), and Denmark (1985).[278] The third wave came after 1989, the year several countries in Central and Eastern Europe began the transition from one-party rule to constitutional democracy.[279] Almost all those countries adopted similar legislation, often in the context of institutional reforms, including Lithuania (1999), Latvia and Estonia (2001), Bosnia and Herzegovina (2002), the Czech Republic (2004), and Bulgaria (2006). Meanwhile, various Western countries adopted one type or another of general legislation on administrative procedure, including Italy (1990), Portugal (1991), the Netherlands (1994), and Greece (1999), while Spain altered its legislation (1992). A common trend thus emerged.[280]

Three indicators may give a better idea of the changing landscape. The first concerns the sample examined in Chapter 4. In the fifty years that followed the Austrian law of 1925, none of the other major administrative systems – those of Britain, France, Germany and Italy – adopted such legislation, though this would change later. Of those nations, Germany was the first to adopt a general legislation on administrative procedure, followed by Italy and, eventually, by France. Britain is a notable exception where the 'unwillingness to codify

277 The laws existing before 1964 were translated into Italian in the volume edited by Pastori (n 232) while C Wiener, *Vers une codification de la procedure administrative: étude de science administrative comparée* (PUF 1975) included excerpts from them, in French, and G Isaac, *La procédure administrative non contentieuse* (LGDJ, 1969) explained administrative procedure legislation before and after 1945.

278 Scandinavian legislative provisions will be examined in section 4. On the German *Verwaltungsverfahrensgesetz* of 25 May 1976, see EJ Eberle, 'The West German Administrative Procedure Act' (1984) 3 Penn St Int L Rev 67.

279 For a comparative analysis, see J Elster, 'Constitutionalism in Eastern Europe: an Introduction' (1991) 58 Un Chi L Rev 447 (for whom those developments can be seen 'as a snowballing process').

280 S Cassese, 'Legislative regulation of adjudicative procedures' (1993) 3 Eur Rev Publ L 15; J Barnès, 'Administrative Procedure' in P Cane, H Hofmann, P Lindseth and EC Ip (eds), *The Oxford Handbook of Comparative Administrative Law* (OUP 2020) 831 (same remark).

reflects [...] dislike of the rigidity that can be attendant upon such reform',[281] though there is government guidance to public administrations with regard to consultation with citizens. The second indicator focuses on EU member States. The vast majority of them, namely twenty-four out of twenty-seven, have adopted some kind of administrative procedure legislation or another. The exceptions include Belgium, where there is general legislation concerning only some particular procedural requirements such as the duty to give reasons, Ireland, and Romania, where a draft code has been drawn up but not adopted. It can be interesting, though, to add that other European nations which have association agreements with the EU have adopted general legislation on administrative procedure, namely Iceland and Norway, which are included in the European Economic Area set up by the Treaty of Oporto (entered into force in 1994), as well as with Switzerland, which has signed a set of distinct agreements with the EU. It may be said therefore that there is a correlation, though not a necessary one, between adhesion to the European single market and the existence of this type of legislation. The third indicator concerns the Council of Europe. After the dissolution of Yugoslavia, all the nations that declared independence adopted their own legislative framework. Ukraine and Moldova did so several years after gaining independence from the USSR. Exceptions include such different polities as Ireland and the UK, on the one hand, and Belarus and Turkey, on the other.

Three brief remarks are appropriate at this stage. In quantitative terms, the existence of general legislation concerning administrative procedure is increasingly the rule rather than the exception. But although apparently similar and to same extent interconnected, these developments also differ in a number of ways, including the purposes and size of administrative procedure legislation. An important explanatory variable is the influence of previous legislation, for example in the area of the former Yugoslavia. Lastly, the legal systems in question present an optimal degree of diversity for comparative analysis: they are neither too similar nor too different. The focus for comparison is twofold. On the one hand, one can examine the processes through which the common trend has emerged. On the other, the outcome of these processes can be analysed and compared.

281 Craig, *Administrative Law* (n 23) 126.

2 Socialist Legal Systems and the Austrian Legacy

The reason for a retrospective on the group of countries – Czechoslovakia, Poland, and Yugoslavia – which adopted administrative procedure legislation along Austrian lines is that they were liberal democracies by the standards of the day (though Yugoslavia had been introducing some authoritarian elements as of 1929), but they underwent a regime change in the wake of WW II, as did Hungary. The term 'regime change' is used here descriptively, to denote that 'socialist' constitutions replaced the previous 'bourgeois' constitutions within the countries that fell under the control of the USSR and only regained full independence after 1989.[282]

The administration and administrative law of communist countries were extremely varied.[283] This diversity also regarded administrative procedure. The legislation of 1920s Czechoslovakia was maintained, although its interpretation gradually changed to accommodate new socialist values by virtue of an executive regulation adopted in 1950. In Yugoslavia, although the new rulers formally abolished all previous legislation, the Constitution of 1946 included 'general administrative procedure' among the matters reserved to federal legislation.[284] Judges and lawyers continued to regard the provisions adopted in 1930 as a frame of reference for solving issues arising between citizens and the public authorities until a new legislative framework was adopted in 1958.[285] In Poland, new legislation replaced that of 1928. Interestingly, the Commission

282 See CE Black, 'Constitutional Trends in Eastern Europe, 1945–48' (1949) 11 Rev of Politics 194 (asserting that those countries would have probably made efforts to re-establish liberal democracy, but fell under the Soviet influence) and H Kupper, 'Evolution and Gestalt of the Hungarian State' in S Cassese, A von Bogdandy and P Huber (eds), *The Max Planck Handbook in European Public Law: vol. I The Administrative State* (OUP 2017) 310 (discussing administrative law under Socialism).

283 For this remark, S Lubman, 'Book review of Z. Szirmai, Law in Eastern Europe' (1964) 64 Columbia L Rev 1364, at 1366 and JN Hazard, *Communists and Their Law: A Search for the Common Core of the Legal Systems of the Marxian Socialist States* (University of Chicago Press 1969) 8 (for whom there was 'room for considerable variation' within the 'family of socialist legal systems'; that is, not only the USSR, the six European countries that were members of the Warsaw Pact, Albania and Yugoslavia, but also China, North Korea, North Vietnam, Mongolia and Cuba). But see also the criticism expressed by HJ Berman – in his review of Hazard's book (1972) 66 Am Pol Sc Rev 249 – for whom that book found difficulties in fitting into its scheme States that were at the opposite spectrum of socialist laws. For a more recent analysis of some of those legal systems, see Scarciglia (n 137) (examining Albania, Bulgaria, Croatia, Serbia and Slovenia).

284 Yugoslav Constitution, Article 44, § 22.

285 NS Stjepanovic, 'The new Yugoslav law on administrative procedure' (1959) 8 AJCL 358, at 359.

tasked with preparing the new legislative framework was explicitly ordered to end 'a real risk of the persisting influence of bourgeois conceptions',[286] an order which was not fully respected. Where general legislation existed, further differences concerned the exceptions. For example, Polish legislation excluded not only taxation but also any procedure concerning the civil service. It entrusted the executive branch, however, with the power to extend its provisions to other procedure through regulations.[287] Hungary, too, adopted administrative procedure legislation with the Law of 9 June 1957, which unlike the others did not list the basic principles.

Nevertheless, there were some common features. Firstly, as in the Austrian legislation of 1925, administrative procedure legislation was of a general kind. For example, the Polish Code of Administrative Procedure established that if a legal provision referred generically to the provisions of administrative procedure, this had to be 'interpreted as being a reference to the provisions of the Code'.[288] Moreover, the Code provided a similar procedure for the various forms of administrative action, thus ensuring a unified pattern.[289] The Yugoslav APA, too, laid down a presumption of the applicability of its provisions to all administrative matters.[290] Secondly, administrative procedure legislation defined rules similar to the fundamental maxims of natural justice. As Austrian legislation prohibited any 'bias' of administrative officers and laid down detailed prescriptions concerning family, business and other important reasons,[291] the Polish Code established the exclusion of public employees from cases involving family or other connections. The Czechoslovak Act of 1967 provided, more succinctly, for the exclusion of employees from all cases where there was 'a doubt concerning their own unbiased approach'.[292] Moreover, both those laws recognized the right to be heard, as did the new Yugoslav APA, while they did not determine the procedures for rulemaking, unlike the US APA.[293] A further common element was the duty to give reasons. Austrian legislation required the public authorities to deal with all questions of fact and law that had emerged during the procedure,[294] as did the new Czechoslovak

286 C Reid, 'The Polish Code of Administrative Procedure' (1987) 13 Review of Socialist Law 60.
287 Act of 14 June 1950, Code of Administrative Procedure, Article 3.
288 id, Article 5 (1).
289 See Reid, 'The Polish Code of Administrative Procedure' (n 286) 819.
290 Stjepanovic, 'The new Yugoslav law on administrative procedure' (n 285) 360 (citing Article 2 of the Yugoslav APA).
291 Austrian APA, § 7.
292 Polish Code, Article 24; Czechoslovak Act n. 71 of June 29, 1967, part II, § 9.
293 Stjepanovic, 'The new Yugoslav law on administrative procedure' (n 285) 359.
294 Austrian APA, §§ 40–44.

legislation, which required public authorities to state 'the reasons', with specific regard to the 'facts relevant to the decision' and the 'legal rules on whose basis the decision was taken'.[295] The Polish Code, too, specified that an administrative decision had to include 'a factual and legal justification', with explicit reference to the facts proven and the legal authority for the decision.[296] In sum, although the laws of socialist systems differed in several respects, there was still an area of agreement concerning administrative procedure, thus reflecting the principles of the Austrian codification.[297]

The question that thus arises is why administrative procedure legislation endured, notwithstanding the change of regime. An initial explanation is that the diffusion of Austrian ideas and norms after 1925 had more far-reaching consequences than the adoption of individual rules within all those nations. This legislation was viewed as part of the accepted order of things, so it became socially undesirable to abrogate it, even after the regime change. As a variation on the same theme, it can be supposed that, as the new constitutions were in 'sharp contrast' with the political traditions of those countries, keeping administrative procedure legislation was an appeal to tradition.[298] Another explanation is the absence of alternatives in the dominant political system. As a matter of fact, the USSR never adopted legislation on administrative procedure, though a project was drawn up. Nor did the Democratic Republic of Germany do so.[299] A third explanation focuses on the purposes of administrative procedure legislation in socialist countries, which differed from 'bourgeois' legal systems. Whereas in the latter, procedural requirements were regarded as shields against the abuse and misuse of power by public authorities, in the former administrative procedures served to ensure the fulfilment of the goals of the State. This reflects a more general element of diversity. Bourgeois constitutions

---

295 Czechoslovak Act, § 47.

296 Polish Code, Article 107 (1) and (3).

297 Langrod, 'Administrative Legal Procedure and Administrative Law' (n 269) 632 (for the remark that the new laws deviated from the Austrian model only to a limited extent).

298 See Black (n 282) 196 and Stjepanovic, 'The new Yugoslav law on administrative procedure' (n 285) 359. See also Reid, 'The Polish Code of Administrative Procedure' (n 286) 817 (for whom this older stratum lay beneath the mass of socialist laws) and Wierzborski and McCaffrey (n 130) 647 (using the metaphor of 'layers'). These authors also affirmed that Eastern European countries 'still belong[ed] to the civil law world', for example in the sense that it was possible to obtain economic compensation for damage caused by public authorities.

299 See W Gellhorn, 'Review of Administrative Acts in the Soviet Union' (1966) 66 Colum L Rev 1051, at 1054 (noting that a draft code was prepared on the eve of WW 2, but was put aside) and G Langrod, 'La nouvelle loi yougoslave sur la procedure administrative non contentieuse' (1957) 10 Revue adm 631.

recognized and protected the rights of the individual, and imposed some duties justified precisely by the safeguarding of such rights. By contrast, socialist constitutions established citizens' duties with a view to achieving the new society.[300] Following this line of reasoning, administrative procedure legislation can be seen as an attempt to regulate society.

These explanations also appear to be helpful with regard to Hungary. After 1956, although its rulers could not import any rules from the legal system of the USSR, where no administrative procedure legislation existed, they could refer to the laws of the other socialist countries, which were varyingly influenced by the Austrian legislation. However, as will be observed in the next section, a different explanation is appealing, one which considers the relationship between administrative procedure and the rights of the individual.

3 Spanish Legislation and Its Diffusion in Latin America

The Spanish law of 1889, the 'Ley *Azcarate*', has already been mentioned in the previous chapter. The fact that it had to be, and was, implemented by executive regulations[301] does not, however, mean that it was not of fundamental importance, and there are three reasons why this should be so. The 'Ley *Azcarate*' was the first important attempt to state the main principles of fair administrative procedure through general legislation.[302] Secondly, though it protected the individual, it sought to promote administrative efficiency. Thirdly, its significance was confirmed by the new law adopted on July 7 17, 1958.[303] Even later legislation, adopted several years after the new Constitution (1978), was regarded as a continuation of the earlier legislation. It is important to address the debate about this Act for a twofold reason. On the one hand, while there

300 Article 76, Polish Constitution; Article 34 Czechoslovak Constitution. See Langrod (n 299), 632 (noting the emphasis on legality); I Markovits, 'Law or Order: Constitutionalism and Legality in Eastern Europe' (1982) 34 Stanford L Rev 513, at 516 (same remark); Reid, 'The Polish Code of Administrative Procedure' (n 286) 823 (noting that in socialist countries legislation had an educative function).

301 See V Santamaria de Paredes, *Curso de derecho administrativo segùn sus principios generales y la legislaciòn actual de España* (3rd edn, Establimento Ricardo Fé 1891) 824.

302 G Langrod, 'La codification de la procédure administrative non contentieuse en Espagne' (1958) 12 Revue admin 74; E Garcia de Enterria, 'Un punto de vista sobre la nueva ley de régimen juridico de las administraciones pùblicas y de procedimiento administrativo comùn de 1992' (1993) 43 Revista de Administraciòn Publica 205 (same thesis).

303 See the reasons given in the report accompanying the Spanish 1958 Act, published in the Official Journal of 18 July 1958.

is a very considerable literature on constitutional change, there has been less consideration of the dimension of change in administrative law. On the other hand, unlike its predecessor, the Spanish Act of 1958 as relevant and significant well beyond national borders, particularly in Latin America. This is the key to understanding the non-autochthone dimension of administrative law.

The new Act governing administrative procedure, adopted on 17 July 1958 was adopted when Spain had been under Francisco Franco's authoritarian government for almost twenty years.[304] Moreover, the government was building a new social system,[305] though it was not based on the same premises as the welfare states that were emerging in the UK and other countries in Western Europe. Consequently, as several commentators observed, the law on administrative procedure was not isolated. Quite the contrary, it was part of an ambitious set of administrative reforms. Among these was the new legal regime for public servants, as well as a renovated legislative framework for administrative justice. It can thus be said that although the Spanish Constitution of 1931 was not replaced, the political and administrative system was indeed reshaped.

There was both continuity and harmony between the new Act and its predecessor in the pursuit of uniformity. According to its first commentators, uniformity was one of the main goals of the 1889 law.[306] The new Spanish law, too, had the same goal. Hence, its provisions concerned all public authorities and were regarded as applicable in the absence of sector-specific rules.[307] In assessing the impact of the Act, it is therefore important to be aware that it defined a sort of paradigm of administrative procedure, which would serve as guidance. There was continuity, moreover, from the viewpoint of the contents of administrative procedure legislation. Several provisions of the Act sought to achieve the simplification of administrative action, for example by limiting the use of written administrative acts.[308] Last but not least, not all procedural infringements implied the annullability of individual acts and measures, but only those vitiated by absolute incompetence or totally prescinded from

304 For this understanding of the political regime, see G Hermet, 'Spain Under Franco: The Changing Character of an Authoritarian Regime' (1976) 4 Eur J Pol Research 311. Whether, more generally, 'authoritarian' regimes should be distinguished from totalitarian ones is an interesting question that requires separate treatment: they are considered in the same terms in K Kovacs, 'Avoiding Authoritarianism in the Administrative Procedure Act' (2020) 28 Geo Mason L Rev 573.

305 Langrod (n 302) 76.

306 Santamaria de Paredes (n 301) 820.

307 Spanish 1958 Act, preliminary provision.

308 Spanish 1958 Act, Article 41.

existing procedural rules.[309] The features briefly highlighted might support an essentially functionalist and technocratic interpretation of the Act.

There was, however, another side of the coin. The Act defined the essential principles of fair administrative procedure. Among these principles was the individual's right to be heard,[310] granted to all 'interested' persons; that is, on the one hand, those who claimed to have either a right or a legitimate interest and, on the other, those 'directly affected' by the administrative decision which the public authority was likely to adopt.[311] There was also a duty to give reasons for all administrative acts that fell within certain categories, for example, those that limited subjective rights and those which deviated from the criteria followed in previous cases or from the opinions formulated by advisory bodies.[312] There were also rules concerning the notification of individual decisions at their addresses. The existence of these procedural constraints can be explained in two ways. While the first focuses on the appeal to tradition, the other one takes external factors into account. Thirteen years after the end of WW II and the defeat of the Axis alliance, which had supported Franco during the civil war, the authoritarian government sought to obtain external recognition and foreign investment. Laying down a uniform regulation of administrative procedure could be very helpful in this respect.

An adequate awareness of the various purposes of administrative procedure legislation turns out to be helpful for understanding the other feature of the Spanish law of 1958, namely its relationship with administrative procedure legislation in Latin America. Three phases can be observed, the first of which includes the legislative provisions adopted by Argentina (1972), Uruguay (1973), Costa Rica (1978), Venezuela (1982), Colombia (1984) and Honduras (1987). The second wave includes the administrative procedure legislation adopted by Mexico (1994), Brazil (1999), Peru (2001), Bolivia (2002) and Chile (2003). The third wave includes the Dominican Republic (2013), Ecuador and El Salvador (2017). There has been, therefore, a diffusion of general administrative procedure legislation covering practically the whole of South America and part of Central America.[313] In this respect, there is a similarity with Europe, but also

309 Spanish 1958 Act, Article 47, (c).
310 Spanish 1958 Act, Article 91.
311 Spanish 1958 Act, Article 23, (a) and (b).
312 Spanish 1958 Act, Article 43, (a) and (c).
313 For a collection of Latin America laws on administrative procedure, see A Brewer-Carias, *Còdigo de leyes de procedimiento administrative en Iberoamérica* (Editorial Jurìdica Venezolana 2021). The importance of these laws has been highlighted by Bignami (n 45) 155.

diversity with regard to other regions of the world, where only a few nations have adopted some kind of administrative procedure legislation.

These laws are characterized by both diversity and commonality. As regards their scope of application, one technique is to generally define administrative procedure as involving the determination of the rights or interests applicable to particular persons, normally after certain steps have been carried out. Another technique is to make the general provisions governing administrative procedure applicable to the functions of central and local authorities, except those that are excluded (normally the functions of public prosecutors and those concerning taxation).[314] There are other two shared features. On the one hand, all these laws regulate the procedures that give rise to the adoption of an individual administrative act or determination with some also regarding contracts. On the other hand, their principles are fundamentally the same.[315] Featuring among these principles are, on the one hand, legality, procedural fairness and propriety, and publicity; on the other, effectiveness, efficacity, and celerity.[316]

There are three other elements that bear a certain relationship with the Spanish legislation. First, the Spanish Act of 1958 was characterized not only by its generic nature but also by the idea of the existence of a sort of paradigm of administrative procedure rather than numerous particular procedures.[317] Several laws adopted by the Latin American nations share this idea. Thus, for example, the Peruvian legislation focuses on 'general administrative procedure'.[318]

Second, while the Austrian general legislation on procedure employed the concept of party, the Spanish Act used a different one, that of interested persons ('*interesados*') and made a reference not only to rights but also to legitimate interests.[319] This is a concept that was already used in the Italian legislation of 1889. It conveys the idea that there is a variety of interests recognized by the legal order, some of which (legitimate interests) are protected with less intensity than others (rights). Several legislative provisions in Latin

314 See, for example, the Argentinian law of 1971, Article 1 (excluding military and defense bodies, as well as those maintaining public order) and the Mexican law of 1994, Article 1 (excluding the issues concerning taxation and the tasks of public prosecutors).

315 Brewer-Carias (n 313) 102.

316 See the Mexican law of 1994, Article 13 (mentioning, among other things, the principles of economy and celerity).

317 Venezuela, Law on Administrative Procedures (1981), title III, Chapter 1 (concerning the 'ordinary' administrative procedure).

318 Peru, Law No 27444 of 1994.

319 Spanish 1958 Act, Article 23, (a) and (b).

America, sometimes with the further specification that legitimate interests must be both direct and personal use the same wording.[320] The Argentinian and Peruvian laws are strikingly similar, except that the former refers to both legitimate interests and rights in the context of the provision regulating the right to be heard,[321] and the latter does so while giving a definition, that of '*administrado*',[322] which clearly echoes the French concept of '*administré*'. The Venezuelan legislation, too, refers to interested persons.[323]

The Spanish legislation was also influential with regard to the right to be heard. The question as to when a hearing is required as a matter of right is a complex one and the precise meaning of that phrase is not always clear. The Spanish Act made three choices. First, it included the right to be heard within general legislation. Second, it established a relationship between this right and the interests recognized and protected by the legal order, affirming that all interested persons were entitled to present their arguments and evidence on condition that they were relevant. Finally, both arguments and evidence had to be discussed in a hearing ('*audiencia*').[324] This was regarded by many as a model to be followed. In particular, the Argentinian and Peruvian laws were similar to the Spanish model, except that the former included the right to be heard within the broader protection of due process ('*debido proceso adjetivo*') and the latter also referred to the rights and interests of third parties, for instance, in environmental matters.[325]

In conclusion, although each Latin American legal system has developed its own administrative procedure legislation, without formal reception of Spanish law, all these legal systems have adopted some of the general concepts and principles embodied in the Spanish Act of 1958, which became an important vehicle for spreading general concepts and principles. Some argue, therefore, that there is a cluster[326] and that the underlying reason can be found both in the existence of common understandings about law and society as a legacy of a shared past and in the technical level of Spanish legislation. Others affirm that the connection is indirect because the Spanish law has been a source of

320 Venezuela, Law of 1981 Article 48 (2).

321 Argentina, Law 19459 of 1972.

322 Peru, Law No 27444/1994, Article 51; A Brewer-Carias, 'Administrative Procedure Regulation in Latin America: First Decade of General Administrative Procedure Law in Peru' (2011) 67 Derecho Publico 47.

323 Venezuela, Law of 1981 Article 59.

324 Spanish Act of 1958, Article 91 (1) and (2).

325 Peru, Law No 27444/1994, Article 182 (1).

326 Garcia de Enterria, *La formación del Derecho Público europeo tràs la Revolución Francesa* (n 41) 205.

inspiration but has not been imitated except in a very few cases, and there have been borrowings and transplants among Latin American laws.

4 The Scandinavian Standard of Fair Procedure

There is another group of countries where administrative procedure legislation was adopted during the 1960s and later, ie, the Scandinavian area. Similarly to *Mitteleuropa*, this area was characterized by both commonality and diversity. In the forefront, above all, stood the historical relationships between the various nations of Scandinavia (Denmark, Finland, Iceland, Norway, and Sweden), which was confirmed by the establishment of the Nordic Council in 1952. Given the importance of these elements of commonality between Nordic legal systems, what matters is to establish the nature of possible relationships between their laws. A first possible event is that each legal system developed a different type of legislation. Another is that one system derived its norms from another one, probably with modifications, or, to use a less strong term, was influenced by another one, which would probably have been the first to adopt administrative procedure legislation. A third possible event is that the initial influence was exerted from a further system, outside the area, for example, Austria or the US.

Herlitz rejected the first hypothesis in the late 1960s. He observed that when a 'rather comprehensive' administrative procedure legislation was enacted in Norway in 1967, in Sweden an 'even more comprehensive draft administrative procedure act' had been presented in 1964, hence the possibility of establishing a 'common standard of fair procedure'.[327] Such commonality, he added, was reinforced by the existence of shared ideas and principles, as the Norwegian Act established several requirements 'reminiscent of Swedish law'.[328] This is a helpful starting point. It is, however, necessary to look closer at the legislation adopted by the various nations of Scandinavia, including Sweden (1971), Denmark (1984), Iceland (1993), and Finland (2003). Several illustrations can be made of the common and connecting elements existing between their laws. Three of them will be elaborated on here. Although they are not exhaustive, they are important because each of them involves a policy choice, with broad implications.

---

327 N Herlitz, 'Legal remedies in Nordic Administrative Law' (1968) 15 AJCL 687, at 691. See also Ragnelman (n 137) (explaining that the 1986 Act had a broader scope than that of 1971).

328 id, 694.

This is evident, in particular, as regards the first element; that is, the choice of a general and comprehensive legislation on administrative procedure, in discontinuity with the past.[329] Thus, for example, the scope of application of the Norwegian legislation of 1967 includes all administrative activities, with the exclusion of the functions of the courts of law, even those not of an intrinsically judicial character.[330] Similarly, the Danish legislation applies to 'all branches of the public administration' in relation to the cases in which a decision has been or will be made by an administrative authority.[331] The legislation adopted by Iceland in 1993 applies to all administrative bodies, both national and local, as far as they adopt decisions impinging on the individual's rights and obligations.[332] Finally, the more recent legislation, adopted by Finland, covers all 'administrative matters' and thus applies to all public authorities.[333] In all these cases, therefore, the choice of a general and comprehensive legislation was made by considering administration both institutionally and functionally. At first sight, the Swedish APA of 1986 seems to have made a different choice, because it applies not only to 'handling of matters by the administrative authorities', but also to what pertains to the courts. However, it does so simply because it applies to administrative activities in their entirety, regardless of the nature of the bodies which perform them.[334]

Herlitz's idea of a 'common standard of fair procedure' is confirmed by the particular emphasis that all Scandinavian legislative provisions lay on the impartiality of public officials and the resulting disqualification, which come soon after the delimitation of the scope of application. The starting point is that a public official must be disqualified from preparing an administrative decision or adopting it if certain circumstances occur. Among such circumstances there is, invariably, direct involvement as a party to the case or matter.[335] There is also indirect involvement, based on marriage, family affiliation, and position. There is, lastly, a reference – in almost the same words – to other special circumstances which may weaken the public's confidence in the impartiality

329 Herlitz, 'Swedish Administrative Law' (n 77) 231 (highlighting the absence of codification).

330 Norway, Act of 10 February 1967 relating to procedure in cases concerning the administration, §§ 1 and 4 (b).

331 Denmark, Public Administration Act of 19 December 1985, §§ 1 and 2 (1).

332 Iceland, Administrative Procedures Act n. 373/1993, Article 1.

333 Finland, Administrative Procedures Act n. 434/2003, Articles 1 and 2.

334 For Sweden, the provision laid down by the Administrative Procedure Act (1986), Section 1 is confirmed by the Administrative Procedure Act (2017), Section 16.

335 Norway, § 6; Denmark PAA, Section 3 (1); Iceland, APA, Article 3; Finland APA, section 28 (1).

of an official.[336] It might be argued that similar rules exist in other parts of Europe and elsewhere and that they can have a different effect. However, our first concern here is with the existence of the general principle (impartiality) and the mechanism that ensures its observance (disqualification).[337]

A common standard emerges, too, with regard to the other fundamental maxim of natural justice, *audi alteram partem*. Norway and Sweden were the first to affirm it in their general legislation and the latter's more recent legislation contains a particular provision regulation the information that a private party wants to give orally. Iceland, too, recognized the right to be heard, in connection with the right to information.[338] This shows a more general feature; that is, the importance accorded to openness. Sweden was a precursor in this respect.[339] Finland has adopted similar legislation since 1950. Denmark has done so in its APA, by recognizing the right of access to files and protecting it with particular intensity against the use of provisions on secrecy.[340] Likewise, the administrative procedure legislation adopted by Iceland affirms the right to have access to the 'documentation … bearing on the case' and specifies that laws on secrecy 'shall not limit the duty to grant access' to it.[341]

In conclusion, like *Mitteleuropa*, the Nordic area is characterized by the existence of a common standard of fair procedure, notwithstanding the fact that judicial review has been differently shaped, because it has been assigned to either generalist or specialized courts, as is respectively the case in Norway and Sweden.[342] But, unlike *Mitteleuropa*, the existence of a common standard is not the product of the spread of ideas and norms from one legal system to the others. It is, rather, the product of countries with a longstanding tradition of open government. Another type of diffusion thus emerges.

---

336 Norway, § 6 (if other special circumstances 'impair confidence in his impartiality'); Sweden, APA, Section 11 ('some other special circumstance that is likely to undermine confidence in his impartiality in the matter'); Iceland, APA, Article 3 (6) ('if such circumstances … are likely to cast reasonable doubt upon his impartiality').

337 For a similar remark, see Watson (n 19) 20.

338 Iceland, APA, Articles 13 and 15.

339 The Swedish Freedom of the Press Act, establishing citizens' right to freely seek information, was approved in 1766. See N Herlitz, 'Legal remedies in Nordic Administrative Law' (n 339) 691; id., 'Swedish Administrative Law' (n 77) 228.

340 Denmark, PAA, Section 9 (1) and (2).

341 Iceland, APA, Article 15.

342 Herlitz, (n 339) 687.

5 Types of States and Administrative Procedure Legislation

Two final remarks can be made at this stage. They concern the differentiation between the legal realities examined and the correlation between variables.

The analysis of administrative procedure legislation confirms the existence of a vast area of agreement between legal systems because when a State adopts one type of legislation or another, it establishes at least a few minimum requirements concerning adjudication and sometimes other forms of administrative action. There is diversity at the same time. Obviously, context matters, and in more than one way. In this respect, it can be fruitful to consider Damaška's essay on public proceedings.[343] He provides an analytical framework within which legal systems that present very different procedural arrangements can be compared.[344] To this end, he argues that all procedural systems are shaped by two types of factors or variables: first, whether the structure of the legal order is basically hierarchical or coordinate, ie, characterized by several *loci* of authority, and, second, whether the goal of justice is viewed as the resolution of conflicts arising from individuals and social groups (what Damaška called the 'reactive State') or the implementation of public policies (the 'activist State'). Though these traits are not to be found in a 'pure' sense, they do provide a range of combinations, which is much more flexible and helpful than the traditional distinction between civil law and common law systems.[345] They explain, for example, that there is a much greater difference between these and the legal systems of the USSR and China, viewed as a 'pronounced activist and hierarchical system' and as the extreme concrete example of this model or type.[346] This approach shows that there can be, and there are often, tensions within a single variable or a pair of variables.

In our case, two variables seem to have influenced the evolution of administrative procedure legislation; that is, the type of State and the conception of the rule of law. Damaška's paradigm of the activist State does much more than promote certain policies, because it strives for a comprehensive vision of the good,[347] helping us to understand the emergence of a different vision

343 MR Damaška, *The Faces of Justice and State Authority* (Yale University Press 1986).

344 For similar remarks, see the book reviews by A von Mehren, 'The Importance of Structure and Ideologies for the Administration of Justice' (1987) 97 Yale L J 341, at 346 and M Shapiro, 'Review of *The Faces of Justice and State Authority* by MR Damaška' (1987) 35 AJCL 835 (1987).

345 Damaška (n 344) 17.

346 id, 198–199.

347 id, 80.

of administrative procedure. The Austrian codification of administrative procedure contained principles and rules which corresponded to the liberal state. The shift from a reactive State, based on the principles of political liberalism, to the activist State, accounts for the reluctance to accept that any infringement of procedure rules could determine the annulment of an administrative decision if obtained through the infringement of procedural rules.[348] There is, thus, a correlation between the advent of the active or social State and the development of the policy implementation type. The socialist legal systems which have retained, in some way, their pre-existing administrative procedure legislation have had to adjust it to the new functional necessities. To a limited extent, a similar development occurred within a legal system at the other end of the political spectrum, that of the US.

This explains the importance of the other variable, concerning conceptions of the rule of law. There is a range of options, which can be included between two extremes.[349] At one extreme, there is a 'thick' conception of the rule of law, such as that of Austria in 1925. At the other extreme is a 'thin' conception of the rule of law, such as that which dominated in Spain under Franco and in socialist systems soon after 1948. Various solutions fall between these extremes, such as those of France and Prussia in the second half of the nineteenth century. In this respect, we may gainfully draw on the retrospective analysis elaborated by a specialist of French administrative law, Auby, with regard to standards of administrative conduct defined by the *Conseil d'État* between 1850 and 1870. Auby observed that it might be surprising that those standards, and the creative techniques used by the administrative judge, saw the light 'under a political regime stamped with authoritarianism', as the French leader of that era, Napoléon III, had obtained power through a coup d'*état*.[350] Auby's answer was not, however, limited to France under the Second Empire. He argued that 'imperial leaders … conscious of the popular reactions that the reduction of political liberties might lead to … wished, as a counterpoise, to accord citizens the satisfaction of having a government respectful of law and free of arbitrariness', a sort of 'safety valve' policy.[351] In other words, procedural requirements could be viewed as a compensation for the loss of political freedom in France and its absence in Prussia, where the dominant authoritarianism excluded

348 id, 180.

349 For further discussion, see P Craig, 'Formal and Substantive Conceptions of the Rule of Law: an Analytical Framework' (1997) 42 Public Law, 467.

350 JM Auby, 'Abuse of Power in French Administrative Law' (1970) 18 AJCL 549, at 551.

351 id, 551.

neither procedural safeguards against administrative arbitrariness nor, incidentally, the delivery of social benefits to individuals and groups.

This line of reasoning implies that the necessary condition for ensuring compliance with these procedural safeguards was the existence of courts that enjoyed a certain margin of autonomy from the other branches, the executive in particular. The courts were, in effect, the guarantors – and partly the creators – of those principles, which corresponded to the values shared by those societies. In the absence of this condition or variable,[352] which was necessary for a set of procedural principles and rules established by legislation to become effective as a barrier against not only arbitrariness but also maladministration, codes of administrative procedure could have only limited effects. It is highly significant that socialist regimes abolished administrative courts where they existed, notably in Czechoslovakia, Hungary and Poland, and they did so because there was a concern that 'aggrieved individuals might attack' administrative actions taken by government officials by seeking judicial review.[353] The fact that Yugoslavia had a more comprehensive and effective system of judicial review of administrative action explains why its legislation of administrative procedure, too, was more effective.[354] At one extreme were the German Democratic Republic and the USSR, which had no administrative procedure legislation governing the conduct of public authorities that impinged on the lives of individuals[355] and where judges did not seem to be actively involved in their control.[356]

In this chapter, greater focus on administrative procedure has shown that, in contrast with the autochthonous view of administrative law, some shared standards of conduct for public authorities have emerged within some clusters, such as *Mitteleuropa*, the Scandinavian area, and the Ibero-american one. The discussion in the next chapter will shift to the interaction between

---

352 For further discussion of the role of variables within the 'most similar cases' logic, see Hirschl (n 105) 134 (referring to a variable or potential explanation which is not central to the study).

353 See Wierzborski and McCaffrey (n 130) 647 and Reid (n 286) 821 (same remark).

354 See N Stjepanovic, 'Judicial Review of Administrative Acts in Yugoslavia' (1957) 6 AJCL 94 (illustrating the law on administrative disputes which became effective in 1957) and W Gellhorn, 'Citizens Grievances against Administrative Agencies: the Yugoslav Approach' (1966) 64 Michigan L Rev 385, at 399 (noting that most judicial decisions were favourable to citizens).

355 Gellhorn (n 354) 1054.

356 id, 1053. See also J Mathews, 'Minimally Democratic Administrative Law' (2016) 68 Adm L Rev 605 (discussing the role of the duty to give reasons and judicial review within modern 'minimally democratic' regimes).

commonality and diversity in today's administrative procedure. This will be followed by a 'factual' analysis concerning legal systems with and without general legislation on administrative procedure.

PART 2

A Synchronic Comparison

CHAPTER 6

Commonality and Diversity in Administrative Procedure Legislation

General legislation on administrative procedure legislation is a fundamental focus of our inquiry. Many European legal systems – including the vast majority of EU member States – have adopted one type of administrative procedure legislation or another. The question that thus arises is whether there are common and connecting elements, not just differences, among these legal systems. There are two different aspects to this topic. There is a strategy underlying the adoption of administrative procedure legislation, manifest first of all at constitutional level and, second, in the determination of the purposes of such legislation. There are also issues concerning the principles of administrative procedure. Both aspects will be considered in the following discussion.

1 The Diversity of Constitutional Foundations

It is fitting from the outset to look at national constitutions because they 'constitute' and limit the powers of government; they are higher law and are justiciable, also playing a symbolic role.[357] That is not to say that written constitutions are the only source of principles. Indeed, sometimes there is no actual written document self-qualifying as a constitution, notably in the UK, and when there is one, it is often complemented either by custom or by reference to other sources, such as the principles of 1789 in France. A constitution is nonetheless one of the best starting points. This can help us to understand the ideas and beliefs about public law that shape the framework for administrative procedure, and from this angle, some ways of dealing with administrative functions and powers may be discerned.

First, a constitution may not lay down any provision concerning administrative procedure and content itself with the definition of broad principles. Article 18 of the Austrian Constitution of 1920 (reinstated in 1945) establishes that 'the entire public administration shall be based on law', from which the necessity of pre-existing standards of administrative conduct can be deduced.

357 B Constant, *Cours de politique constitutionnelle* (1836; Sklatine 1982) 8–9.

The constitutions of the peoples in the former Yugoslavia adhere to the same vision of administrative action and lay down the same principle, with slight modifications: Article 198 of the Serbian Constitution provides that administrative action and individual acts 'must be based on the law'; Article 19 of the Croatian Constitution requires that the decisions of all bodies 'vested with public authority ... shall be grounded on law'; Article 120 (2) of the Slovenian Constitution establishes that administrative bodies 'perform their work ... on the basis of laws'. A relationship between these norms may be based, above all, on the historical relationship between the legal systems that were characterized by the diffusion of Austrian ideas and norms after 1925, which had more far-reaching consequences than the adoption of individual rules. It may also reflect the existence of certain shared values, such as respect for the rule of law and fundamental rights, also with a view to joining the EU.

Second, a constitution may either define some general principles of administrative procedure or certain process rights or do so indirectly by empowering political institutions to do so. Interestingly, these techniques have been used by three constitutions which have entered into force after the fall of the authoritarian regimes in the 1970s: those of Greece (1975), Portugal (1976) and Spain (1978). Article 20 of the Greek Constitution guarantees that '*the right of a person to a prior hearing also applies in any administrative action or measure adopted at the expense of his rights or interests*'. This right is shaped in broad terms, and the courts may not only annul administrative measures that are found to be in contrast with it, but also invalidate primary legislation.[358]

Thirdly, a constitution may give a mandate to parliamentary institutions with a view to adopting general legislation on administrative procedure. This is exemplified by the Spanish Constitution. Its Article 105 establishes that legislation will regulate citizens' participation in the process of elaboration of administrative provisions, their rights to be heard within administrative procedure and the right to have access to the documentation held by public authorities.[359] Though the constitutional provision plainly imposes a duty on the legislator, this may not accomplish it. However, as has been seen earlier, general legislation on administrative procedure existed before the Constitution's entry into force. Accordingly, the new constitutional provision reinforced existing rights. Likewise, Article 267 (5) of the Portuguese Constitution provides that

358 See E Spiliotopoulos, 'Judicial Review of Legislative Acts in Greece' (1983) 56 Temple L Q 463.

359 Spanish Constitution, Article 105. For further analysis, see S Munoz Machad, 'General Principles of European Law and the Reform of the Spanish Law on Administrative Procedure' (1994) 1 Maastricht J Eur & Comp L 231.

the discharge of administrative activities 'shall be the object of a special law' with a view to ensuring that citizens may participate in the adoption of decisions or deliberations concerning them.

Lastly, especially the constitutions adopted after 1989 reveal the influence of supranational charters of rights. This is the case with the new Hungarian Constitution (of 2011, as amended in 2016). Its Article XXIV (1) practically reproduces the provision of the EU Charter of Fundamental Rights concerning the right to a good administration ('every person has the right to have his or her affairs handled impartially, fairly and within a reasonable time') and specifies that this right shall include the requirement to give reasons 'as determined by law'.[360] A broader influence has been exercised by Article 6 ECHR, concerning the right to a fair trial, of which there are several equivalents within national constitutions.[361]

The above shows, broadly speaking, that a difference emerges between less recent constitutions and those adopted in the last four or five decades, which devote more attention to the discharge of administrative functions and powers and sometimes require institutions to adopt general legislation on procedures. Not all recent constitutions, however, lay down what could be conceptualized as a general principle of fair administrative procedure. It must be seen, therefore, whether any common trend emerges from national administrative procedure legislation, as well as whether the courts interpret national laws in the light of supranational principles.[362] The first task will be accomplished in the rest of this chapter, the other in the following three.

2 The Heterogeneity of Administrative Procedure Legislation

Previous scholarly works have lain emphasis on the goals legislators seek to achieve. It is readily apparent that this is an important viewpoint. Parliaments often seek to promote change by defining priorities and strategies, and administrative procedure legislation can be part of such strategies, sometimes in conjunction with reforms of the civil service or of judicial review.

360 Hungarian Constitution, Article 24 (1).

361 See, for example, Article 111 of the Italian Constitution and Article 92 of the Latvian Constitution and, for further analysis, A Stone Sweet and H Keller (ed), *A Europe of Rights. The Impact of the ECHR on National Legal Systems* (Oxford University Press 2008).

362 E Schmidt-Aßmann, 'Structures and Functions of Administrative Procedures in German, European and International Law' in J Barnes (ed), *Transforming Administrative Procedure* (Global Law Press 2008) 43.

Different legal systems may, and often do, have different strategies. For example, the German codification of administrative procedure was often portrayed as an attempt to increase administrative efficiency. Quite to the contrary, the adoption of general legislation in Italy was mainly seen as an attempt to protect and promote citizens' rights *vis-à-vis* the public authorities. This reflects a more general distinction because procedural provisions may have an instrumental or a non-instrumental rationale.[363] They may have an instrumental rationale in the sense of clarifying the steps that have to be taken in order to achieve the desired purpose. By clarifying how the administrative procedure must be carried out, legislation makes life easier for government officers, practicing lawyers, and citizens.[364] It also relieves the legislator from the need to define procedural rules for every sector. The purpose is, thus, to avoid an 'unworkable government'.[365] There can be also a non-instrumental rationale. In the absence of a framework for the exercise of discretionary powers, individuals are left in a Kafkaesque situation,[366] which is detrimental to their autonomy and dignity.[367]

Another dichotomy is between parliamentary legislation and executive or delegated norms. Three decades or so ago, Cassese observed that 'administrative procedure can be self-regulated by administrative agencies … or determined by judicial review. The source of the regulation is more than important, it is crucial'.[368] In the last decades, the balance seems to have favored parliamentary legislation. However, this statement requires twofold qualification. On the one hand, the argument whereby parliamentary legislation circumscribes executive regulation neglects the importance of delegation. The French case shows this as it was the executive branch that defined the rules on the basis of parliamentary authorization, and those rules were drafted by experts who codified the settled case law of the administrative courts.[369] Moreover, primary legislation is also used to limit the powers of state or regional authorities, thus leading to centralization. This was the case in countries with different

363 For this distinction, see P Craig, 'Procedures and Administrative Decisionmaking: A Common Law Perspective' (1992; special issue) Eur Rev Publ L 55, at 58.

364 For this remark, see Eberle (n 278) 70.

365 M Shapiro, 'APA: Past, Present, Future' (1986) 72 Virginia L Rev 447.

366 On process values, see RS Summers, 'Evaluating and Improving Legal Processes – A Plea for 'process values'' (1974) 60 Cornell L Rev 1.

367 For this approach, see Mashaw (n 52) 179–180; DJ Galligan, *Due Process and Fair Procedures. A Study of Administrative Procedures* (Clarendon 1999).

368 Cassese, *La construction du droit administratif* (n 7) 16.

369 See D Custos', The 2015 French Code of Administrative Procedure: An Assessment', in Rose-Ackerman, Lindseth and Emerson (n 159) 284.

administrative traditions, such as Poland in 1930, or under authoritarian governments, such as Spain in 1958. More recently, the legislation adopted by States, such as Italy and Spain, which entrust regional authorities with legislative powers, requires these to comply with the principles laid down by national legislation, thus leaving a margin of appreciation to the courts in the event of conflict.

This is an interesting debate, part of the more general discussion concerning the advantages and disadvantages of codification, but it should not divert attention from the issue at the heart of this essay, the relationship between commonality and diversity. In this respect, it is important to look at how administrative procedure addresses general principles. This task is not unproblematic. One difficulty encountered in identifying those principles is that sometimes legislation uses the term 'principle' as an equivalent of general rule. Another problem is that sometimes what is effectively the same principle may be known by more than one name.

Administrative procedure legislation deals with general principles in more than one way. Three mechanisms can be distinguished: list, definition, and *renvoi*. There is often an initial provision defining a list of general principles. Both the Swedish APA of 1986 and the Italian legislation adopted few years later define general requirements and principles, respectively. Included between these general standards are legality, efficiency, and economy of administrative action.[370] More recent administrative procedure legislation is replete with longer lists, sometimes followed by a definition of each principle. Thus, for example, Section 4 of the Latvian APA includes and defines the following principles: the respect of individual rights, equality, the rule of law, reasonableness, non-arbitrariness, confidence in legality, lawful basis, democracy, proportionality, the priority of laws and procedural equity. The APA of another Baltic state, Lithuania, includes the same principles, sometimes with slight modifications: for example, it refers to the supremacy of law and to efficiency.[371] Moreover, it lays down the principle of proportionality, which is defined in terms of the necessity and reasonableness of the goals pursued by the administration. Proportionality is increasingly recognized by administrative procedure legislation, though with some variants. For example, the Dutch legislation

370 Swedish APA, Section 7; Italian Law No 241/1990, Article 1.

371 See also the Bulgarian APA, Articles 5–13 (defining the principles of lawfulness, commensurability (which refers to good faith, fairness and reasonableness), truthfulness, equality, independence and objectivity, promptness and procedural economy, accessibility, publicity and transparency, and, finally, sequence and foreseeability) and the Bosnian APA (2012) (defining the principles of legality, due process, transparency, and cost-effectiveness).

requires public authorities to prevent the adverse consequences of an order being 'disproportionate' in relation to the purposes served by such an order.[372] Lastly, there is sometimes a *renvoi* to principles that are established elsewhere. Thus, Article 1 (1) of the Italian APA contains a *renvoi* to the principles of EU law, whose scope of application is, therefore, not limited to the implementation of EU law and policies but has a general reach.[373]

The above confirms that there are differences between the various legislative frameworks on administrative procedure. While the legislation adopted by Nordic legal systems is fairly reduced, the codes of administrative procedure adopted by the Baltic countries, as well as by Bulgaria and some countries of the Balkans tend to be much longer. For example, that of Latvia spans over one hundred pages and includes almost four-hundred articles. We ought now to broaden our analysis in order to ascertain whether the contents of administrative procedure legislation reveal not only diversity, but also commonality.

3 An Area of Agreement: Administrative Adjudication

Our comparative inquiry has shown, first of all, an area of agreement between legal systems concerning adjudication. This area emerges, on the one hand, from the ways general legislation on administrative procedure circumscribes its ambit or scope of application by way of both exclusions and inclusions. On the other hand, a common concern in administrative law regards the process by which an agency reaches a decision.

Most national legislative provisions exclude the functions that pertain to the other branches of government, namely legislation and judicial adjudication. For example, both the Dutch and the German legislation exclude parliamentary and judicial bodies.[374] It is often the case, moreover, that national legislative provisions exclude public prosecutors. Inclusions are of even greater relevance and significance. The baseline in each national legislation is the necessity to ensure that it applies to administrative authorities, though more than one legal technique is adopted for delimiting the scope of application.

---

372 Dutch APA, section 3:4 (2). See also the Croatian APA (2009), Article 6.

373 Italian law on administrative procedure (1990), Article 1. For further remarks, see G della Cananea, 'A Law on EU Administrative Procedures: Implications for National Legal Orders' in A Varga and others (eds), *Current Issues of the National and EU Administrative Procedures (the RENEUAL Model Rules)* (Pazmany Press 2015) 283.

374 Dutch GALA, Section 1:1(a); German APA, Article 1.1. See also the Finnish legislation, section 4 and the Norwegian law, §4(a).

Thus, for instance, when the Dutch and the German legislative provisions give a definition of 'administrative authority', they do not refer simply to the existence of an authority or body but specify that it must have been 'established under public law'.[375] Likewise, the Greek legislation extends its application, in addition to the State and local authorities, to 'other legal entities of public law', and the Finnish one applies to central and local authorities as well as 'institutions governed by public law'.[376] A similar technique is used with regard to administration in the functional sense. When giving the definition of an 'order', the Dutch general legislation clarifies that it is a 'ruling of an administrative authority constituted under public law' and that it 'is not of a general nature'. Similarly, the German APA defines an administrative act with regard to the exercise of sovereign powers in the sphere of public law.[377] Thus, in line with a traditional school of thought in public law, the exercise of power by public authorities is viewed from the angle of the individual administrative act or determination.

All these legislative provisions are based on the traditional element of administrative law; that is, the existence of a public administration or authority.[378] Others establish that administrative procedure legislation applies to private bodies when they are vested with public authority[379] or carry out activities that are mainly funded by public finances.[380] A functional conception of administration thus emerges. Such a functional conception is coherent with EU law, where there is a consolidated concept of a 'body governed by public law', notably in the directives concerning public procurements.[381] While the terms 'public law' and 'private law' may be used either descriptively or prescriptively, in this case the latter form prevails. The underlying idea is that an administrative authority discharges functions and powers under public law, which need to be subject to special burdens or requirements, including the

---

375 Dutch APA, Section 1:1(a); German APA, § 1.1.

376 Greek APA, Article 1; Finnish APA, section 2.

377 German APA, § 35 ('an administrative act shall be any order, decision or other sovereign measure taken by an authority to regulate an individual case in the sphere of public law and intended to have a direct external effect').

378 M Shapiro, 'Administrative Law Unbounded: Reflections on Government and Governance' (2000) 8 Ind J Global Legal Stud 369.

379 Spanish APA, Article 2(2); Dutch APA, Article 1: 1 (1) (a); Croatian APA, Article 1; Serbian APA, Article 2; Latvian APA, Article 1(1).

380 Danish APA, section 1(2) (referring to activities mainly covered by public funds); Czech APA, section 1(1); Polish APA, Article 1.

381 See MP Chiti, 'The EC Notion of Public Administration: The Case of the Bodies Governed by Public Law' (2002) 8 Eur Public Law 473.

duties of legality, fairness and rationality on the part of decision-makers. The underlying assumption is that those tasks and duties are different from those that characterize private bodies *tout court*. In the last analysis, all these mechanisms serve to individuate the boundaries for applying administrative procedure legislation to one class of regulated action; that is, adjudication. If a case fits within that class or category, all of the legislative provisions governing adjudication regulate that procedure. A common concern, then, is the process by which public authorities and bodies reach a decision. What must be seen is how this process is shaped.

A first requirement concerns compliance with the pre-established administrative procedure. This requirement is very clearly set out in Spanish legislation, as it rests on consolidated tradition. The Spanish norm, as defined by Article 53 (1) of the law adopted in 1992, provides that administrative acts, whether they are adopted upon request of the interested person or *ex officio*, will be adopted on the basis of the 'established procedure'. Similarly, Section 3 (10) of the Dutch general law on administrative procedure requires the procedure for the preparations of orders to be followed either if legislation so provides or if an order of the authority does so. A similar requirement lies at the basis of every type of administrative procedure legislation, whether it provides a uniform paradigm of procedure or more than one. It is precisely for this reason that administrative procedure legislation invariably gives autonomous legal relevance to the initiative, or first step, whether it is taken *ex officio* or by the interested person(s) and requires public authorities to render the final decision on the basis of the evidence they have collected. It is within this area of commonality that variants can be better appreciated. For example, the German *Verwaltungsverfahrengesetz* is very clear in requiring the authority to determine the facts of the case, as well as in specifying that it is not bound by the parties' submissions to admit evidence, while the Italian legislation requires the authority to take the evidence and arguments brought by the parties into due account, provided that they pertain to the case. The Croatian law is similar to that of Germany, except that it requires the authority to determine the 'facts and circumstances which are essential' for the decision, while the Dutch law refers to the 'relevant facts and the interests', which must be gathered and weighed.

4 The Closest Things to Invariants: Hearings

Two other requirements will now be considered, namely, the right to be heard and the duty to give reasons. Both have been affirmed by the European Court of

Human Rights in its settled case law concerning Article 6 ECHR.[382] Moreover, both are defined by Article 41 (1) of the EU Charter of Fundamental Rights, according to which the right to a good administration includes, among other things, the 'right of every person to be heard, before any individual measure which would affect him or her adversely is taken', as well as the 'obligation of the administration to give reasons for its decisions'. However, as will be seen, while the former provision defines what may be regarded as a minimum requirement, the latter delineates a requirement that goes beyond the common denominator of national laws.

Many national laws, more or less literally, reproduce the maxim *audi alteram partem.* The German law ('before an administrative act affecting the right of a participant may be executed, the latter must be given the opportunity of commenting on the facts relevant to the decision') is similar to the Charter, except that it does not apply only to the acts and measures that might give rise to effects unfavorable either to their addressees or to other persons. However, it provides for some exceptions. Other national provisions express the same concern in similar, if not the same, words. Thus, for example, Article 9 of the Serbian APA provides that 'before adopting a decision, the parties must be allowed to make a statement concerning the facts and circumstances of relevance for decision-making', Article 10 of the Bosnian AOA establishes that 'prior to taking a decision, a party must be given an opportunity to provide his position on all the facts and circumstances important for taking a decision', and Article 6 (1) of the Greek Administrative Procedure Code requires administrative authorities to invite interested parties to express their opinions, but with regard to all issues, not only those of fact. The Dutch legislation (section 3.13) does not require the hearing, but it does ensure that the parties may state their views on the draft administrative decision or determination. The Swedish legislation (revised in 2017) conceives the right to be heard as the foundation for a number of process rights, such as access to documents and legal assistance.[383] The fact that the requirement established for the right to be heard is higher than the minimum requirement established by the EU Charter may also be appreciated with respect to other norms. French legislation provides an enlightening example, because the hearing requirement applies not only to the issuance of individual decisions that must be reasoned because they either adversely affect the individual's interest or derogate from general rules, but

382 ECtHR, Judgment of 20 October 2009, in *Lombardi Vallauri v Italy* (Application No 39128/05) (finding that Italy failed to ensure compliance with procedural guarantees by a private university in a case concerning termination of a professor's contract).

383 Swedish APA (2017), Sections 9 and 14.

also to decisions that concern an individual.[384] The above shows that a common standard exists, though sometimes it is expressly regarded as a principle, for instance in the Bosnian law just mentioned, while in other cases – including Italy – legislation does not set out a general concept, but requires that some types of process rights be respected, including the right to notification, to have access to all the documents held by the public authority entrusted with the power to decide, and to submit opinions and evidence.[385]

There is nonetheless a variety of ways in which the right to be heard manifests itself. One is a general statement about the duty of the public authorities to deliver notice about the commencement of a procedure. The other is a – varyingly detailed – description of the various steps to be followed. Between these two methods, again, lies a broad spectrum. Often, administrative procedure legislation requires public authorities to deliver notice not only to the individuals to whom the final act or measure will apply, but also to those who are potentially affected by it in an adverse manner. Increasingly often, procedural norms specify that notice must be given in a timely manner. Some take account of other factors in deciding on the notice that must be given, including the type of act being issued and the number of people who are affected by it. Another element of differentiation between national procedural rules concerns the nature of the hearing. Many norms, especially those of Central and Eastern European countries, are based on the assumption that the hearing will normally be oral.[386] Others so provide either if private parties request a hearing,[387] or if a written procedure would cause inconvenience to them, as in the Scandinavian countries.[388] However, there is no general rule that this must be so. There can, for example, be a general requirement that an oral hearing take place unless the law provides otherwise, due to an urgency, for example. In other cases, included the Italian legislation, the general norm is constructed so as to dispense with an oral hearing, which is required by sector-specific rules, for example for disciplinary procedures. In brief, as observed by Schlesinger in the field of private law, it is evident that 'the areas of agreement

384 French Law of 2016, Article L122–1, ('*décisions qui … son prises en considération de la personne*').

385 Italian Law No 241 of 1990, Articles 7–11.

386 Bosnian APA, Article 10 (1) Croatian APA, Articles 4(1) and 54(1); Slovenian APA, Article 154; Serbian APA, Article 144; Hungarian APA, sec. 74(1)(a)-(c); Slovak APA, § 21(1); Estonian APA, § 45(1); Czech APA, section 36(2). Lastly, the Polish APA, Article 89 provides that a hearing shall be held whenever it would simplify or expedite the procedure.

387 Dutch APA, Section 3:15.

388 Swedish APA, sections 9 and 24; Norwegian APA, § 11 (d); Finnish APA, Section 37. See also the Albanian APA, Article 88 (1).

and disagreement are interlaced, often in subtle ways, and that it is quite impossible to accurately formulate an area of agreement without staking out its limits and thus demarcating an actual or potential area of disagreement'.[389]

Nonetheless, the structure of these national norms is the same. There are two related, but distinct, aspects. On the one hand, legislation defines and regulates a broad class or category of agency adjudication, ie, single-case decisions, with some exceptions established by law. On the other hand, this class or category of adjudication is characterized by a common requirement, which concerns what the public authority has to do before it makes its final decision. Such a class or category of administrative adjudication is legally required to be determined by an agency only after an opportunity for a hearing, in the absence of which the whole agency action would not only appear less scrupulous than necessary but would be irremediably unfair. It is in this sense and within these limits that the right to be heard in adjudication can be considered one of the closest things to an invariant in administrative action.

5 The Closest Things to Invariants: Giving Reasons

In the context of administrative adjudication, the other closest thing to an invariant is the duty to give reasons. In this respect, Article 190 of the Treaty of Rome laid down a requirement that attracted the interest of American scholars, including Mashaw and Shapiro,[390] largely due to the fact that the requirement was shaped in very broad terms. Its scope of application included not only decisions adversely affecting the individual's rights or interests, as was then the case, for example, within the French and Italian administrative laws. Moreover, that requirement applied not only to individual decisions, but also to regulations and directives; that is, to acts laying down rules. The requirement established by Article 41 of the EU Charter is narrower in scope, as it refers to decisions alone. Even in this more limited sense, it remains to be seen whether this requirement can be regarded as a common denominator. Two aspects will be considered in turn: whether there is a general duty to give reasons, and the stringency of the duty.

National provisions increasingly require public authorities to state the reasons for their administrative decisions. However, this in itself is not sufficient

389 Schlesinger, 'Introduction' (n 2) 39.

390 See Shapiro, 'The Giving Reasons Requirement' (n 243) 179; JL Mashaw, 'Reasoned Administration: The European Union, the United States, and the Project of Democratic Governance' (2007) 76 George Wa L Rev 99.

to say that there is always a general duty to give reasons, though there is evidence that most national laws are moving in that direction. To provide a more specific idea of the scope and content of national provisions, it is helpful to compare three of them, which can be regarded as representative of a more general pattern. The first is the French legislative provision, which does not contain a general duty to give reasons. In fact, reasons must be provided in certain circumstances, including whenever a decision either adversely affects the individual's freedoms and rights (or, anyway, constitutes a police measure) or deviates from general rules. In brief, reasons are not always due, but only when liberty or equality are at stake. The historical origins of the norm can be found in the case law of the French administrative judge and diverge from the norm that has constantly been applied for the judiciary, as some statement of reasons was required within judgments rendered by the courts.[391] The underlying assumption is that the administration should not be overburdened by a general duty. Whatever its intrinsic soundness, this solution is by no means isolated. Quite the contrary, it is shared by the general laws adopted by Austria (1991) and Spain (1992).[392] Moreover, and interestingly, there is no general duty for public authorities to provide reasons in common law in the UK, though some sector-specific norms require public authorities to give their reasons for a decision that adversely affects the rights or interests of the individual.[393]

The opposite choice can be exemplified for its clarity and conciseness by the Dutch general legislation. Its Section 4 (16) provides that 'a decision shall be based on proper reason'. Leaving aside for the moment the propriety of the reasons, it should be observed that this norm applies to every decision, meaning 'an order not of general nature' (as specified by Section 1 (3) (2)). Interestingly, in the legal literature, there is no indication that this solution has impaired the exercise of discretion. Whatever its merits, the same solution has been adopted by administrative procedure legislation in various parts of Europe, Greece, Italy, and numerous countries in Central and Eastern Europe.[394]

Lastly, a somewhat intermediate position can be found where there is a general requirement, albeit subject to exceptions. This can be exemplified

391 See G Bergholtz, '*Ratio et Auctoritas*: A Comparative Study of the Significance of Reasoned Decisions with Special Reference to Civil Cases' in V Gessner and C Varga (eds), *European Legal Cultures* (Aldershot 1997) 123 (tracing the development of the duty to give reasons).

392 French code (2016), Articles L121–1 and L211–2 and 3; Austrian law (1991), §58; Spanish APA, Article 54.

393 P Craig, 'The Common Law, Reasons and Administrative Justice' (1994) 53 Cambridge LJ 288; C Harlow and R Rawlings, *Law and Administration* (3rd edn, Cambridge UP 2017) 611.

394 Italy, Law No 241/1990, Article 3.

by Germany, where Article 39 of the APA requires public authorities to state the grounds for any written administrative act, but there are six exceptions, including when the act grants an application to someone and does not infringe upon the right of another person, as well as when the authority issues 'identical administrative acts in considerable numbers'. The underlying rationale is different, because in the former case the idea is that there is no adverse effect for anyone, an idea that is shared also by other national legal systems such as Denmark and Sweden,[395] while in the latter there is a balancing between the individual's interest and that of not overburdening the administration.

The other relevant aspect is the stringency of the duty to give reasons. The stringency of the duty will, of course, depend to the same extent upon the language of the particular national legislation and the broader context, ranging from a purely procedural requirement to give reasons to a much more structured one. The German norm is, again, exemplificative of a basic and clear requirement. Under Article 39, the statement of grounds 'must contain the chief material and legal grounds' which led the authority to take its decision. Similar norms exist, for example, in Italy and Spain.[396] What characterizes these norms is the existence of a giving-reasons requirement that is conceived as a purely procedural requirement, in the sense that the public authority is required to give reasons, so as to enable the individual to understand why the authority has acted in a certain manner and to assess whether the decision can be challenged. But there is no further indication as to the scope or quality of the reasons. The Greek Code goes beyond this as its Article 17 does not simply require a 'justification' for every individual administrative act, but establishes that such justification should be 'clear, specific, sufficient and derived from the particulars of the file'. An important distinction, underlined by Shapiro,[397] thus emerges between a procedural conception of the requirement to give reasons and a substantive one. By virtue of the latter, a generic statement of reasons would not meet the legislative requirement. The Dutch APA goes one step further from the viewpoint of both negative and positive circumstances. According to Section 4 (17) (3), if the reasons supporting a decision have not been stated on the grounds of celerity, whenever an interested party so requests, they 'shall be notified as quickly as possible'. There is also, as observed earlier, a requirement that any decision be based on 'proper reasons'. This is obviously a more demanding requirement. By requiring the public authority

395 The Danish APA, Section 22, provides an exception, if the decision 'is in every particular in favour of the party concerned'. The Swedish APA includes a list of exceptions.

396 Italy, Law No 241/1990, Article 3; Spain, law of 1992, Article 52.

397 Shapiro, 'The Giving Reasons Requirement' (n 243) 181.

to provide proper reasons, the procedural requirement is converted into a substantive one, in the sense that if the decision-maker chooses to furnish only a concise or stereotyped statement of reasons, then the justification for its action is exposed to risk. The court could assume that no adequate or proper justification has been provided and, accordingly, reach the conclusion that the contested decision is illegal.[398] Such a conclusion would not be in contrast with the discretionary nature of the exercised powers, because it is a corollary of the discretion conferred upon the public authority that the latter has the duty to set out the reasons in sufficient detail to allow the affected parties and the courts to understand the choices that it has made.[399] Last but not least, a legislative provision that refers to the elements of fact and law that emerge from the preliminary fact-finding activities carried out by the public authority goes beyond the mere duty to provide reasons because it creates a sort of requirement for dialogue,[400] in the sense that the public authority must show that the arguments and evidence brought by private parties have been taken into due account.

The remarks thus made with regard to the scope of the duty to give reasons and its stringency should now be considered together. What follows from them is that the requirement established by Article 41 of the EU Charter can in part be considered indicative of a common standard. Public authorities are required to set out the reasons either for a decision that adversely affects the rights or interests of the individual or for one that deviates from existing rules or criteria. More generally, an analysis of administrative procedure legislation shows that in more than one respect there is a spectacular approximation or assimilation between national administrative laws.[401]

6 Diversity: Rulemaking

The individual's interests, as well as those of social groups (families, associations, firms) may be affected not only through single-case decisions (that is, individual adjudication), but also through the application of rules. In the

398 Bosnian APA, Article 193(1); Bulgarian APA, Article 7; Croatian APA, Article 98(5); German APA, sec 39(1) (which reinforces the duty to give reasons with regard to discretionary decisions); Slovenian APA, Article 214.

399 This line of reasoning would be accepted by the courts in the UK: see Craig, *Administrative Law* (n 23) 286.

400 See Shapiro, 'The Giving Reasons Requirement' (n 243) 186.

401 Fromont (n 4) 9.

past, this aspect of administrative action was neglected, because the idea that dominated legal thinking was that rules were adopted by political bodies.[402] But, with the growth of government, administrative agencies have increasingly defined rules. Sometimes, these rules aim to pre-determine the exercise of discretion in individual cases, but nevertheless strongly influence their outcome. In other circumstances, these rules would lead directly to a certain result, for example when public authorities define prices and tariffs. In both guises, the use of administrative rulemaking expanded dramatically, among other things, to protect health, the environment, and safety. Hence the increasing demand for public participation in rulemaking procedures.

Before examining the solutions found by European legal systems, it may be helpful to consider the options at our disposal when thinking about rulemaking. All legal systems must make two choices. First, they have to decide on the conceptual foundation for including rulemaking within their general legislation on administrative procedure. If they decide to do so, then the other choice which must be made is how such legislation can regulate rulemaking by agencies. Of course, different legal systems will devise differing solutions, and what is of interest is not only the final choice, but also the reasons underlying it.

With regard to the first option, in Europe, very few States have defined rules on administrative rulemaking within their general legislation. This is the case with Bulgaria, Norway, and Spain. For example, the Norwegian procedural legislation applies to administrative activities in the broad sense.[403] It thus regulates every action taken by a public authority which 'generally or specifically determines the rights or duties', including both individual decisions and regulations, the former relating to 'one or more specified persons' and the latter to an 'indefinite number or an indeterminate group of persons'.[404] Similarly, Bulgarian legislation makes a distinction between various types of individual administrative acts on the one hand and 'general administrative acts' and regulations on the other.[405] In these few instances there is an explicitly established duty to give reasons with regard to rulemaking.[406]

The opposite choice has been made by most European legal systems. The German case is enlightening in both its clarity and conceptual foundation.

402 See MH Bernstein, 'The Regulatory Process: A Framework for Analysis' (1961) 26 L & Cont Probl 329 (observing that research and discussion have focused primarily on administrative adjudication).

403 Norway, Public Administration Act of 1967 (amended in 2003), section 1.

404 id, section 2 (a), (b) and (c).

405 Bulgarian Code of Administrative Procedure (2006), Article 2.

406 Bulgarian APA, Articles 66(2), 73 and 75; Czech APA, Article 172; Spanish APA, Article 129.

Its general legislation defines an administrative procedure as the 'activity of authorities […] directed to the […] preparation and adoption of an administrative act or to the conclusion of an administrative agreement under public law'.[407] The conceptual foundation is still Mayer' definition of the administrative act as the one that declares what the is law for a particular person.[408] The only deviation from Mayer's paradigm of the administrative act is the provision of an alternative option, in the form of an agreement under public law. Every form of administrative action that exceeds the individual dimension is left out of this definition. Similar choices are made by other legal systems, such as that of Slovenia, where the general provisions on administrative procedure do not take rulemaking into account.[409]

The other choice to be made regards the ways in which administrative rulemaking is governed by general legislation. In this respect, we find a limited area of agreement between legal systems. Thus, for example, in Norway, there is a requirement that the agency ensure 'that the case is clarified as possible before an administrative decision is made', the agency is entrusted with the power to define the procedure for notice and comment, and there is a requirement that every regulation be published.[410] In Bulgaria, there is a variety of forms of participation of interested persons and organizations. These include written proposals and objections and participation in advisory bodies and hearings.[411] Interestingly, there is a legislative provision allowing the application of the rules governing adjudication for the matters that are 'unsettled'.[412]

The Italian legislation on administrative procedure makes a different choice, because it establishes that the provisions regarding citizens' participation 'shall not apply' to the action directed to the adoption of regulations, general administrative acts, and plans, which 'shall continue to be governed by the specific rules regulating their framing.[413] Thus, ironically, the only general norm is that there are no general norms. The underlying reason is, however, one of comparative interest. The reason is that, while public participation in the rulemaking process is desirable and has been so recognized by several sector-specific provisions (typically with regard to regulatory agencies in liberalized public utilities and urban planning), a general requirement in respect to

407 German law on administrative procedure, Article 9.

408 See Hauriou, *Précis de droit administrative* (n 267) and Mayer (n 143).

409 Bugaric (n 248) 30.

410 Norwegian APA, sections 37 and 38.

411 Bulgarian Code of Administrative Procedure (2006), Articles 65–73.

412 id, Article 74.

413 Italian law on administrative procedure, Article 13 (1).

popular participation seems highly undesirable. The making of administrative rules and regulations, so the argument goes, involves very different economic, legal and social circumstances. Accordingly, a general requirement concerning citizens' participation may be either over-or under-inclusive and thus may either over-burden the administration or be insufficient. It seems much more advisable to tailor it on the basis of particular circumstances.

As a final remark, the European legal area, considered as a whole, differs from the US experience, where the federal APA requires each agency to adopt its procedural rules, in addition to a general requirement that all rulemaking shall be accompanied by notice and comment and, finally, that there be proper publicity for administrative rules that are likely to affect the public.[414] Similar requirements have been embodied in the Model State APA. As a result, in the US, general legislation on administrative procedure is characterized by a set of requirements concerning rulemaking, while in Europe it is the exception rather than the rule. This may be seen as indicating that, if a common core of European administrative laws exists, it is limited to adjudication, with the exclusion of rulemaking. This working hypothesis must, however, be further tested. It is now time to consider, through a factual analysis, whether national solutions are similar or different in the daily business of government.

---

414 For further analysis, see E Gellhorn, 'Public Participation in Administrative Proceedings' (1972) 81 Yale L J 359 (observing that participation serve to the presentation of various, otherwise unrepresented views) and S Rose-Ackerman, *Democracy and Executive Power. Policymaking Accountability in the US, the UK, Germany, and France* (Yale UP 2021) 6 (pointing out the distinctiveness of US rulemaking procedures).

CHAPTER 7

A Factual Analysis: Adjudication

In the previous chapters we have examined administrative procedure legislation. This does not, however, constitute a sufficient test for our initial conjecture. There are two orders of reasons why it is not sufficient. The first concerns the area of comparison. Not all European legal systems have administrative procedure legislation of one type or another. Legislation of this kind is notably absent from the English legal system, which is traditionally reluctant to have recourse to codification. But it is also absent from the Belgian legal system, which does have a tradition of codification. We must, therefore, seek to understand how citizens and firms live without a code of administrative procedure. The other order of reasons why legislation does not constitute an adequate test requires a more extended explanation, which will be illustrated in the next section, followed by an analysis of some hypothetical cases.

1 Hypothetical Cases

As mentioned previously,[415] in various fields of law, it has been found that legislation is only one of the factors that shape the daily working of legal institutions. Other legal formants – including judicial decisions and background theories – concur in shaping the solutions given for the problems that arise. This is necessarily so in the field of administrative law, because legislation has been less extensive for so long. Moreover, governmental practice plays an important role. As a result, it is necessary to go beyond what used to be called *legislation comparée*.

The question that concerns us here can be expressed as follows. In two or more legal systems there is a range of goods on which public authorities impose control, because they are potentially risky for some users or they might be controversial from a moral viewpoint, and so on. Those who want to import such goods, therefore, need permission from the competent administrative agency, which is entrusted with the power to allow the importation of controlled goods on the basis of certain criteria. So far, those legal systems may have adopted similar, if not the same, rules notwithstanding their institutional

415 Above, Ch 1, Para 3.

diversity, for example if one is a liberal democracy and another an authoritarian government. But those rules must be enforced, and here lies our problem. In most circumstances, when the agency receives an application for a permit, it will simply look at its precedents and seek to behave accordingly. In other cases, the agency will have to take a decision, which may consist of various factual, legal, and discretionary elements.

Various questions thus arise. If the agency has omitted either to consult a technical body or to give the applicant a possibility to be heard, can it be said that it has acted outside its powers or that it has misused them? If a court of law or other public institution is seized to deal with the legality of the agency's conduct and decision, as distinct from its correctness, will it take only existing rules into account, or will it apply some judicial doctrine, such as those concerning general principles of law? It is for this reason that various administrative scholars at different times have called for greater attention to empirical research.[416] Others have argued that this type of research, 'focusing on specific legal situations', might be particularly helpful for comparative purposes.[417] The discussion that follows focuses on four procedural requirements concerning administrative adjudication,[418] while rulemaking will be examined in the following chapter. These requirements are freedom from bias, the right to be heard, the duty to give reasons, and the duty to consult.

2 Freedom from Bias

The maxim *nemo judex in causa sua* (or *in re sua*) expresses the principle that no person can judge a case in which he or she has an interest. Thus intended, such prohibition is very old. As a precept of Roman law, it was codified in the Code of Justinian (529).[419] In English law, it was applied in the famous *Dr. Bonham's Case*: the Court of Common Pleas, presided by Coke, ruled against the College of Physicians, holding that "the Censors cannot be judges, ministers, and parties;

416 See PH Schuck and D Elliott, 'Studying Administrative Law: A Methodology for, and Report on, New Empirical Research' (1990) 42 Admin L R 519 (observing that academic specialists often neglect how judicial review affects administrative agency decision-making).

417 Morstein Marx (n 156).

418 By 'adjudication', the US APA, 5 USC. § 551 (7), refers to 'agency process for the formulation of an order'. The definition thus shifts from the action to final act or measure. For further analysis, see M Asimow, 'Five Models of Administrative Adjudication' (2015) 63 Am J Comp L 3 (considering both the decisions taken by agencies and judicial review).

419 The Code's section 3.5.0 provides that: "*Ne quis in sua causa iudicet vel sibi ius dicat*" (that is, "let no one pass judgement in his own cause, nor speak the law unto himself").

judges to give … judgment; ministers to make summons; and parties to have … the forfeiture".[420] The same rationale underlies James Madison's assertion in *Federalist* No. 10 that "no man is allowed to be a judge in his own case" and the decision of the *Conseil d'État* according to which no judge can pronounce a judgment on an earlier decision which he has contributed to adopt.[421] In our epoch, freedom from bias is one of the main instruments to uphold standards in judicial life. It is established by several modern constitutions and codes of civil and criminal procedure. It is defined by both universal and regional charters of rights, such as Article 6 ECHR, which requires "an independent and impartial tribunal, established by law", and the Strasbourg Court has clarified that it applies to public law disputes such as those concerning judicial offices.[422] However, freedom from bias can be intended in more than one way. Within the same legal order in some cases the principle is very strictly applied to any appearance of a possible bias, in the sense that "justice must not only be done, but must be seen to be done",[423] while in others evidence of bias, or at least of a real danger, is required. There are also variations across different legal orders concerning the infringement of the principle, because in some cases any breach of the principle renders the judgment invalid, while in others the case may be remitted.

Differences emerge also with regard to administrative adjudication. As a matter of principle, an independent adjudicator is regarded as an essential requirement of procedural justice. In the UK, it is one of the fundamental maxims of natural justice. Elsewhere, written constitutions – including those of Italy and Spain-[424] define a general principle of impartiality of administrative action. In still other continental legal systems, the principle is established either by general legislation governing administrative procedure or by the courts. Thus, for example, in France, the principle was affirmed by the *Conseil d'État* in 1949, when it dealt with some cases concerning the previous regime of Vichy. It was later codified by the Code governing the relationship between public administrations and citizens, which requires the former to pursue the general interest and to respect the duty of neutrality.[425] Other APAs, such as

---

420 *Bonham v College of Physicians* (1610).

421 J Madison, A Hamilton and J Jay, *The Federalist Papers* (1788; Penguin, 1987); *Conseil d'État*, 11 August 1864, *Ville de Montpellier*.

422 Eur. Ct. H.R., Grand Chamber, Judgment of 25 September 2018, case of *Denisov v Ukraine* (application n. 76639/11); § 52.

423 House of Lords, *R v Sussex Justices, ex parte McCarthy*, *per* Lord Hewart [1923] All ER 233.

424 Italian Constitution, Article 97 (2); Spanish Constitution, Article 103 (2).

425 French APA, Article L 100–2.

the Swedish one, reinforce impartiality by requiring all persons who are disqualified, either on personal grounds or because their impartiality may be questioned, to abstain from participating when the matter is discussed, but there is an exception if "it is obvious that the question of impartiality is of no importance".[426] Similarly, in Switzerland the government officer who elaborates a decision must abstain if he or she may give the impression to have a bias. More generally, the question that arises is whether the principle applies in the same manner to administrative agencies and courts. In some legal systems, the prohibition of bias is intended rigorously especially when a government officer has either any personal or financial interest in the outcome of a certain procedure (planning permissions provide, again, an instructive example) or when he has any personal animosity or prejudice towards an individual or a group. Within the research team, therefore, it was thought that the aspect of bias or prejudice against a group or category of individuals could provide an interesting terrain for testing whether the principle of freedom from bias governs administrative procedure and, that being the case, whether the threshold differs from that which concerns the judicial function.

In our hypothetical case, we suppose that Fatima is a Sudanese national who fled away from her country in order to save her life and entered illegally into a European country that has signed several international treaties imposing duties of assistance and asylum to those who escape from wars, civil wars, and revolutions. When she applies for asylum, her request is rejected by a three-members board, presided by a man who often gives interviews to newspapers alleging that the board's role is to stop the invasion of African migrants, whatever their reasons for seeking asylum. Fatima contests the rejection of her request before the competent court, holding that the president had a clear bias, that he influenced the whole procedure and the final decision should be annulled. The board objects that there is no provision, in the legislative framework that established the board and the asylum procedure, which obliges its members to refrain from expressing their thoughts outside the official procedure. Nor is there any provision obliging them to abstain from taking part in any decision after so doing. Two questions thus arise. The first is whether the legal systems define a general principle against bias, which in our case is not of a specific type, in the sense the adjudicator has a monetary or personal interest, but is of the type which is often referred to as 'prejudice'. The second is whether any infringement of such principle would lead to the annulment of the contested decision. This is, in some sense, an 'extreme' consequence, as it

---

426 Swedish APA (2017), Sections 16 (4) and 17.

implies that any deviation from the standard would imply the annullability of the individual decision.

National reports show more than a difference concerning administrative procedure and judicial mechanisms. Most legal systems have adopted sector specific rules governing the asylum procedure. Thus, for example, France has a "Code for the entry and residence of foreigners and the right to asylum" since 2005. Sector specific rules are, however, variably interpreted in light of general principles, such as those established by Articles 6 and 10 ECHR, as well as by administrative procedure legislation, for example in Italy and Switzerland. Moreover, in the majority of the legal systems examined the courts may only annul an unlawful decision, while in others – such as Austria – they could replace the board's decision.

That said, there are three ways in which our hypothetical case would be handled. The first, which is exemplified by the UK, is to hold that the president's public pronouncements show his apparent or actual bias, thus tainting and discrediting the entire decision-making process. There are two sides of the coin. One is the common law test for "apparent bias", through which the reviewing court must consider whether an informed observer, having considered the relevant fact, would conclude that there was a real possibility that the panel's president was biased.[427] In this case not only is the appearance of bias reinforced by its racial dimension, but Fatima might even be able to argue that the decision was affected by actual, rather than apparent, bias.[428] The other side of the coin concerns statutory law. It cannot be excluded that Parliament intends to derogate from common law principles, including the rule against bias, but such intent should be expressly declared, which is not the case. Interestingly, the jurisprudence of French and Italian administrative courts would reach a very similar conclusion, in the sense that the prohibition to publicly express ideas that would be prejudicial to the proper exercise of authority is deduced from the principle of impartiality. Outside the EU, Serbian courts, too, would be most likely to enforce the obligation to refrain from taking part in a procedure if there facts which raise doubts about impartiality.

The second way in which Fatima's claim could be considered is exemplified by the German legal framework. The interviews with newspapers and other public pronouncements would not justify, in themselves, the annulment of the

427 House of Lords, *R v* Gough [1993] AC. 646. For further analysis, see S Atrill, 'Who is the "Fair-minded and informed observer"? Bias After Magill', (2003) 62 Cambridge LJ. 279.

428 G Anthony, 'UK', in G della Cananea and JB Auby, *General Principles and Sector specific Norms in European Administrative Laws* (OUP, 2023, forthcoming). Also the other national reports mentioned in this paragraph are published therein.

contested decision. They would be regarded as justifying a suspect of partiality. The bottom line is the general principle according to which procedural weaknesses invalidate an administrative decision only if they influence its content. The same conclusion would be reached, among others, by Austrian, Greek, and Romanian courts. Austrian courts would not hesitate, though, to hold that a statement expressing fear of an "invasion of African migrants" raises a reasonable doubt about the board president's bias. Another similarity between Austria and Germany is that the freedom of speech of government officers under Article 10 ECHR would be recognized. However, its exercise is subject to conditions, including the obligation to abstain from cases in which the decision taken by the public authority may be influenced by personal or political opinions. Failure to respect such conditions would inevitably affect the validity of the final decision, which would be annulled.

The Spanish legal system provides an example of a third solution. As observed earlier, the Constitution defines a general principle of impartiality and objectivity, which is reinforced by the prohibition of bias on grounds, among other things, of race and other personal or social conditions. However, an apparent bias would not suffice to set aside the contested decision. The connection with Fatima's case should be demonstrated. Moreover, as the decision is taken by a board, it is necessary to show that the president's public pronouncement, regardless of their inopportunity, have actually influenced the decision. As a result, even though administrators are required to act impartially, the courts would be unlikely to set aside that decision on the sole grounds that the president has made those pronouncement, though they would be very likely to give raise to a disciplinary procedure.

It may be helpful to relate the hypothetical case to one of the main themes of this book; notably the importance of standards of good administrative conduct, also in light of the values recognized and protected by supranational legal orders, including dignity, freedom, respect for the rule of law and fundamental rights. While in other cases the countervailing interests of public bodies, including order and security, would be weighed in balance by the courts, this is not the case when the impartiality of the adjudicator is at stake. The individual's interest to an unbiased adjudicator trumps even the latter's freedom of thought. The underlying rationale is that it is inappropriate for the member of a board – *a fortiori* for its president – to make assertions that are racially connotated concerning the administrative decisions to be taken. Although the various legal systems give different weight to apparent bias, if the courts find that the rejection of the request of asylum is influenced by prejudice, they will either quash it or vary the administrative authority's decision.

This common ground is strengthened by both the ECHR and by EU law. Under Article 13 ECHR, states are required to independently and rigorously examine claims that the applicants' right to life and to be subject to torture (protected by Articles 2 and 3) would be jeopardized upon return. Since *T.I. v. the UK* and *Jabari v. Turkey*, two case decided in 2000, the trend has been very much in the direction of excluding any form of arbitrariness in the handling of asylum procedures.[429] While leaving a certain margin of appreciation to the States, more recent rulings hold that procedural weaknesses, such as an excessively short time-limit for filing an application and for appealing against a removal decision, may render the procedure ineffective and thus in breach of Article 13.[430] Within the more limited scope of EU law, national authorities are required to take decision "objectively and impartially" and it is for this purpose that reasons must be given if the decision has unfavorable effects for the applicant.[431] These standards are interpreted by the Court of Justice as preventing national authorities from adopting measures based on general considerations, without any specific assessment of the conduct of the person concerned.[432]

3 The Unfair Dismissal of a Civil Servant

Public employment is of particular importance for procedural protection also in another respect; that is, administrative due process of law. Traditionally, the dividing line is between the area of what is regarded by the law as an office and the area of politically appointed employees. However, the legal relevance of that stark division should not be overestimated, especially from the viewpoint of a traditional power of the State, that of punishing officials' misconduct (*ius puniendi*) by suspension and dismissal. This justifies Wade's remark that if there is an administrative power that requires an impartial decision-maker and a fair procedure, it is precisely the disciplinary one.[433] This is, therefore, a type of case that is likely to generate interest across national borders, as happened in the British Commonwealth after the House of Lords' ruling in

429 Eur. Ct.H.R., judgments of 7 March 2000, Case of *TI v. UK* (application No. 43844/98), and 11 July 2000, *Jabari v. Turkey* (application No. 40035/98).

430 Eur. Ct.H.R., judgment of 2 February 2012, Case of *IM v. France* (application No. 9152/09), §§ 136–150. The concept of margin of appreciation was defined by the Court in its judgment of 7 December 1976, *Handyside v United Kingdom* (Application No 5493/72).

431 EU Directive 2013/33, Article 7 (4).

432 CJEU, judgment of 14 January 2021, *KS. v Minister for Justice and Equality & MHK. v. Minister for Justice and Equality*, Joined cases C-322/19 and C385/19, § 91.

433 W Wade, *Administrative Law* (Clarendon 1967) 183.

Ridge v. Baldwin.[434] There is still another element of interest, the possibility of invoking the application of Article 6 ECHR.[435] However, the content of procedural protections and the intensity with which their respect is ensured by the courts varies from an area to another. In other words, procedural requirements depend upon the facts of the particular case.

In our hypothetical case, a police officer, Alvin, receives notice of the commencement of a disciplinary procedure for his alleged professional misconduct (ie, related to his office). However, when he asks for legal representation, the officials who conduct the hearing do not allow him to be accompanied by a lawyer on the grounds that this is not required by existing regulations and would make the procedure longer than necessary. Alvin thus defends himself during the hearing. A few days later, the Police Department issues a disciplinary penalty suspending Alvin from service for six months without salary. He then challenges the disciplinary sanction before the competent court, arguing that the hearing was unfair because the refusal to admit legal representation did not allow him to fully show the insufficiency of the evidence against him, and that, when such unfairness occurs, the courts must provide a remedy to redress the consequences. The issues that thus arise are, first, whether the court would give weight to the arguments based on due process of law, notwithstanding the absence of express rules and, if so, whether it would be willing to quash the challenged measure.[436]

The answers given by experts to the hypothetical case reveal significant differences. They concern the rules governing the exercise of disciplinary powers, some procedural aspects, and the nature of the court that adjudicates the official's complaint. There is a complex relationship between general and sector-specific rules, which are sometimes particularly detailed. Trade unions have varying possibilities to impose adjustments to the rules adopted by public authorities. In some legal systems, the disciplinary procedure is preceded by either mediation or conciliation. The deadlines for completing the procedure are more or less stringent. While in some legal systems the dismissal must be challenged before the ordinary courts, in others, there are specialized

434 See W Wade, *Constitutional Fundamentals* (Stevens 1980) 63.

435 See R Chapus, *Droit administratif général* (Monthcrestien 1985) 255 (for the thesis that the difference is that disciplinary procedure concern jobs and professions, while criminal proceedings impinge on the individual's liberties).

436 The same case is discussed, with slight variations, in two edited books: G della Cananea and R Caranta, *Tort Liability of Public Authorities in European Laws* (OUP 2020) 92; G della Cananea and M Andenas (eds), *Judicial Review of Administration in Europe. Procedural Fairness and Propriety* (OUP 2021) 173.

administrative courts. Whatever their nature, some courts would be likely to consider whether legal representation would make the whole procedure unnecessarily long and complex. Others would distinguish between suspension and dismissal and would take a hard look at respect for procedural safeguards only in the latter case.

There is, however, an area of agreement between the legal systems considered. The disciplinary procedure everywhere has a pre-established pattern that must be followed. It begins with the issuing of the notice, it continues with the relevant facts being gathered, and proceeds to the hearing; it comes to an end with the final decision, which must be notified. Moreover, the courts take procedural safeguards seriously, as the following findings show. Powers must be exercised with reasonable care. The right to be heard is recognized and protected. Even the legal systems where there is no general requirement of an oral hearing provide it when an official may be subject to suspension or dismissal. A record of the hearing must be elaborated and kept. Technical assistance is granted, either through lawyers or through experts working in trade unions. There is yet another safeguard concerning the final decision: it must be reasoned. All legal systems, therefore, conform to the maxim *audi alteram partem*, in the strict sense, as well as to the giving-reasons requirement.

What remains to be seen, however, is how those legal systems deal with failure to respect a certain procedural requirement or another. This can be exemplified with regard to an official's hearing. It may be helpful to observe that at the level of general rules there are variants even between neighboring legal systems, such as Austria and Germany. While the former takes procedural infringements very seriously, the latter adheres to the doctrine whereby these do not necessarily determine the illegality of the final administrative act or measure. On the contrary, in this case the German Constitutional Court has ruled that this right forms an essential part of the right to a fair trial under Article 20 of the Basic Law.[437] In the light of this decision, the general rule can be interpreted in the sense that it cannot be categorically ruled out that the decision might have been different if the official had been assisted by a lawyer. Comparatively, what emerges is that there is not simply a common concern for the niceties of administrative procedure but, more concretely, there is the court's willingness to hold that, if the decision-making process is not characterized by an accurate gathering of the relevant elements of fact and law, as well as by fairness in the form of a hearing, the final decision must be quashed. This confirms the conclusion reached by the European Court of

437 German Constitutional Court, decision of 8 October 1974, No 747/73.

Justice in *Alvis*, a case concerning the dismissal of a servant of the EC. The Court followed the opinion of advocate-general Lagrange, for whom the failure to inform the official of the allegations against him had not to be considered decisive in that particular case because the facts were undisputed,[438] but nevertheless expressed its thoughts regarding the right of defence in broad terms, which deserve full quotation:

> according to a general accepted principle of law in the member states of the EEC, the administrations of these States must allow their servants the opportunity of replying to allegations before any disciplinary measure is taken concerning them. This rule which meets the requirements of sound justice and good administration, must be followed by Community institutions. The observance of this principle is even more important when, as in this case, the allegations are capable of resulting in the dismissal of the servant concerned.[439]

This is another example of the judicial development of general principles common to the legal systems of the member States. It is reinforced by the Court's holding that this principle 'meets the requirements of sound justice and good administration', a language that echoes that of Austrian and Italian administrative courts in the last decades of the nineteenth century. Of course, nothing in the above implies that other European legal systems, in other moments of their development, will necessarily endorse the reasoning of the ECJ. Moreover, the national courts' reasoning would differ as to whether it would put the emphasis on instrumental rationales, as opposed to non-instrumental ones, such as those based on dignity. National legal cultures and judicial doctrines would thus be of importance. However, Article 6 ECHR, too, would play an important role. Where the outcome of disciplinary procedure would lead to dismissal and thus exclude an employee from the chosen professional area (unlike other jobs which can be found both in the public and private sectors, such as the medical profession), this could trigger Article 6. This is confirmed in the case law of the European Court of Human Rights, according to which the States – 'in their function as guardians of the public interest' – retain discretionary powers as to the maintenance or establishment of a distinction between criminal proceedings, which are always subject to Article 6, and disciplinary procedures, but

438 Advocate-general Lagrange, Opinion issued on 26 March 1963, in Case 32/62, *Alvis v Council*, § II.

439 ECJ, judgment of 4 July 1963, Case 32/62, *Alvis v Council*, § 1 (A). On the importance of gathering facts, see E Schmidt-Aßmann, 'Conclusions' in Ruffert (n 141) 197.

only subject to certain conditions, so as to exclude results incompatible with the Convention.[440]

4 A License Revocation *Inaudita Altera Parte*

While a disciplinary procedure such as the one just examined concerns action internal to public authorities and gives rise to the exercise of power without any prior decision, in other cases their action produces external effects on individuals, social groups, and legal entities. This is the case, among others, with expropriations and sanctions, as well as with authorizations and licenses. The latter have become increasingly important within that are of government authority initially known as police power and has, in recent years, come to be called 'regulation'. The effects of licenses differ, as occupational licenses imply restraint on the freedom of individuals to pursue their chosen professions, while others allow individuals to use public resources. The classic example is concessions for the individual use of a part of the public domain, such as a beach or waterfront. These measures give rise to the problem of balancing individual and collective interests not only when they are issued for the first time but also when they are modified or terminated. While public welfare may require a summary revocation of the various licenses, the interests of the licensees demand impartial and accurate consideration: may the licensing authority take only public welfare into account, or must it accord the licensees the safeguards of notice, an opportunity to be heard, and the benefit of reasons?

There is more than one reason why this question has become of growing interest from the comparative perspective. One aspect concerns the individual's legal position. Is the licensee's interest considered a privilege, which in some legal systems (for example, in the US) is traditionally distinct from a right and therefore not eligible for the procedural protections associated with rights? Another aspect is whether issuing a license should be distinguished from renewal or revocation as licensees should enjoy greater protection in the latter scenario. It was in a case of this type that the French *Conseil d'État*

440 Eur Ct H R, judgment of 8 June 1975, *Engel and others v the Netherlands* (applications No 5100/71 and others), § 85. See also the judgment of 25 February 1993, *Funke v France* (Application No 10828/84), § 57, where the Court found that the conditions governing the exercise of powers by the tax administration appeared 'too lax' and thus unable to prevent disproportionate interference with the individual's rights.

explicitly enounced for the first time its doctrine of the general principles of law,[441] a case which was cited with approval by Wade to show that similar problems arose on both sides of the Channel and that French administrative courts had 'striven to raise the control of administration'.[442] Moreover, a revocation of the unlawful administrative measures granting economic benefits to the servants of the ECSC was at the heart of the ECJ ruling in *Algera*.

Our hypothetical case comes very close to the French case just mentioned, which regarded a license for selling newspapers and maps at a kiosk. We suppose that Mrs Tramp has a license for selling certain products for those who practice sports, which are not reserved to pharmacies. One day the licensing authority decides to withdraw her license because it intends to renew the offer of such services (without any charge of misconduct), but without giving her any opportunity to be heard. The licensee thus challenges the revocation before a court of law, arguing that the decision was taken in breach of duties of fairness and rationality in decision-making, and asks the court to annul it. While the licensing authority objects that no procedural due process is owed to the licensee, would the court contest unfairness and breach of rationality? In either case, would Mrs Tramp's action be successful? In other words, the hypothesis we seek to test is not so much whether, where a statute or municipal ordinance authorizes the withdrawal of licenses and specifies that notice and hearing to the licensee are requisites for the exercise of the administration's power, but whether compliance to these conditions is essential for a valid revocation. The difficulty arises where the statute or ordinance is silent on the subject of notice and hearing, as well as on the reasons to be given.

On one initial proposition there is an area of agreement between the legal systems included in our comparison; that is, the licensee has a sufficient interest to seek to obtain judicial protection. But, after this, the courts fall into disagreement as to the nature of the interest that is recognized and protected by the legal order. There is disagreement also as to whether the renewal and revocation of licenses are governed by sector-specific legislative rules, as distinct from those of general legislation on administrative procedure, as happens, for example, in Germany, Italy, and nowadays in France. The general rules differ, moreover, as the ECJ observed in *Algera*, with regard the time limit within which the revocation may be decided. Last but not least, the courts disagree as to the breadth of the discretionary power exercised by the licensing authority

441 *Conseil d'Etat*, Judgment of 5 May 1944, *Dame veuve Trompier-Gravier*. For further analysis, see Y Gaudemet, *Droit administratif* (23rd edn, LGDJ 2020) 293.

442 W Wade, *Administrative Law* (Clarendon 1961) 8.

since policy or standards must sometimes be defined beforehand, an issue we will return to in the next chapter, when discussing regulation.

This area of divergence, however, coexists with an area of agreement. While in earlier periods some courts sustained revocation without notice or hearing afforded to the licensee, the decisions assuming the converse position with regard to the process rights related to a license have become the rule rather than the exception. In all legal systems the licensee's interest to carry out a lawful business is regarded as a valuable interest, recognized and protected by the legal order. This entails a twofold consequence. Although public authorities are entrusted with discretionary powers, these can be exercised only in view of all the relevant facts of the particular case. Thus, to offer an example that differs from our case, if the revocation of a license is alleged to be the consequence of the violation of legislative or regulatory provisions, there must be evidence supporting such an allegation. Moreover, the license cannot be revoked without notice and a hearing relating to the licensee. She must be granted access to the preliminary investigations and assessments that induced the licensing authority to commence the procedure, and she must be allowed to present documents and evidence supporting the request that it desist from revoking the license. If it eventually revokes the license, it must give reasons. If it fails to do, and more generally in order to respect procedural requirements, it exposes itself to a twofold risk; that is, its decision may be annulled (in the UK, the licensee may also obtain a remedy by *mandamus* against arbitrary exercise of authority) and the authority may be held liable for damages. In many legal systems – including those of Hungary, Poland, and Romania – when the courts receive claims challenging the revocation of licenses without notice and comment or without reasons, they simply assert that the procedure infringes the principles of fair administrative procedure, and the revocation is, therefore, invalid.

Once again, the existence of a common standard is confirmed from both the substantive and procedural viewpoints by the case law of the European Court of Human Rights. The Court took into consideration the right or interest related to a business license and reached the conclusion that it constitutes 'possession' for the purposes of the protection of property under Article 1 of Protocol No 1 to the ECHR.[443] Procedurally, although the Court recognizes that national authorities have a wide margin of appreciation, one of the cases in which it has found no public interest justifying interference with such a right

443 See the judgment of 18 September 2007, *Paeffgen Gmbh v Germany* (Applications Nos 25379/04, 21688/05, 21722/05) (concerning an internet domain name).

or interest is precisely the annulment or revocation of a license to run a business without any of the reasons relied on by the authorities in the relevant decision.[444]

Outside this area of agreement, other differences re-emerge. Thus, for example, in some legal systems it is affirmed that the holder should not be deprived of the license without being offered an opportunity, with timely notice, to defend it. Conversely, in other legal systems, the infringement of procedural requirements could be justified if an overriding public interest so requires, which however cannot be simply asserted but must be justified. There are yet other legal systems where time is particularly relevant as the licensee's legitimate expectation to be able to continue her business enjoys greater protection considering the time passed since the license was issued. Lastly, our hypothetical case must be distinguished from the circumstance in which a licensing authority decides, as a matter of policy, to revoke all existing licenses, as opposed to a particular one. If individuals seek judicial review of the decisions affecting their interests, they would probably rule that action under the policy was a proper exercise of discretion, though other procedural requirements would apply.[445] In conclusion, a public authority must respect procedural requirements, but these are understood and applied in a flexible manner.

5 Administrative Detention without Reasons

Thus far, we have considered rights relating to businesses, including the deprivation of office and the revocation of licences. But procedural requirements are often invoked also with regard to individual freedom. There is one kind of case concerning detainees subjected to administrative measures that would result in a loss of liberty without a fair hearing, and there is another line of cases regarding suspected terrorists. This is an area of public law which has become increasingly important and, at the same time, controversial. On the

444 Judgment of 28 July 2005, *Rosenzweig and Bonded Warehouse v Poland* (Application No 51728/99) § 62. The earliest case in this line is the judgment of 27 October 1987, *Pudas v Sweden* (Application No 10426/83) (absence of adequate reasons for revoking the license). See Stirn, (n 81) 67 (mentioning various cases in which the Court has recognized a wide margin of appreciation).

445 See, with regard to the rulemaking procedure in the US, DM Bridges, 'Discretion to Revoke and Suspend Licenses: Evasion of the Rule-Making Procedure of the Administrative Procedure Act' (1960) 48 California L Rev 822.

one hand, especially after 2001, national authorities have widely exercised their traditional powers over persons, including the freezing of funds and the deportation of persons where this is said to be conducive to the public good. They have occasionally asserted that they are not bound to grant a hearing or give reasons prior to adopting a deportation order. On the other hand, after some hesitations, national and supranational courts have reacted against what was perceived as a total disregard of due process of law. The *Kadi* ruling of the ECJ is perhaps the best known of these cases.[446] The questions that arise in this respect include whether the absence of a right to enter, and stay in, a country implies the absence of procedural protections, and – as has been observed with regard to the revocation of licenses – whether a person whose permit is revoked should have greater procedural protection than one who applies for asylum for the first time.[447]

To discuss these issues, we imagined a somewhat 'extreme' hypothetical case, as we will explain later. We suppose that a non-European citizen, Fatima, enters a European country legally and obtains a permit of stay for three months, renewable for a maximum of six years, for study reasons. However, on the basis of information gathered by the host country's Department of Internal Affairs, the Minister finds that she poses a threat to national security and prohibits her to leave the house where she resides for three months, a measure that is provided for in national legislation in cases where national security is under serious threat. The Minister's order simply says

> whereas I have reasonable cause to believe that Fatima to be a person of hostile association and by reason thereof it is necessary to exercise control over her, by prohibiting her to leave the flat where she leaves for the next ninety days.

446 ECJ, Judgment of 3 September 2008, joined cases C-402/05 P and C-415/05 P, *Kadi and Al Barakaat International Foundation v Commission and Council*. For further remarks, see JHH Weiler, 'Editorial' (2008) 19 Eur J Int L 895 (holding that the ECJ's decision in Kadi is 'destined to become a landmark in the annals of international law'); G della Cananea, 'Global Security and Procedural Due Process of Law between the United Nations and the European Union' (2009) 15 Columbia J Eur Law 511 (arguing that this ruling maximized procedural due process); G De Burca, 'The EU, the European Court of Justice and the International Legal Order after Kadi' (2010) 51 Harv Int'l L J 1 (for the remark that the ruling weakened the unity of international law).

447 see Craig, *Administrative Law* (n 23) 451. See also the opinion of Judge Friendly in the judgment of the US Court of Appeals for the Second Circuit, *Wong Wing Hang v Immigration Naturalization Service*, 360 F.2d 715 (1966) (holding that there was no obligation to provide a reasoned decision).

Fatima brings an action against the order claiming that it does not state the grounds for the decision and is unreasonable. The Minister responds that, unless a particular legislative provision so prescribes, there is no need to disclose the basis for his decision and that his actions are not justiciable in a court of law. The questions that thus arise are whether the court would endorse the Minister's response and treat the action as non-justiciable and, if not, whether it would be willing to side with Fatima on the merits, particularly as regards procedural protections.

Once again, there is disagreement among the legal systems examined in more than one respect. There are different divisions of power between central and local authorities, such as those of the prefects in France and Italy. There are also different degrees of detail in legislative provisions governing the exercise of administrative power. Moreover, there are different scopes of judicial review against measures such as administrative detention. Thus, for example, in the UK, the norms governing the issuing of control orders under anti-terrorism legislation provide for limited rights of appeal, which has often been contested by the courts. Elsewhere, for example in Belgium and Hungary, there is a pronounced judicial deference *vis-à-vis* the executive determination that 'national security is under serious threat'. In countries that adhere to the ECHR, aliens have a right to obtain judicial review, including the use of interim measures if necessary. Before national courts, in the majority of cases, an administrative act without reasons would most probably be regarded as annullable, while in others – including Italy and Spain – it might be regarded as null. Lastly, in some legal systems, notably Germany, the court would probably give the executive the possibility to State its reasons before the end of the judicial trial. In others, this would be regarded as a posthumous statement of reasons in contrast with the principle of effective judicial protection, as the claimant would not be able to understand the reasons on which the order is based and, therefore, to establish the grounds for appealing against it. Perhaps the strongest criticism has been expressed by Lord Stein, according to whom

> a constitutional state must accord to individuals the right to know of a decision before their rights can be adversely affected. The antithesis of such a state was described by Kafka: a state where the rights of individuals are overridden by hole-in-the-corner decisions or knock on doors in the early hours.[448]

448 House of Lords, *Regina v. Secretary of State for the Home Department and another ex parte Anufrijeva* (2003), § 28. For further analysis, see S Nason, 'The UK' in della Cananea and Andenas (n 436) 185–186.

The diversity in the ways the rule of law is understood is thus confirmed.

That said, a significant area of agreement between those legal systems has emerged. It concerns three requirements. The first is the necessity to respect the pre-established procedure. This requirement is reinforced by supranational norms, namely EU directives for its member States, and the ECHR for the rest of Europe. Article 5 ECHR recognizes the States' discretionary power to restrict the freedom of foreigners, with a view to deportation or extradition. However, this power is not unlimited. It must be exercised in compliance with 'a procedure prescribed by law'. As a second requirement, discretion cannot subside into arbitrariness or unreasonableness. It is precisely because administrative authority is neither unbounded nor permitted to be exercised unreasonably that it is subject to the duty to assess all relevant facts, in order to justify its action. Thirdly, there is a requirement to provide reasons, which requires one or two words of explanation. We have already seen, in Chapter 6, that this requirement, which previously applied only to judicial decisions as opposed to legislation and administration, is nowadays a general feature – a sort of invariant – of administrative procedure legislation in its essence, ie, when an administrative decision adversely affects the individual's rights or deviates from existing rules.[449] A distinction can be made between the two rationales that underlie the duty to give reasons, either non-instrumental (that is, dignity) or instrumental (good administration). But, ultimately, at the root of this duty lies a conception of authority that must not be taken as a synonym of power, let alone of force. In fact, it implies a particular kind of power: that which is justified or 'rightful'. The whole idea of justification refers to the issue of why people accept authority.[450]

In this sense, our hypothetical case is 'extreme' because of the absence of any specific reason except the stereotyped assertion that an administrative measure is required by national security. Since there is no indication that Fatima poses a serious threat to public security, the requirement to give reasons is infringed because there is no justification for the power that is exercised. Accordingly, the courts would allow the appeal and annul the order. Whether

449 ECtHR, Judgment of 22 September 1994, Case *Hentrich v France*, § 56 (for the remark that 'in administrative proceedings the reasons given by the administrative authority were too summary and general to enable the appellant to mount a reasoned challenge to their assessment; and the tribunals of fact declined to allow the applicant to submit arguments in support of his case').

450 CJ Friedrich, 'Authority, Reason, and Discretion' (1958) 1 Nomos 28, at 30 (referring also to Theodore Mommsen's analysis of *auctoritas* in Roman law, regarded as supplementing the act of will by adding reasons to it).

administrative detention – as suggested by some national reports – might also be vitiated by unjustified discrimination against a particular ethnic group or nationality is another possibility which deserves treatment on its own. Lastly, it may be interesting to add that the three requirements mentioned just now are not exclusive to Europe but are shared in another region of the world: Latin America.[451]

6 Consultation: The Role of Experts

The fact that the total absence of reasons, or at least of any reason bearing on the specific facts of the case, constitutes an extreme scenario suggests that less extreme circumstances should be considered in order to have a better understanding of the area of agreement between legal systems. It might therefore be helpful to test the commonality and diversity among these legal systems from another point of view, distinct and distant from the traditional requirements of natural justice and, at the same time, close to the reality of the daily business of government, ie, consulting with technical bodies. These bodies have multiplied rapidly during the last century. They are used widely for administrative functions and differ according to the nature of the problem they are called upon to examine. In areas of scientific uncertainty, they will, for example, be called upon to assess the level of risk posed by a certain substance in the environment (for instance, the chemicals that can be used in a gold mine) or its effect on human beings (eg, in relation to the approval of a new pharmaceutical product). In other cases, there might not be a problem of imperfect information, but there will be diverse views about the impact of a factory on the landscape. There is diversity, moreover, as to the terms under which these bodies are consulted (a duty may be established by legislative or regulatory provisions, but a public authority may decide to consult before adopting a certain decision) and their effects, which can be more or less binding.

In our hypothetical case, we suppose that legislation has established that certain buildings that are particularly important for artistic or historical reasons are protected. They are included in a list. A listed building may not be altered or demolished without special permission from the local planning authority, which must consult the relevant central government's technical committee. This is the case of an old castle. When receiving the application for prior approval sent by a private corporation that has bought the castle and intends

451 See A Brewer-Caris, 'Latin America' in della Cananea and Andenas (n 436) 181.

to alter it for use as a hotel, the local municipality makes its decision without consulting the competent technical committee. The municipality decides that the application cannot be approved, except for some very limited parts. As this decision adversely affects the interests of the private corporation, it brings an action before the courts on the ground that the procedure established by law was not respected, and this did not allow an adequate understanding of either the facts or the interests involved. The question that thus arises is not only whether the court would endorse this argument, but also whether it would be willing to quash the contested decision.

Our case thus differs from what is perhaps the most frequent situation, in which local authorities fail to consult experts before deciding because they wish to grant the permit on the assumption that this will promote the creation of new jobs and increase local revenues. Anyone seeking simple answers might be disappointed. There is great diversity concerning both substantive and procedural aspects of the legal protection accorded to such buildings. The substantive rules have changed throughout the years, most notably in the countries of Central and Eastern Europe, such as Hungary. They differ in part even within the same legal order, notably in the UK. Administrative functions and powers are divided, in various ways, between central and local authorities, with the result that sometimes – notably in Spain – two distinct procedures must be carried out. Furthermore, in some legal systems, the rules governing protected buildings provide that technical bodies must be consulted only when the owner of a protected building intends to destroy it, while in others the duty to consult is generalized, and the opinion of technical bodies is binding to different degrees. Lastly, the type of review which would be carried out by the courts is also variable. Thus, for example, in Austria the administrative court would consult the central government advisory board and consider its technical assessment of the facts before handing down a judgment,[452] while in Germany the administrative court would not quash the contested decision if the procedural error is remedied before the end of the judicial proceeding.[453]

For a better understanding of this case, it is important to bear in mind the differences between it and the previous ones. What is at stake is not one of the traditional requirements of due process – the unbiased adjudicator and *audi alteram partem* – but the duty to consult an advisory body. The very existence of such a duty in the various legal systems examined here is both relevant a significant. It confirms that there is a shared concern for both fairness and

452 See L Mischensky, 'Austria' in della Cananea and Andenas (n 436) 132.

453 See L Weidemann, 'Germany' della Cananea and Andenas (n 436) 137.

propriety. The legal consequences of failure to consult, however, remains to be clarified. The stringency with which the courts have exercised judicial review has varied in different countries and over different periods of time. In more than one legal system, there has been an unwillingness to declare administrative decisions invalid simply because the applicant could point to one relevant element of fact that the authority had not taken into account. Moreover, legislative provisions – for example in Germany – establish that not all procedural infringements constitute illegalities and do not, therefore, lead to invalidity.

It is precisely because of this differentiated legislative and judicial approach to the infringement of procedural duties that it is interesting to see how failure to consult is treated. Thus, for example, the Belgian *Conseil d'État* has held that consultations with the Commission, which must deliver advice on projects that intend to transform protected buildings, constitutes an 'essential formality'.[454] Elsewhere, for example in Hungary, there is a distinction between absolute and relative procedural errors, but the underlying idea changes little. There are, however, two underlying rationales. One is that this is a legally established duty and should not, therefore be conceived as a mere formality. Following this line of reasoning, in the Lithuanian legal order for instance, the duty to consult is associated with the principle of legality. The other rationale is that technical expertise is essential for an accurate and objective decision-making process. People may well disagree as to whether, for example, a certain building deserves to be protected, among other things, using public money. This is a discretionary decision. But it is another thing to ascertain whether a certain building possess the characteristics to be included in the list of protected buildings, as well which characteristics do not alter the essence of such characteristics. In this respect, the intensity of judicial review – for example, in France, Italy, and Spain – would be minimal, because the courts defer to the assessment of those characteristics made by experts, with the exception of deviations from existing criteria. By contrast, an alleged failure to consult is subject to more intense scrutiny and would give rise to the annulment of the contested decision.

7 An Area of Agreement

The procedural requirements imposed on public authorities discharging administrative functions and powers have formed the subject of this chapter,

454 See D Renders, 'Belgium' della Cananea and Andenas (n 436) 134.

and we have touched upon some of the problems regarding the exercise of these powers, focusing in particular on adjudication.

The main point that emerges from our comparative analysis is that, although there is no inflexible principle whereby any infringement of procedural requirements gives rise to invalidity, any breach will normally be taken into account by the courts in the light of the general principles of legality, non-arbitrariness, due process, and transparency. This is not to say that the system of review has become unproblematic. There have been new problems resulting from an excessive demand for procedural justice. Moreover, both EU law and the ECHR have exerted a growing influence. The point being made here, however, is more general. In the field of administrative adjudication, the hypothesis at the basis of this essay can be said to have been confirmed. In brief, there is indeed a common core.

It remains to be seen whether a similar conclusion or a different one may be reached with regard to rulemaking.

CHAPTER 8

A Factual Analysis: Rulemaking

The discussion thus far has been concerned with administrative adjudication. It is now time to examine another administrative function of increasing importance in the business of government, rulemaking.[455] Two types of administrative action, contracts and the exercise of police powers, will be considered in the following chapter. Administrative rulemaking has a twofold importance from the perspective of the common core. On the one hand, the procedural issues that it poses are distinct from those concerning administrative adjudication.[456] While adjudication is based on the paradigm of the judicial proceeding, with the principles of due process rooted in European laws, rulemaking is akin to legislation and requires distinct procedural tools, such as consultation and participation. On the other hand, there is the question of whether the factual analysis confirms the diversity – pointed out in Chapter 6 – that characterizes general legislation on administrative procedure. As a first step, we will take a closer look at the whole problem of rulemaking. Next, our factual analysis will focus on three cases concerning the existence of the power to adopt rules in the absence of a specific legislative basis, citizens' consultation before a policy change adversely affecting them and, lastly, the publication of rules. The final section of the chapter will briefly touch on the more general issue of the significance of rulemaking for the common core.

1 Variety of Administrative Rules

In the past, it was often taken for granted that a fundamental division existed – and had to be maintained – between rules and decisions as a consequence of separation of powers. Rules had to be both general and abstract, in the sense of defining standards of conduct for a pre-defined class or category of persons and legal relationships. They had to be adopted by parliamentary bodies, which at the beginning of the twentieth century were regarded as being

455 See RF Fuchs, 'Procedure in Administrative Rule-Making' (1938) 52 Harvard L Rev 259 (for the characterization of rule-making as a function, as distinct from a mere activity); S Croley, 'Making Rules: An Introduction' (1995) 93 Michigan L Rev 1511, at 1512 (same thesis).

456 Fuchs (n 455) 259.

 | DOI:10.1163/9789004549579_009

broadly representative of all parts of society, though beyond the term 'representative democracy' there were very different realities.[457] Accordingly, executive rulemaking had to be authorized through delegation. On the contrary, an individual decision affected the individual or a pre-defined class or category of individuals or legal entities. It had, therefore, to be adopted by the executive.

With the growth of government, this clear-cut division blurred. Already in the first half of the last century, legislators adopted single-case decisions. Sometimes, they even retrospectively validated unlawfully adopted decisions. This was criticized in orthodox legal scholarship, including German public lawyer Ernst Forsthoff, on grounds that it infringed the principle of *Rechtsstaat*.[458] The same trend emerged in other legal systems, including those of France and Italy. The huge increase – in number and kind – of the rules adopted by administrative agencies had an even broader reach, including common law countries. The reason is that the challenges governments face lead to the use of intrinsically incomplete legislative provisions because they set out the objectives of administrative action without establishing priorities among them or without defining the procedures agencies must follow. A US Court illustrates it in the following manner:

> Congress passes a broadly worded statute. The agency follows with regulations containing broad language, open-ended phrases, ambiguous standards and the like. Then as years pass, the agency issues circulars or guidance or memoranda, explaining, interpreting, defining and often expanding the commands in the regulations.[459]

In Europe, the importance of administrative rules was confirmed in the late 1950's by the Treaty of Rome with a view to legal harmonization.[460] Its norms

457 See KC Davis, *Discretionary Justice. A Preliminary Inquiry* (Greenwood Press 1969) 46 (criticizing, among others, the views of judge Henry Friendly); R Baldwin, *Rules and Government* (Oxford University Press, 1995) (focusing on the legitimacy of governmental processes); A von Bogdandy, *Gubernative Rechtsetzung. Eine Neubestimmung der Rechtsetzung und des Regierungssystems unter dem Grundgesetz in der Perspektive gemeineuropäischer Dogmatik* (Mohr 2000) (comparing the main European legal systems).

458 E Forsthoff, *Rechtsstaat im Wandel: verfassungsrechtliche Abhandlungen, 1950–1964* (Kohlhammer 1964).

459 US Court of Appeals, District of Columbia, *Appalachian Power Company v EPA* (2000), § 11. See also, for a comparison between the US and France, S Rose-Ackerman and T Perroud, 'Policymaking and Public Law in France: Public Participation, Agency Independence, and Impact Assessment' (2013) 19 Columbia J Eur L 225, at 227 (for the remark that rules 'cannot be the sole responsibility of the legislature').

460 For further discussion, see Chapter 11, § 5.

are now reproduced in Article 114 (1) TFUE by virtue of which EU institutions may adopt 'the measures for the approximation of the provisions laid down by law, regulation or administrative action in member States' in relation to the establishment and functioning of the internal market. What matters, thus, is not the legal status of the provisions adopted by national authorities but whether such provisions or rules affect the European single market.

Administrative rules are highly differentiated. There are interpretative rules (which explain the contents and effects of legislative and regulatory provisions), policy statements, procedural rules, and others governing the organization of an agency such as codes of practice and guidelines for enforcement officers. Moreover, whereas in several legal systems – such as Germany and Italy – public authorities may adopt regulations only if authorized to do so, this is not the case for administrative rules. Sometimes these rules are adopted on the basis of enabling legislative provisions. Other rules are adopted by agencies themselves as an alternative to achieving policy goals through individualized adjudication, which can be controversial.[461] Rules will have sometimes have to be applied on a case by case basis, but they will often nevertheless 'be determinative of the result and will strongly influence the outcome'.[462] Other times, they will be directly binding, like regulations.[463] The question that thus arises is how administrative rules can be discerned. Various elements appear to be of legal relevance in this context, including the general applicability of a precept and its future effects. A precept is regarded as being general when it applies to a pre-defined class of persons or legal entities, though they are still relatively few. It must also be prospective, in the sense that it applies not only to legal relationships or situations existing at the time of the enactment but also to those that come into existence later.[464]

From the practical point of view, there are various advantages associated with the increase of administrative rules but also some drawbacks. Rulemaking serves to organize the work of government officers, thus promoting efficiency.

461 See DL Shapiro, 'The Choice of Rulemaking or Adjudication in the Development of Administrative Policy' (1965) 78 Harvard L Rev 921 (criticizing the agencies' reluctance to use rulemaking procedures) and A Scalia, 'Back to Basics: Making Law Without Rules' [1981] Regulation 25 (calling for attention on procedural burdens imposed on rule-making).

462 See see Craig, *Administrative Law* (n 23) 398 (on the 'tremendous variety' of administrative rules); P Cane, *Controlling Administrative Power. An Historical Comparison* (Cambridge UP 2016) 269.

463 See SA De Smith, 'Sub-Delegation and Circulars' (1949) 12 Modern L Rev 37, at 43 (for the remark that 'many circulars do affect the rights of the public').

464 For further discussion, see § 3.

It also provides decision-makers with the possibility to proceed according to a clear statement of the policy regarding the intended course of action[465] as opposed to the exercise of *ad hoc* discretion. However, the procedure to be followed may be difficult and time-consuming. On the other hand, opening procedures may serve to ensure their legitimacy, which is particularly clear in the field of environmental protection. There are national legal systems, such as France, where legislation has been amended to provide for greater transparency and public input.[466] Moreover, the majority of European legal systems have acceded to the Aarhus Convention of 1998.[467] Lastly, rules provide for a clear warning of the consequences to be imposed on individuals, social groups and legal entities, though this raises the question of their publication. These quick remarks may give an idea of some of the issues raised by administrative rulemaking. Three of them will be discussed in more detail in the following sections.

2 Standardless Discretion?

Some words should be said to explain the choice of the first issue, which is of particular importance from the perspective of the common core. Until some decades ago, in Europe there were two opposite visions of the relationship between rules and discretion. One was reflected in the no-fettering rule, while the other required public authorities to rigorously limit and structure their discretionary powers.

The first position prevailed in Britain and other Westminster-type democracies. It was clearly expressed by the House of Lords in the well-known *British Oxygen* case.[468] What was established was that a public body may not unlawfully fetter a discretionary power granted by statute. The underlying basis was, ultimately, the doctrine of parliamentary sovereignty. Thus, even if Parliament

465 Whether rules may also reduce litigation is still another question.

466 See S Rose-Ackerman and T Perroud (n 459) 306.

467 *Aarhus Convention on Access to Information, Public Participation in Environmental Decision-making and Access to Justice in Environmental Matters*, adopted in 1998 and entered into force in 2001. On the Convention's status, see the ruling of the CJEU in Case C-240/09, *Lesoochranárske zoskupenie VLK v Ministerstvo životného prostredia Slovenskej republiky* (holding that, though the Convention has no direct effect in domestic law, national courts must interpret rules concerning administrative and judicial proceedings in accordance with the Convention's objectives, as set out by Article 9).

468 *British Oxygen Co Ltd v Board of Trade* [1971] AC 610. This precedent has been cited, among others, by *R. (Sandiford) v Foreign and Commonwealth Secretary* [2013] EWCA Civ 581, § 59.

had granted a public authority, such as a government minister or an agency, the discretion to determine the best course of action in individual cases, the holder of such discretion was not authorized to transform it into a duty to exercise it in a particular way. Fettering administrative discretion would amount, in Wade's words, to *ultra vires*.[469] His analysis was regarded as exemplary by Giannini in his preface to the Italian translation of Wade's textbook. Giannini took a positive view of this doctrine precisely because it left public administrations considerable leeway.[470]

Conversely, in both Germany and Italy, administrative courts held that if legislation did not define standards for exercising discretion in individual cases, the public authority was required to predetermine the canons of conduct.[471] Otherwise, there was the risk that discretion could be used very differently from case to case and thus degrade into arbitrariness. The phrase coined by German lawyers, '*Selbsbindung der Verwaltung*', expresses the idea that the administrative authority must, first, adopt a binding rule governing its action and, second, respect it. The bindingness of the rules adopted by public authorities was justified, also in other European legal cultures, by the principles of coherence and legal certainty expressed in the maxim *patere legem tuam quam ipse fecisti* (that is, you are bound by your own rule).[472]

On the other side of the Atlantic, in his essay on discretionary justice, Davis' dissented from Dicey. He also dissented from 'European writers [considering] what they call 'the principle of legality' to mean that discretion must be guided by rules'.[473] Empirically, he found that both police and border control officers, as well as prosecutors, exercised very broad discretionary powers and argued that, in order to avoid arbitrariness, they had to limit their discretion, structure its exercise, and thus make it accountable.[474] This was an important step beyond the simplistic ideals that dominated the liberal period, according to which discretion had to be eliminated, and opened up the field for new thinking about the relationship between rules and discretion.

---

469 Wade, *Administrative Law* (n 442) 60.

470 MS Giannini, 'Prefazione' in W Wade, *Diritto amministrativo inglese* (Giuffrè 1965) xv-xvi.

471 This doctrine emerged in the 1930s in the case law of Italian administrative courts. As regards Germany, for a recent reappraisal, see the judgment of the *Bundesverwaltungsgericht* (Federal Administrative Court) of 17 January 1996, 11 C.95, Neue Juristisches Wochenschrift, 1996, 1766.

472 See C Perelman, *Logique juridique* (Dalloz 1976) 147 (discussing also the other maxim *venire contra factum proprium*).

473 Davis, *Discretionary Justice* (n 457) 31 (referring, in particular, to Duguit).

474 id, 219.

For a better understanding of the real terms of the question of interest here, it is important to be aware of the deficiencies of the alleged contrast between the administrative laws of Continental Europe and the British scenario. Some of the shortcomings of the traditional model have already been touched on in the discussion of fact and theory in Chapter 1. Two further difficulties can be identified at the prescriptive and descriptive levels.

Prescriptively, Dicey was a liberal and was thus concerned with what was later called administrative despotism,[475] while Giannini was a public lawyer who developed a functionalist approach to public law in the interwar period and beyond. They opined that, with the widening of the sphere of government, the use of discretionary powers was simply necessary for the efficient conduct of business and, ultimately, for the promotion of social change. Several consequences followed on from this. Social interests, rather than legal rules, lay at the heart of the legal order, and the courts of law were deemed ill-equipped to control the exercise of discretion, particularly with regard to the issues arising under social legislation. The no-fettering doctrine thus appeared to him as one the most striking differences between the English legal system and what he called 'the continental system'.[476] In the former, if a public authority relinquishes exercise of statutory discretionary power, its conduct is incompatible with the law. Referring to the no-fettering doctrine was, in sum, a way of expressing greater faith in administrative bodies than in courts. However, the more legislation was characterized by broad, open-textured provisions, the more it became necessary to discipline the exercise of discretion, as will become clear from the discussion to follow.

Descriptively, things differ from the way in which they were portrayed. In the UK, the fact that an agency does not have express power to adopt standards of administrative conduct does not, *per se*, imply that they are invalid if it adopts them. Invalidity would be sanctioned by the courts when a standard works as an inflexible or invariable rule, in the sense that it prescribes the conduct of administrative officers rather than assisting them in their exercise of discretionary power. In other words, exercising such power must not be determined automatically by a rigid choice made in advance. This is the context in which the no-fettering doctrine has been seen in relation to public law values of fairness and transparency. Thus, for example, in *Bushell*, the House of Lords held that ministers, in exercising their discretion, 'as in exercising any other administrative function …, owe a constitutional duty to perform

---

475 See Lord Hewart, *The New Despotism* (Benn 1929).

476 Giannini (n 470) xvi.

fairly and honestly'.[477] It is in the light of these values that, according to Daly's comparative analysis, the no-fettering doctrine should be viewed as a principle, as opposed to a rule, operating as a means of judicial control 'over the *degree of structuring* of discretion' appropriate to particular contexts.[478] Within the legal systems of Continental Europe, too, things are more complex than Giannini described them. In France, the traditional dichotomy between discretionary power and bound administrative action ('*administration discretionnaire ou liée*') has been enriched by the definition of a third type of action, called '*ligotée*', tied in such a way as to leave some measure of reasonable discretion.[479] Similarly, Italian administrative courts have required decision-makers to discipline the exercise of their discretion through guidelines, in the absence of which executive action may be prone to excess of power, as distinct from illegality.

While the above contributes to clarifying the substantive side of the question concerning the admissibility of rules aiming to structure the exercise of discretion, their effects can only be discerned by looking at the relevant legislative provisions granting a public authority discretionary power, in addition to observing governmental practice and judicial interpretation. There is, moreover, a procedural side concerning the ways a public authority may make rules. Various mechanisms can be used to control it, including parliamentary scrutiny, consultation, and judicial review.

Our hypothetical case regards the rules regulating the disbursement of public money. We assume that parliamentary legislation enables public money to be granted to toy manufacturers that promote a particular social goal: greater environmental awareness in children under the age of ten. According to this legislation, the Department of the Environment can award grants to the producers of the new games. The Department decides to establish some rules of practice, including one whereby it would not award grants for any game costing more than a certain amount of money. When a producer applies for a grant for a new game, its application is rejected on the grounds that the sale price of the game exceeds the amount of money established in advance. The producer thus brings a claim before the court, claiming that, before defining its rules of practice or standards, the Department should have consulted the stakeholders, instead of acting unilaterally. The public authority objects that there is no legislative provision requiring it to consult stakeholders before adopting any rule

477 *Bushell v Secretary of State for the Environment* (1981). For further remarks, see Jowell (n 217) (delineating the contours of the "principle … of consistency").

478 P Daly, *Understanding Administrative Law* (Oxford University Press 2021) 57 (emphasis in the original).

479 On this distinction, see L Di Qual, *La compétence liée* (LGDJ 1964) 368.

or policy. What is at issue is, firstly, whether the court would give any weight to the claim based on the lack of consultation with stakeholders and, secondly, whether, this being the case, it would either strike down the disputed rejection of TW's application or require the public authority to re-open the consultation phase or stage.

The distinction just made between the two limbs of our hypothetical case is helpful from a comparative perspective. As far as the first limb is concerned, all the legal systems examined recognized the existence of legal rules that do not directly affect the rights and interests of individuals, but confine and structure the discretionary powers granted to public authorities. They admit the adoption of rules of this type and distinguish. One thing is whether administrative rules are inflexible, insofar as they leave no measure of discretion to decision-makers, for instance by indicating a mandatory process rather than a recommended but optional one. Another thing is whether rules are conditional or flexible, for example by allowing officials to do something if a certain circumstance is fulfilled, which comes close to the idea of how discretion should be exercised 'normally' but not invariably. Moreover, the importance of consultation is recognized.[480] There are, obviously, variants concerning, for example, the existence of a general duty to predetermine the standards of administrative conduct (which in Italy has been codified by administrative procedure legislation but does not exist elsewhere),[481] a duty to consult stakeholders before adopting rules aiming at interpreting or implementing legislation, and the binding nature of implementing rules. It is for the courts, therefore, to define the possible role of consultation.[482]

There are three relevant aspects for this purpose: legislative intent, precedents, and general principles. Courts look at the language of legislative provisions in order to see if it there is an explicit or implicit support for consultation. In the former case, the absence of consultation will be regarded as a procedural infringement. In the latter, it will be regarded as a choice that requires appropriate justification. The courts will also consider past government practice. Thus, for example, if in other cases the same public authority has consulted

480 See, for example, in the UK, the ruling of the House of Lords in *R. v Secretary of State for Health, ex parte US Tobacco International Inc* (1992), in which a ban on tobacco was held invalid because during the procedure the company was not told the scientific grounds on which the ban was based.

481 Article 12 of the Italian APA requires public authorities to predetermine the 'criteria and ways' in which they will act.

482 For example, the French *Conseil d'Etat* held that certain acts of general applicability, such as circulars and guidelines, may not be contested judicially if they have no binding effects: judgment of 12 June 2020, No 418142, *GISTI*.

stakeholders before making rules, this would be a *prima facie* argument in favor of consultation. Lastly, the courts will apply the general principles governing the exercise of discretionary decision-making. Their willingness to invalidate an administrative rule of the type under examination here on the grounds of, for example, accuracy or unreasonableness may depend on whether the producer can give evidence that, had the Department consulted stakeholders, it would have been manifest that the amount of money it intended to establish was incompatible with the legislative intent. This incompatibility may depend, for instance, on the fact that the established price is excessively low or that it excludes some toys for which a considerable effort has been made to develop environmental awareness. There is still another ground on which the producer's claim might have good chances of success; that is, the argument that an administration consistent with the principles of good governance must hear what the individual has to say about the relevant facts, though a general obligation to consult with stakeholders prior to the adoption of administrative rules exists in some legal systems, but not in others (including Switzerland). It is in this sense and within these limits that an area of agreement exists and can be said to be significant.

Conversely, as regards the other limb of our hypothetical case, namely judicial reaction, there is disagreement between the legal systems included in our comparison. In some of them, notably in the UK, unless there is something in the wording of the statute that indicates Parliament's intent to grant the public authority the authority to issue guidelines or rules, the courts will most probably quash the challenged rule. The reason is, that the rule is used not as a flexible but as a mandatory tool and, consequently, leaves no margin of discretion to government officials; in other words, it is entirely binding on the decision-makers.[483] Conversely, in other legal systems such as those of Italy and Serbia, the judge will probably be satisfied with ascertaining that a standard of administrative conduct has been pre-determined and has been respected in the particular case. Though the latter feature does not focus on the rule itself, but on its application, it must not be neglected because it evokes the existence of an enforceable legitimate expectation. In still other legal systems, a court will deem that, if there is a procedural weakness, it can be remedied and will require the public authority to carry out a consultation before the end of the judicial process.

---

483 This is the case with the UK, which however is not isolated: see the answer provided in the Belgian report in the case discussed in the next section: Renders (n 454) 273.

The existence of a persisting and significant area of disagreement between the legal systems examined should not, however, prevent adequate understanding of the development of the law across time. It is clear that the control of discretion has not remained static. It has changed, and it has done so in a way that escapes the rigid distinction between a no-fettering (inflexible) rule and the duty to pre-determine criteria and standards in the absence of which individual administrative acts are invalid.

3 Consultation before Policy Change

Given the importance of the administrative choices that affect the public at large, the analysis of another case has been deemed advisable. It concerns consulting the public before a decisive policy change. The previous discussion is also relevant here, as is general legislation on administrative procedure. There are, however, some distinctive traits, which will be discussed shortly after setting out the hypothetical case.

We imagine that under national legislation local authorities are required to provide a comprehensive library service. The term 'comprehensive service' is not defined in the legislation, however. It is the responsibility of local authorities to determine how to deliver public library services in the light of local needs and available funding. But there is a legislative duty to consult users, and the Ministry for culture and media can order an inquiry when there is a concern that a local authority is failing to fulfil its duties. When a local authority announces on its website that it is going to close three of its five public libraries and drastically reduce the opening hours of the remaining two libraries, a consumer association challenges this change of policy and argues that it ought to be consulted before a final decision is taken. The local authority simply asserts that its decision is due to financial difficulties and adopts the decision. The consumer association then brings a case before a court on the grounds that: a) the duty to consult users should be taken very seriously when a decision is likely to deprive them of existing benefits; b) consultation should thus occur when proposals are at a formative stage rather than on the point of being adopted; c) the local authority should consider more than one option, weighing up their advantages and disadvantages, also in the light of the users' observations. As in the previous case, we seek to understand whether the court would endorse any of these arguments and, if so, whether it would be willing to quash the challenged decision.

At least two distinctive traits between this case and the previous one deserve a mention. The first is that in this case the focus is on determining a policy, rather than on the rules. Secondly, whereas in the previous case it was the legislator who made the main decisions, in this one, legislation allows the local authority to take into account a wide variety of factors in determining the public interest, including maintaining certain standards in the delivery of public services and promoting the interests of users, as well as maintaining an appropriate balance between the various types of expenditure and thus seeking to reduce costs. The function that the local authority must discharge is financially and socially complex. Financially, closing one or more public libraries might be justified, for example, because it may produce economies of scale, though in our hypothetical case there is no such justification. Socially, closing libraries inevitably provokes discontent among actual and potential users. Where the range of relevant factors is broader, then the problem of administrative discretion becomes less manageable. However, all legal systems have to decide on the mechanisms for exercising some degree of public control over them, including consultation and judicial review. It is not, therefore, only substantive aspects that matter, but also procedural ones.

It is clear from our comparative analysis that legal systems differ as to how services must be performed, as well as whether interested individuals and groups should be given an opportunity to submit statements and produce evidence supporting or opposing the proposed policy change.[484] Several consequences flow from this difference, including whether the public authority should make public a concise general statement about the purposes of its action. There is, first of all, divergence concerning the existence of national legislative provisions governing the organization of public libraries. Lithuania has legislation of this type, while other nations do not. Secondly, there are differences in procedural requirements. While our hypothetical case supposes that a legislative duty to consult users exists and then goes on to ask what the consequences of its infringement would be, in reality such a duty does not exist outside but a few legal systems. This is not the case, for example, with Hungary, while in Germany the rules governing local planning might be applied, by way of analogy. Spain is at the opposite end of the spectrum as it has legislation requiring public consultation before a public service may be severely reduced or dismantled. Thirdly, judicial attitudes towards consultation differ remarkably. The Spanish legal system is, again, illustrative of increased participatory rights, because courts will annul an act which implements policy change carried out

484 See T Ziamou, 'Public Participation in Administrative Rulemaking: the Legal Tradition and Perspective in the American and European (English, German, Greek) Legal Systems' (2000) 71 Heidelberg J Int L 42 (2000).

without prior consultation.[485] In the UK, too, it is likely that the courts would hold that the duty to consult users should be taken very seriously. Moreover, they would affirm the general common law principle that consultation must take place at a formative stage.[486] Similarly, in Germany, administrative procedure legislation has recently been amended by introducing what is called the duty of early public participation. Furthermore, the administrative court would probably hold that users have not been provided with sufficient information, although this failure could be remedied if the local authority carries out a proper consultation before the end of the judicial process.[487] This is not the case in Austria, where it is unlikely that the courts would affirm a duty to consult at an early stage.[488] Fourthly and finally, judicial attitudes differ as to how the exercise of discretion should be controlled. Thus, for example, courts in the UK would take the asserted necessity of austerity measures into due account, but would nevertheless require local authorities to consider the product of consultation before finalizing any proposals.[489] By contrast, in Hungary and Lithuania the courts would refrain from discussing how discretion has been exercised, especially with regard to financial difficulties.[490]

However, there is an area of agreement between almost all those legal systems on two general points. First, with the notable exception of Hungary, there is an emerging propensity of both legislators and judges to promote the citizens' right to be provided with a meaningful opportunity to make their voices heard before a public authority makes a policy change which may adversely affect them. General legislation on administrative procedure would be applied, for example, within the legal systems of Italy and Ukraine. Second, *if* there is a legislative duty to consult users before making a policy change, as is supposed in our hypothetical case, then the local authority is required to take it seriously everywhere. Thus, for example, in the UK the courts enforce the duty to act fairly, also in the light of the democratic principle that the public must be involved in policy choices affecting it. Similarly, in Italy, the administrative court would most probably endorse the applicant's claim that if the local authority is unable to prove that the decision severely cutting services was the only possible one in view of financial difficulties, and annul it.[491] In Belgium,

485 O Mir Puigpelat, 'Spain' della Cananea and Andenas (n 436) 283.

486 Nason (n 448) 285.

487 Weidemann (n 453) 277.

488 V Neubauer, 'Austria' della Cananea and Andenas (n 436) 272.

489 See again Nason (n 448) 285, noting the similarity of the fact of our hypothetical case with *R(WX) v Northamptonshire County Council* [2018] EWHC 2178 (Admin).

490 A Andrijauskaite, 'Lithuania' della Cananea and Andenas (n 436) 280.

491 DU Galetta and P Provenzano, 'Italy' della Cananea and Andenas (n 436) 279.

too, the administrative court would consider consultation an essential formality; as a result, if the duty to consult is infringed, the final measure will be quashed.[492] Interestingly, in a neighboring nation, France, the administrative court would probably develop a different line of reasoning but would reach the same conclusion. Its reasoning would be different because the French administrative courts would review the local authority's action from the perspective of the traditional principles upon which the *service public* is based; that is, equality and continuity.[493] However, they would quash the contested decision.

4 Partially Unpublished Rules

Another controversial issue concerning administrative rules is information. This is controversial because administrative rules are governed by different norms from those that govern administrative adjudication and legislation. Briefly, the most basic requirement is that decisions regarding individuals must be notified to their addressees, though some legal systems have set a higher standard in the sense that identifiable third parties must also receive notification, for example when the issuance of a building permit for a factory impinges on the interests of neighbors. As regards legislation, a traditional feature of liberal democracies is that it must be published in some form if it is to be obeyed and respected. It normally comes into operation either on the date it is published (as distinct from the date on which it is made) or on a subsequent date. The underlying rationale in France is the principle dating back to the Revolution that legislation must be accessible to the public.[494]

It is much more difficult to find administrative rules than it is to gain access to legislation. Part of the problem depends on the fact that there is no uniform approach to the nomenclature of administrative rules. Another part of the problem regards publication. On the eve of the adoption of the US APA, an American observer pointed out that not only were individuals no longer able to readily inform themselves about the numerous rules applicable to their conduct, but government officers too were 'unable to find their

492 Renders (n 454) 273–274.

493 D Costa, 'France', in della Cananea and Andenas (n 436) 276.

494 This is amply illustrated in a report by the Conseil d'Etat, *Publication et entée en viguer des lois et de certains acts administratifs* (La documentation française 2001) 15. In other legal systems, such as Spain, the retroactivity of administrative acts is explicitly prohibited by administrative procedure legislation: S Muñoz Machado, *Tratado de derecho administrative y derecho pùblico general* (2nd edn, BOE 2019) 93.

way in the labyrinth of regulations accumulated in different bureaus without adequate systematic registration or publication'.[495] In Europe, too, unpublished rules proliferated. For example, a Belgian commentator observed that while legislation required the publication of regulations, other acts containing administrative rules, such as circulars and general orders were not published.[496] A similar problem emerged in France, where Parliament opted for a drastic solution, consisting in depriving unpublished circulars of any effect, but numerous circulars have subsequently been adopted without being published. Like in France, in Italy a general statutory norm requires the publication of all acts of a general nature. The UK has made a different choice, as delegated legislation comes into force after it is published, and the Statutory Instruments Act 1946 is regarded by some commentators as confirming the common law rule,[497] but there is a plethora of administrative rules subject to differentiated requirements as to their publication. There is yet another part to the problem, one which derives from technological progress. Although legal norms require public authorities to keep a hard copy of the rules they adopt, the question that arises is whether it makes sense to do so, when all rules can be published and be immediately accessible on the internet, thus reducing the secrecy of administrative law,[498] as do the freedom of information acts adopted by many European legal systems. There remains, lastly, the question of whether agencies should be bound by their own rules, regardless of whether these are published in the official journals. This is an important aspect of what it means to have a government of laws, where the citizenry seek to hold those who govern to the respect of rules they make because they may have acted on the basis of those rules.[499] The same rationale is at the heart of the prohibition of retroactive rules.[500]

Among all these issues, our hypothetical case focuses on the question of publication. Suppose that during a pandemic, the Minister of Health defines the prices of various types of face masks in an order that also establishes

495 AK Kuhn, 'The Administrative Procedure Act and the State Department' (1946) 40 Am J Int L 784. See also LA Jaffe, 'Publication of Administrative Rules and Orders' (1936) 24 Am Bar Ass. J. 393, at 394 (same remark) and, for the UK, De Smith, 'Sub-Delegation and Circulars' (n 463) 42 (observing that 'it is unsatisfactory that the public may be without means of access' to rules).

496 A Buttgenbach, *Manuel de droit administratif* (3rd edn, Larcier 1966) 23.

497 See DJ Lanham, 'Delegated Legislation and Publication' (1974) 37 Modern L Rev 510.

498 PL Strauss, 'The Rulemaking Continuum' (1992) 41 Duke L J 1463, at 1464.

499 See Davis, *Discretionary Justice* (n 457) 79 (for whom regulations should be published and readily available).

500 See L Fuller, *The Morality of Law* (Yale University Press 1969) 51.

pecuniary sanctions in the event of non-compliance with the price limits. The Minister announces that the order will be published in the official journal, as required by existing legislation. But the order is published only in part, without mentioning the specific prices for the various types of face masks. Moreover, it is published on the Health Department's website rather than the official journal. When a chemist is sanctioned by the local administration for selling the masks at a different price, she challenges the penalty before the competent court. She argues that without full publication of the order, it is either invalid or unable to produce any legal effect because her freedom to do business may not be limited outside the cases and forms established by law. The Health Department responds that the order is valid, despite its failure to publish it on the official journal, because in today's world, a government website can potentially reach more persons than the official journal. The questions that thus arise are, first, whether the court would endorse the chemist's arguments based on the failure to publish and, second, whether it would deem that the partially unpublished order is either ineffective or invalid.

At first sight, in this case, the area of disagreement between the legal systems examined seems broader than in those examined earlier. It would appear, in particular, that there is a profound difference between the legal systems where publication is required as a condition for the validity of the rules, and the other legal systems, where publication is regarded as a mandatory requirement and the breach of which inevitably invalidates the act to which it relates, and, lastly, the systems in which it is considered a directory requirement, in the sense that its breach does not necessarily have this effect. Greece, France, and the UK exemplify these differing solutions. In Greece, the courts do not accord weight to the label of an act as a circular or guideline. If these acts impose duties on government officials or impinge on citizens' lives, be it favorably or unfavorably, courts require publication as a condition for validity, like regulations.[501] In France, after an attempt to eliminate circulars *en masse*, the general norm established by administrative procedure legislation[502] is that government guidance, including circulars and instructions that interpret legislation or define administrative procedures, must be published. In the absence of publication, they are abrogated. But the Code also clarifies that unpublished circulars are not applicable, and public authorities are prevented from using them in their relationships with citizens. Accordingly, whether or not an unpublished rule is still valid, it cannot have legal effects. Lastly, in the UK the facts of the leading

501 Ziamou (n 484) 49.

502 Article L 312–2 of the Code adopted in 2016.

case, are very similar to those in our hypothetical case. When an act of delegated legislation was published without the annex, and a firm was charged with infringement of the rules contained in it, it challenged the action due to the lack of publication. The Court held that the lack of publication or partial publication does not, in itself, invalidate the act, because the general common law rule is that only delegated legislation us required to be published, but this requirement is not mandatory. However, it ruled out that anyone could be held guilty of a contravention of an unpublished rule.[503]

It must be observed, however, that the area of disagreement is considerably narrowed if one takes into consideration the criteria defined by the courts. In this regard, it has been found that, according to the French administrative courts, the norm of the Code does not apply, for example, to a circular determining the standard of conduct for certain government officials. As a result, the fact that the circular was unpublished has not determined its abrogation. Moreover, and more importantly for our purposes here, it has been found that an unpublished rule cannot be applied adversely to individuals in the decisions directly and adversely affecting them.[504] This comes close to the solution adopted in the UK, as well as in other common law systems, including the US, where a person may not be required to resort to, or be adversely affected by, an unpublished rule, unless that person has actual knowledge of it.[505] This shows, in contrast with the first impression, that, in terms of the actual results reached in our factual analysis, the area of disagreement becomes less significant if one considers not only the ready applicable norms but also a host of other rules and doctrines decisive for their interpretation. Underlying this area of agreement is a common concern for legal certainty, which is not seen as a general ideal but a principle that prevents public authorities from applying unpublished rules.[506]

---

503 House of Lords, *Regina v Sheer Metalcraft Ltd* (1954). For further comments, see Lanham (n 497) 512 (suggesting that there is a presumption that Parliament does not intend its delegates to make rules which come into force before they are published).

504 *Conseil d'Etat*, decision of 19 December 2016, Application No 405471, *association La Cimade*. See also the decision of 7 July 2019, Application No 427638, *Ligue des droits de l'Homme et Conféderation Générale du travail*, concerning the interpretation of the provision of the Code.

505 US APA, § 552. For further remarks, see Strauss (n 498) 804.

506 See Muñoz Machado (n 494) 93; Lanham (n 497) 516.

5 An Unexpected Area of Agreement

Turning from the specific findings to the broad over-all picture, two aspects should be considered: what could be expected and what has been found. As observed in Chapter 6, administrative procedure legislation is characterized by diversity in two ways: most, but not all, European legal systems have adopted one kind of administrative procedure legislation or another, and even among those legal systems that have one, only a few have defined general norms on rulemaking. One could, therefore, expect that the area of disagreement would be much larger than what has emerged with regard to administrative adjudication. In some instances, our findings confirm what a public lawyer with an adequate knowledge of other legal systems would have expected, for example, with regard to consultation.

However, other findings are at least partially unexpected.[507] These refer, in particular, to the power to pre-determine the standards of administrative conduct. The supposed contrast between common law and civil law systems concerning the relationship between discretion and rules was found to produce fewer differences than expected. *In lieu* of the expected distinctions, there are interlaced areas of agreement and disagreement. To mention one further example, concerning the publication of rules, there is obvious divergence among the legal systems examined as to whether the absence of publication impinges either on the validity of rules or on their effectiveness. But all these legal systems adhere to the same norm that unpublished rules may not be applied against individuals and legal entities. Underlying this norm is the principle of legal certainty. The area of agreement is, therefore, qualitatively at least as significant as the area of disagreement. This reveals an improvement for society as a whole. 'Citizens are better off' if they can have adequate knowledge of the rules that, directly or indirectly (that is, through individual administrative decisions applying those rules), impinge on their interests, and can thus more easily verify whether they receive equal treatment.[508]

---

507 See F Moderne, 'Préface' in A Brewer-Carias, *Les principes de la procedure administrative non contentieuse* (Economica 1992) 2.

508 Strauss (n 498) 808.

CHAPTER 9

Governmental Wrongdoing

This chapter will, as mentioned earlier, be concerned with another type of consequence for public authorities arising from the claim that their administrative action is unlawful on the grounds of procedural fairness and propriety. We shall now move on to look at government liability. According to a (diminishingly important) strand in public law, liability was at the heart of the divide between common law and civil law systems. There are further reasons suggesting that liability is fertile terrain for legal comparison, in view of European integration. The next step will be to discuss the results of our factual analysis of four cases considering the consequences of procedural impropriety and unfairness in two of the cases we have already examined: the dismissal of civil servants and the revocation of licences. Two further cases concerning forms of administrative action other than adjudication, contract, and physical coercion, will then be discussed.

1 A Worst-Case Scenario

There are three reasons for considering government liability a fertile topic for comparison. Every system of law must face and solve problems concerning the liability of public authorities and public officers.[509] The solutions can be similar or different, but legal scholarship has, until now, focused on their diversity, making government liability a 'worst-case scenario'. However, over the last seven decades, the autonomy of the State, of every State when addressing issues concerning liability has been limited by the obligations stemming from membership of both the EU and the Council of Europe. Both these aspects will be addressed in turn. Dicey stretched the contrastive approach when he criticized

> 'the opposition specially apparent in the protection given in foreign countries to servants of the State or … of the Crown, who, while acting

509 D Fairgrieve, *State Liability in Tort: A Comparative Law Study* (Oxford University Press 2003) 269.

> in pursuance of official orders, or in the bona fide attempt to discharge official duties, are guilty of acts which in themselves are wrongful or unlawful'.
>
> 'the fourth and most despotic characteristic of *droit administratif* lies in its tendency to protect from the supervision or control of the ordinary law courts any servant of the State who is guilty of an act, however illegal'.[510]

The problem was that he focused on less recent French norms, essentially as they were before 1848, whereas they had been changed in 1875. Well before the first edition of his treatise, much had already been done through the jurisprudence of the *Conseil d'État* concerning liability. Moreover, for all the prestige of French administrative law, in other parts of Continental Europe, lawyers and judges were used to thinking of tort law as preeminently private law. Dicey's account of English law also failed to acknowledge the fact that the English law of the day accorded extensive immunities from being sued in tort to the Crown, even if government officials did not benefit from them. In a similar vein, as early as the 1950s, Davis cast doubt on 'whether English courts at any time would have held the Prime Minister liable personally on account of exercise of discretionary powers'.[511] However, for some, government liability is still marked by differences.[512] It can, therefore, be viewed as a sort of worst-case scenario in the sense illustrated by Shapiro, ie, as the 'body of known legal phenomena most likely to falsify' a conjecture or position, in our case, the hypothesis that a common core exists and does not consist only in vague ideals.[513]

This is all the more interesting in the light of European integration because the choice of solutions to the problems concerning public authorities is no longer entirely left to each individual State. The measures adopted by both the Council of Europe and the EU influence this choice. After issuing various acts concerning the exercise of administrative powers, the CoE Committee of Ministers adopted a recommendation on public liability.[514] Although the recommendation was not binding on the member States, it was interesting for two reasons. The first of these was the intent to increase the liability of public authorities as evident in the first principle laid down by the

510 Dicey, *Introduction to the Study of the Law of the Constitution* (n 22) 329 and 345.

511 KC Davis, 'Administrative Officers' Tort Liability' (1956) 55 Michigan Law Rev 201, at 202.

512 P Gonod, 'Les tendances contemporaines de la responsabilité administrative en France et à l'étranger: quelle convergences?' (2013) 147 Rev fr adm publ 720.

513 Shapiro, *Courts. A Comparative and Political Analysis* (n 67) vii.

514 Committee of Ministers, Recommendation No R (84) 15, of 18 September 1984, relating to public liability.

Recommendation: reparation should be ensured 'for damage caused by an act due to a failure of a public authority to conduct itself in a way that can be reasonably expected from it in law', with the presumption that a failure occurred 'in case of transgression of an established legal rule'. The EU has also adopted some measures that have had an impact on national systems of liability. Some of these measures are sector-specific as they concern a given field, such as public procurement. Since 1989, EU directives require member States to ensure that if those who participate in government procurement suffer unjust damage arising from the conduct of public authorities, they can seek financial compensation. A more general limitation to the autonomy of the member States derives from the Court of Justice's assertion of the general rule, 'inherent in the system laid down by the treaties', whereby a State that fails to respect the rights stemming from EC legislation is financially liable for the damage caused to those rights and cannot claim the sovereign immunity.[515] By virtue of the vertical effect of this rule, EU tort law upholds individuals' interests against the State by imposing the respect of legality. Secondly, the legal system of the EC/EU is interesting due to its own regime of liability. The Treaty of Rome made the EEC liable for all the torts it or its agents committed, and rested liability on the 'general principles common to the laws of the member States'.[516] This could be interpreted as implying that the six founding States shared a general principle of tort liability. Its existence was implicit, too, in the *renvoi* to the shared general principles.

2 Further Consequences of Procedural Unfairness in Adjudication

We have already examined two cases concerning claims of procedural impropriety and unfairness; that is, the dismissal of a civil servant and the revocation of a license *inaudita altera parte*. They deserve further consideration because due to their 'extreme nature' in that government action is affected by 'egregious procedural failings'.[517] The point of interest here is whether the

515 Case C-6/90, *Francovich, Bonifaci e.a. v Italy* and Joined Cases C-178/94, C-179/94, C-188/94, C-189/94 and C-190/94, *Dillenkofer and others*. For further analysis, see R Caranta, 'Governmental Liability After Francovich' (1993) 52 Cambridge LJ 272.

516 Article 215 EEC Treaty, now Article 340 TFEU. See Lorenz (n 54) 24.

517 G Anthony, 'UK' in della Cananea and Caranta (n 436) 124.

arguments brought by the applicants can be endorsed by the courts also from the viewpoint of damages.

Our first hypothetical case concerned a disciplinary procedure ending with the dismissal of a policeman, Maurice. In this case, it was found that some standards generally associated with public law are relevant in the legal systems included in our comparison. An employee subjected to such a procedure is entitled to a clear statement of the charges against him and to a meaningful opportunity to make his case in a hearing, assisted by either a lawyer or an expert. The authority is also required to take into account all relevant considerations. If the final decision adversely affects the employee, and all the more so in the event of dismissal, the public authority must give a statement of reasons. There are cases where the misbehavior of the civil servant is so serious, and the facts are so manifestly clear, that a judge may take the view that whatever the description of the facts and related events the employee may give, it would make no difference. This was the standard, from a comparative perspective, set by the ECJ in *Alvis*. As for reasons, in various legal systems, these might be furnished in another document, so long as a reference is made to it. Moreover, in various legal systems, including Germany and the UK, interest would be payable, but this would not be the case in France. It is equally uncertain whether Maurice would be able to obtain damages for loss of reputation. This would be so in Spain and Switzerland but not in Austria and Poland, while in the UK it would depend on whether the procedural failings were due to the inadequacy of sector-specific rules rather than an act of discretion.[518]

That having been said, an area of agreement between legal systems can be found where none would have been expected on the basis of the ideas and beliefs about public law widespread until some decades ago. For example, though there is no general duty to provide an oral hearing in Italy, it would be required in a case of this kind. Similarly, in the UK, the common law does not impose a general duty to furnish reasons, but it would do so in this case. If the dismissal infringes these standards, which are associated with the public law values of propriety, fairness and transparency, also in the light of Article 6 ECHR,[519] it will most probably be annulled. The area of disagreement becomes even less significant if one considers that not only does the annulment produce its effects retrospectively, but it also implies that the public authority must pay

518 See E Nieto-Garrido, 'Spain', in della Cananea and Caranta (n 436) 121, T Tanquerel, 'Switzerland', ibid. 122, S Storr, 'Austria', ibid. 98, M Wierzborski, 'Poland', ibid. 112, and Anthony, ibid. 125.

519 R Vornicu, 'Romania' in della Cananea and Caranta (n 436) 118.

compensation. However, this cannot be established simply in terms of the net wages Maurice would have earned without unfair dismissal, as would be the case in Germany.[520] Especially in France, this is not permitted due to a principle stemming from public finances: public money cannot be given for a service that has not, in reality, be rendered.

The other hypothetical case concerns the revocation of a license or concession *inaudita altera parte*. The distinguishing elements of this case can be briefly mentioned. There is no concept of the employer's prerogative, but a discretionary power related with the distribution of government largesse, in this case through the attribution of the reserved use of a part of the public domain. More importantly, the facts of the case confront us with an exercise of power in absence of any notice and hearing, as well as reasons justifying the decision taken by the public authority.

In this respect, at least two elements of diversity must be noticed. First, in some legal systems, including Austria and Germany,[521] a claim against government liability has a subsidiary nature and is, accordingly, only permissible if other legal remedies have failed to protect the claimant's interests. Accordingly, only a limited space remains for a claim for damages. Second, in some places – for example, in Poland – both losses and lost profit would be included in the compensation the court may award, whereas in Austria, lost profit would be recognized only where the conduct of the public authority is characterized either by willful intent or gross negligence, and in France it would not be granted on the basis of the principle of the precariousness of any license concerning the public domain.[522] There is thus a disagreement among the compared legal systems, and not just regarding questions of detail but also the applicability of the provisions established by civil codes, if they exist.

However, from a comparison of the actual results from the viewpoint of judicial enforcement of the requirements imposed on public authorities, an area of agreement among legal systems can be found. First and foremost, all the legal systems adhere to the principle that administration is not exempt from liability. The point Wade made in the early 1960s – 'if an authority exceeds it powers […] if its act, being without justification, constitutes a tort' then it is liable for an action for damages – was thus of general importance for administrative law.[523] Whether their functions, notably legislation, can still be considered immune outside the area governed by EU law is another question.

520 F Wollenschlager, 'Germany' in della Cananea and Caranta (n 436) 107.

521 Storr (n 518) 216; Wollenschlager (n 520) 220.

522 See T Perroud and R Del Pilar Trujillo, 'France' in della Cananea and Caranta (n 436) 219.

523 Wade, *Administrative Law* (n 442) 82.

Secondly, it emerges that procedural requirements such as the right to be heard and the duty to give reasons are everywhere deemed necessary in order to protect people from arbitrary interference by those who wield power over them. Infringement of these requirements entails the invalidity of the revocation due to the impossibility to understand how administrative action can be justified. The area of agreement is, therefore, more significant than expected.

3 Contracts: The Unlawful Exclusion of a Tenderer

We turn now to other ways in which administration is discharged, namely through contracts and police powers. We observed in Chapter 3 that the close of the nineteenth century saw a growing number of requests for judicial review of police power by individuals claiming that they had undergone abuse of power in the ways in which limitations were imposed either on personal liberty or freedom to do business, and we suggested that the development of procedural requirements permitted the courts to control the exercise of power through judicial review. The topic thus has a bearing on our argument that procedures can provide a better terrain for testing the existence of a common core.

Things are partially different as regards contracts, which normally enhance the opportunities for individuals and firms to achieve their own goals.[524] As contracts are increasingly used by public authorities, which define therein the terms for spending a very large sum of public money, there are issues of fairness and propriety concerning their making.[525] At first sight, the law governing administrative action appears to be characterized by both commonality and diversity. Whereas in some legal systems public authorities are subject to the general law of contract, albeit with some adaptations as a response to the specific needs of administrative activities, in others there is a more or less separate body of government contract law, concerning what the French call administrative contracts ('*contracts administratifs*'). On the other hand, the solutions are largely influenced by international and supranational norms. There are international treaties, such as the Agreement on Government Procurement adopted in the context of the WTO.[526] There are EU directives, which are binding for its

524 G Langrod, 'Administrative Contract: A Comparative Study' (1955) 4 AJCL 325.

525 See D Lemieux, 'Fair Procedures and the Contracting State' (2009) 61 Admin L Rev 115 (discussing the US and Canadian experience).

526 The Agreement, adopted in 1994 and subsequently replaced in 2012, has forty-eight WTO members, including the EU, its twenty-seven States and other European States (Moldova, Montenegro, Norway, Switzerland, Ukraine and the UK). The US, Australia, Japan and South Korea, too, are parties to the GPA.

member States, as well as on the others that have stipulated agreements with the EU, such as Norway and Switzerland. These directives establish the general principles to be respected, including free competition and transparency for acquiring goods and services, and the specific types of procurement procedures, such as open tenders and private auction. They define detailed prescriptions concerning the phases or stages of such procedures.[527] As a result of all these requirements, when public authorities make contracts, their freedom of choice is much more limited than that of private parties in order to ensure the respect of the principles of fairness and transparency so as to avoid any bias among parties and the mismanagement of public money.

In our hypothetical case, we seek to shed light on how contracting authorities exercise their powers in the context of public procurement law: the exclusion of participants from a tender procedure if they are considered unreliable and therefore unsuitable to be awarded a contract. Contracting authorities can exclude from a procurement procedure any operator who has been convicted for professional misconduct, including the failure to pay social security contributions. We thus imagine that during the procurement procedure initiated by the municipality of Mandeville, it receives information from the Department of Social Security (DSS) showing that a bidder, Alphagroup, has systematically failed to pay social security contributions. Mandevilles' officials use the information received from the DSS, which is not informed about it, and drop its offer. It is only after the conclusion of the tendering procedure, when Alphagroup has access to the documentation held by the municipality, that it discovers that its offer had been dropped because of its alleged systematic failure to pay social security contributions. It then seizes the national court, arguing that: (i) the municipality had no right to use information against it without giving it a real opportunity to challenge it; and (ii) factually, the DSS had made a mistake, insofar as the economic operator that failed to respect the obligations stemming from social security legislation was not Alphagroup but another one named 'Alpha Group Ltd'. Alphagroup then brings an action for damages against the Mandeville municipality before the court. The municipality objects that if anyone is liable, it should be the DSS. The questions that thus arise are, first, whether Alphagroup's action based on procedural fairness would be likely to be endorsed by the court, and, if so, whether the court would conclude that the participant lost the chance to win a contract and, lastly, if the municipality is found liable, whether it can turn to the DSS, in order to place the burden on them, or at least share it.

527 EU Directive 2014/24 of the European Parliament and of the Council of 26 February 2014.

It is necessary to make a preliminary remark concerning the remedies available against the exclusion of a tenderer. All the national reports point out that the legal systems examined provide for interim relief, which is a requisite for EU States that was laid down as early as 1989 by directive 89/665.[528] Some reports add that the request for immediate judicial protection constitutes a requisite, in the sense that if the applicant has not sought to obtain it, a judge will normally be unlikely to allow an action on grounds of liability. The underlying assumption is that if the tenderer had sought to obtain interim relief, the contracting authority would have an opportunity to rectify its decision. This is important in itself. It may also give rise to further consideration from the point of view of the question concerning the respective positions of the local and national authorities because the former had no reason to suspect that the information provided by the latter was wholly inaccurate. Alternatively, it might be argued that had the contracting authority correctly followed procedural requirements and thus heard the applicant, it would not have excluded it only on the basis of the information received from the Department. However, in our hypothetical case, we suppose that the participant has not been duly informed in a timely manner of the reasons supporting its exclusion precisely because we seek to understand whether the infringement of procedural requirements can give rise to government liability.

Not surprisingly, the results reached are largely those that experts in government procurement with a comparative background would have anticipated. The distribution of judicial powers is even more differentiated than in other cases. In the UK, for example, the firm's action would obviously have to be brought before the ordinary courts. Other legal systems, including France and Italy, apply the general rule that action taken by administrative authorities must be challenged before administrative courts, though there are sometimes particular rules governing this type of judicial proceeding, in order to ensure its speed. There are still other legal systems, for example Austria and Poland, where, unlike the action for annulment, the action for damages falls within the jurisdiction of the ordinary courts. Moreover, as regards the standards of administrative conduct, in Germany the duty to accurately consider all the relevant facts is established by legislation, while elsewhere – notably in the UK – it is a judicial construction. Another crucial factor of diversity concerns the conditions for affirming governmental liability. There are differences depending on whether the liability is governed by the general rules, established either by

528 For further analysis, R Caranta, 'The interplay between EU legislation and effectiveness, effective judicial protection, and the right to an effective remedy in EU public procurement law' (2019) 12 Rev Eur Adm L 63.

civil codes or the courts (as in Germany and the UK, respectively) or is subject to a special legal regime, notably as in France. In Germany, for example, liability is sometimes imposed on the basis of illegality, and this solution can also be found in EU law, where there is no real discretion (otherwise, the breach would have to be sufficiently serious).[529] In other legal systems, including France and Romania, authorities are liable if an administrative action is characterized by either fault or intentional wrongdoing, and the general understanding is that fault denotes illegality.[530] Further differences arise in the field of public procurements. Within the EU, this field is the subject of both EU directives and the national legislation implementing them, while in Switzerland some cantons do not have special provisions, and others rule out compensation for lost profit.[531] In Germany, compensation for loss of profit might be awarded if the participant can show that if the error of assessment had not been made, it would have been ranked in first position, while in Italy it would be sufficient for the participant to show that it had a good chance of winning the award.[532]

However, some findings emerged that came as a surprise at least to some, while others were unexpected by the majority of participants in our seminar. Starting from the standards invoked by the applicant, the general position in domestic laws is that both the right to be heard and the duty to accurately consider all the relevant elements of fact would be important and enforceable for the purposes of judicial review. It is clear that a claimant who seeks to rely on a breach of procedural requirements will have to prove their existence. In terms of procedural fairness and propriety, however, the courts would most probably consider that there was a failure to inform the participant of the cause of exclusion, a breach not justified by any overriding public interest (as might be the case, for instance, in a criminal investigation). They would hold that, had the local authority duly informed the participant, it would have been able to show that there had been an error of fact. They would reach the conclusion that there was evidence of misconduct and that the participant consequently lost its chance of being awarded the contract. There is, thus, a causal link between the infringement of procedural requirements and the damage suffered by the participant. The participant would be awarded compensation for the costs incurred for preparing the offer and participating in the procedure. Lastly, everywhere, including in the legal systems in place under socialist

529 See Wollenschlager (n 520) and B Marchetti, 'The EU' in della Cananea and Caranta (n 436) 163.

530 See Vornicu (n 518) 178.

531 Tanquerel (n 518) 181–182.

532 See Wollenschlager (n 520) 171–172.

governments until 1989 (such as Hungary, Poland and Romania), the responsibility of both local and national authorities would be recognized in the sense that liability should be shared. In conclusion, there is an area of agreement between legal systems that can be explained by the presence of two forces. Modern governments face similar challenges[533] and often devise similar solutions. Similarity is further accentuated by the common standards defined by EU law.

4 The Violent Police Officer

Thus far, we have looked at various forms of administrative action that give rise to the adoption of legal acts, including administrative decisions, contracts, and acts of general applicability. But administrative functions and powers are not discharged only through legal acts. There is a wide range of activities consisting in the delivery of goods and services, such as free books in schools, and medical treatment in hospitals, respectively. This area is a manifestation of the 'positive' State. There is also a vast area of police powers that – manifesting the 'negative' State – implies interference with an individual's rights. The latter area, which has seldom been examined from the comparative point of view,[534] will be considered here.

Three preliminary points should be made before presenting our hypothetical case. Firstly, the phrase 'police powers' can be understood in either broad or narrow terms. In the broad sense, the police powers doctrine holds that States have the power to regulate the conduct of all citizens in order to protect a public interest. These powers include, for example, adopting rules concerning goods and other things that may constitute a danger to the public (such as chemical substances and inflammable material), general orders limiting the free movement of persons and goods, and individual measures, such as the confiscation/requisition of goods, or the suspension of a business concern. In the narrow sense, police powers to stop and search individuals are among

533 See Langrod, 'Administrative Contract: A Comparative Study' (n 524) 340 (noting that in common law systems, a 'progressive adaptation of 'normal' contractual procedures emerged, as a response to functional needs'); JDB Mitchell, *The Contracts of Public Authorities. A Comparative Study* (Bell & Sons 1954) (comparing the UK, the US and France and showing some analogies); JB Auby, 'Comparative Approaches to the Rise of Contract in the Public Sphere' (2007) 52 Public Law 40.

534 F Morstein Marx, 'Comparative Administrative Law: Exercise of Police Power' (1942) 90 Un Pennsylvania L Rev (90) 266.

the most contentious aspects of administrative action. They have always been contentious because they impinge on the individual's liberty in a variety of ways, ranging from a request for information ('did you see anyone leave that place?') to the order to leave a place, which, if disregarded, may be followed by arrest for resisting an officer of the law, and a pecuniary penalty, while the most extreme power is to carry out an arrest in the context of a criminal proceeding.[535] Secondly, it is highly problematic to compare the exercise of police powers within two or more States. It is one thing to discuss such powers in the context of a liberal democracy or a well-administered State but quite another to discuss them in the reality of an authoritarian government. Perhaps it may turn out that the degree of comparability varies from sub-topic to sub-topic, for example from police powers to patrol highways to the dispersal of an unauthorized public meeting. As a practical example, it seemed advisable to choose the first type of case. Thirdly, in this case, the exercise of power by public officers implies the use of coercion. This raises a whole host of issues, including when and how coercion may be legitimately used and the limits that must be respected in order to avoid arbitrariness. If these ways and limits are violated, can a police officer be said to be acting to fulfil a public duty, or is he or she acting in the same way as a private individual would? From this viewpoint, police officers are not regarded as law-enforcers and protectors of the peace but as law-breakers. The other question that thus arises is what consequences ensue in terms of liability for damages.

In our hypothetical case, we suppose that two police officers stop a driver, Agatha, and ask her quite ruthlessly to get out of the vehicle and show them her papers. Agatha vehemently protests and resists the officers' request, stating that she is being treated unfairly. One of the two officers, without warning Agatha as required by Police Department rules, moves towards her, grabs her left arm, and twists it into an armlock. The torsion causes Agatha's elbow to crack, and permanent injury ensues. She refuses any assistance from the police officers and is taken to hospital by some witnesses. Subsequently, Agatha sues the two police officers and the State for damages. The questions which arise are, first, under what conditions, and to what extent, would her court case be successful and, second, whether it would be relevant that the two policemen infringed the guidelines set out by the Police Department.

As might be expected, the comparison of police powers is more complex than, say, the adoption of authorization to sell electronic communications

535 See S Williams Cooper, 'Abuse of Police Powers' (1890) 150 North American Review 658 and JM Evans, 'Police Power to Stop without Arrest' (1970) 33 Modern L Rev 438.

services, an area increasingly regulated by EU law. There are both general and particular legislative provisions on police powers. The latter concern, for example, the prevention of terrorism, with a further element of differentiation depending on whether there are also rules established by regional authorities, as is the case for example in Germany but not in Italy. There are also different rules governing government liability. Thus, in Austria, for example, a direct lawsuit against a police officer is not feasible if he or she was acting in the course of duty.[536] On the contrary, in both France and Italy, the action would need to be brought against the State. The underlying rationale is not to accord special protection to public servants but to protect victims from an officer's actions, with the further distinctive trait that the State will then take action against the responsible officer. Moreover, in the UK, as well as in other common law systems, our hypothetical case would be conceptualized as one of strict liability; that is, a case in which a person is legally responsible for the consequences that flow from the action carried out, even in the absence of any intent (*mens rea*). There is still another element of divergence concerning the rules governing the exercise of police powers. While in a legal system – for example in France –[537] the guidelines defined by the Police Department serve to structure and limit the exercise of power, together with regulations, and their violation would entail the officers' misconduct, in another only the latter are both legally relevant and binding, so their infringement gives rise to illegality. Other differences concern judicial review. There would be a different tendency to consider whether the police officers can be said to be acting to enforce the law. This would have an impact on the court's jurisdiction. While in most legal systems the action would have to be brought before ordinary courts, in France the claim would be heard by administrative courts, unless there is misconduct on the part of the police officers, as opposed to '*faute de service*' (that is, a service fault).

With these caveats, it is noticeable that not only is this hypothetical case regarded as potentially relevant to all the legal systems included in our comparison, but it is also soluble.[538] While it is no doubt right in general terms to say that policemen have a duty to prevent crime and that the execution of this general duty involves various powers interfering with personal freedom, at least as far as the use of vehicles is concerned, such powers are not unlimited. If there is an area of public law in which, for all the importance of the ends, they

536 Storr (n 518) 271.

537 T Perroud and Del Pilar Trujillo (n 522) 274.

538 Even 'readily soluble', according to C Harlow, 'France and the United Kingdom' in della Cananea and Caranta (n 436) 305.

do not justify all means, it is precisely that of police powers. First and foremost, not all means are permitted, but only those allowed by the law.[539] Second, the use of coercion must respect some basic requirements, including a clear warning, except when an officer is under attack, which is not the case here. Without this necessary warning, the use of force is illegitimate, also because a warning would have probably avoided the injury. Third, the use of excessive force is prohibited according to a logic of proportionality. Fourth, in all the legal systems examined, an action for damages can be brought against the exercise of police powers, although the court's willingness to uphold it will be different. Finally, if the infringements of the legal requirements just mentioned are proved, in addition to a causal link with the damage, that is the injury suffered by the victim, liability arises, and the damage can only be compensated for in money. This always covers medical expenses and any loss of profit, for example for the period of time in which the injured person is unable to work. It may also cover non-economic losses. The area of agreement is, therefore, broader than could be expected.

It does not rule out, however, the existence of two further differences which deserve a mention. In some legal systems including the UK, but not all, the courts would most probably also accord 'exemplary' damages.[540] Damages of this kind express the court's disfavor towards officers who abuse their powers and are intended to prevent the same officers or others from committing the same offences in the future. In other legal systems, notably in Hungary, the courts would probably be willing to accord more weight to Agatha's conduct, especially her initial refusal to establish her identity and show the papers regarding the vehicle. We can probably see here the legacy of an authoritarian theory of the exercise of State power over the individual.

This is not without problems from the perspective of the ECHR. The point is well illustrated by the recent case of *Vig v Hungary*, in which the European Court showed its willingness to interfere with a refusal by domestic courts to acknowledge that the plaintiff had suffered harm caused by the exercise of police powers.[541] These powers were widely exercised against a group of people in the context of a festival organized by a community centre in Budapest. Police forces carried out 'enhanced checks', asking participants to reveal their identity. The plaintiff did so because he felt intimidated by the police but later brought a claim before the domestic courts. When his claim was

539 Wollenschlager (n 520) 276.

540 Harlow (n 538) 305.

541 ECtHR, Judgment of 14 January 2021, Case *Vig v. Hungary*, (Application No 59648/13).

rejected, he argued that his rights under Article 8 ECHR had been violated. Interestingly, his complaint was not that the police had exceeded their powers under national legislation, but that such legislation was incompatible with the Convention. The Court endorsed his argument in two ways. It observed that interference with the individual's rights must be necessary in view of a certain objective, which was stated when the administrative action was authorized. This was problematic from the viewpoint of the proportionality of the challenged measure. Moreover, as the domestic court itself had affirmed, it had no power to review either the authorization of the enhanced checks or the operational plan defined by the police force.[542] The Court thus held that, in the absence of adequate safeguards offering the individual adequate protection against arbitrary interference, Article 8 had been breached, and awarded non-pecuniary damages to the applicant, in addition to the costs and expenses incurred during the proceeding.[543] This ruling shows the persistence or return of a positivist-authoritarian theory of the exercise of State powers, as well as the Court's willingness to challenge it. This is confirmed by other recent rulings, even in the more contentious area of anti-terrorism legislation. Thus, for example, in cases such as *Gillian and Quinton* and *Vinks*, the Court endorsed the individuals' argument that the powers of authorization and confirmation of stop and search were neither sufficiently circumscribed by existing rules nor subject to adequate legal guarantees against abuse and were not, therefore, 'in accordance with the law', in contrast with Article 8.[544] This is not without consequences, because the member States have a fiduciary duty to revise their legislation and practices when these have been found to be in breach of the Convention.

5 Conclusion

Our analysis of liability in various forms of administrative action has taken into account, on the one hand, 'extreme' cases, where governmental action is affected by 'egregious procedural failings' and is, consequently, more likely to

542 Id, § 56–57.

543 Id, § 62 and 75. For further remarks, see A Sajo, 'On Old and New Bottles: Obstacles to the Rule of Law in Eastern Europe' (1995) 22 J Law & Soc 97.

544 ECtHR, Judgment of 12 January 2010, *Gillian and Quinton v the United Kingdom*, (Application No 4158/05); judgment of 30 January 2020, *Vinks and Ribicka v Latvia* (Application No 28926/2010).

be subject to liability,[545] and, on the other, more ordinary cases, such as the exclusion of a bidder. Our analysis has sought to ascertain whether there are not only distinctive but also common traits. The former not only persist in general terms, but in some cases also appear more significant than they were some years ago. This is illustrated by the Hungarian case just examined, in which the conflict between the common values and principles, in the context of the ECHR, and national legislation and practices, is manifest.

At the same time, there is an area of agreement among the legal systems examined here, and it is not limited to the demise of old ideas and beliefs about public law, 'as administrative authorities have virtually no immunity',[546] but extends to the duties of consideration and procedural fairness that public authorities owe citizens and other individuals, as well as social groups and legal entities. These duties reflect to varying degrees the common values recognized and promoted by the Council of Europe and the EU and support the view being advanced here that it is both factually unrealistic and normatively untenable to assume that domestic administrative laws are characterized only by innumerable differences or are even incommensurable. However, the infringement of these duties does not necessarily imply liability. In this respect, we find a further confirmation of the flexibility of procedural justice.[547]

545 Lochak (n 15) 122; T Heukels and J Tib, 'Towards Homogeneity in the Field of Legal Remedies: Convergence and Divergence' in P Beaumont, C Lyons, N Walker (eds), *Convergence and Divergence in European Public Law* (Hart 2002) 111.

546 Wade, *Administrative Law* (n 442) 39.

547 Harlow and Rawlings, *Law and Administration* (n 393) 621.

PART 3

Commonality and Diversity: An Evolving Relationship

CHAPTER 10

Explaining Diversity

Our initial conjecture about the existence of some shared and connecting elements among European legal systems, as well as numerous and significant differences, has been tested through diachronic and synchronic comparison in Parts 1 and 2. Naturally, the coherence between the initial research choices and the results, as well as their intrinsic relevance, is for the reader to assess. We offer a few general remarks in this final Part. At the beginning of his innovative research, Schlesinger observed that the '*existence* of some kind of common core was hardly challenged', while its etiology 'may not yet be fully explored'.[548] In our case, likewise, there are clearly numerous differences between European administrative laws, but the factors that underlie such differences are less easily comprehensible, so it may be helpful, therefore, to examine them in detail in this chapter, beginning with the question of diversity. We aim to go beyond the mere claim that 'history matters', like culture. It does so, under an umbrella of diversity that gives adequate weight to policy considerations and choices.

1 The Causes of Commonality and Diversity

As we have just observed, it is necessary to explore the etiology of commonality, as well as that of diversity. There are two reasons for beginning with an examination of their etiology. The first is that this way of proceeding corresponds to an established line of thinking. Secondly, an analysis of the causes of commonality has been suggested in the context of earlier studies about the common core because it can offer a better understanding of its significance.

Assessing the causes requires us to clarify the key terms. For the established tradition dating back to Aristotle, causes are not merely antecedent events that produce other events but the reasons things exist and are the way they are. In brief, causes provide explanation. There are two basic reasons to support an investigation of the causes: one concerns the importance of causes considered as a whole; the other the role that different types of causes can play. On the one

548 R Schlesinger, 'The Common Core of Legal Systems: An Emerging Object of Comparative Study' in K Nadelmann, A von Mehren and J Hazard (eds), *Twentieth Century Comparative and Conflicts. Studies in Honor of Hessel Yntema* (Sythoff 1961) 66 (emphasis in the original).

DOI:10.1163/9789004549579_011

hand, a causal analysis is indispensable simply because an adequate comprehension of things involves identifying their origin, *raison d'être* and evolution. This distinguishes scientific knowledge from an accidental or superficial one. On the other hand, there are different types of causes. Aristotle distinguished four types: the material cause (what a thing is made of), the formal (what it is), the efficient (how it came to be what it is), and the final or teleological (what is its purpose).[549] It is important to understand what a certain thing is, in our case for example, whether a certain standard of administrative conduct is an invariable or a variable one, and its substrate. If things were unchangeable, an analysis of their essence would suffice. However, since things can change, and often do, this dimension must be considered too. This requires us to ponder on whether a change was the consequence of a certain cause and whether it was necessary, sufficient, or contributed to with others (concurrent causes).

Although the above may already explain why an analysis of the causes is necessary, another word or two are appropriate in the light of previous studies on the common core, beginning with Schlesinger, Gorla and other scholars in the context of the Cornell Law School seminars.[550] Their research constituted a healthy antidote to the simplistic assumption that two similar legal provisions or institutions should produce similar effects. It stimulated explanation based on social and political settings,[551] as well as the historical roots of the legal institutions examined. It thus promoted new research focusing on parameters that can serve as indicators of efficient causes. In particular, in his studies on judicial decisions in the period of *jus commune* (especially in the seventeenth and eighteenth centuries) Gorla shed light on the adjacency or proximity of legal systems (both conveying the sense of being very near to another), as well as their affinity, ie, their close similarity, often due to the existence of a

549 Aristotle, *Metaphysics*, 1.3. In secondary literature, see WL Benoit, 'Systems of Explanation: Aristotle and Burke on "Cause"' (1983) 13 Rhetoric Soc Quart 41 (observing that Greek philosophy did not intend to discover laws of succession in phenomena but what things themselves are and thus arguing that Aristotle's system of causes is more easily understood as a theory of explanation, rather than a strict theory of causality) and HS Thayer, 'Aristotle on Nature: A Study in the Relativity of Concepts and Procedures of Analysis' (1975) 28 Rev of Metaphysics 725, at 731 (for the remark that purposive causes also include deviations and failures).

550 Schlesinger, 'Introduction' (n 2). The team also included Pierre Bonassies, John Leyser, Werner Lorenz, Karl H. Neumayer, Ishwar C. Saxena and W. J. Wagner.

551 See M Rheinstein, 'Book review of RB Schlesinger, Formation of Contracts: A Study of the Common Core of Legal Systems' (1969) 36 Un Chicago L Rev 448, at 453 (noting, however, the that the aim of viewing law as a social system had not been pursued and probably could not be so in a team composed only by legal scholars).

common core.[552] It is in this sense that, according to Schlesinger, the existence of a common core, viewed as a working hypothesis, derived plausibility from historical studies.[553] On the other hand, where there are no common roots among legal institutions forming parts of legal systems with fairly dissimilar trajectories, a focus on final causes may serve to explain why such legal systems have adopted, for example, a *Conseil d'État* entrusted with both advisory and judicial functions. In addition to factors such as prestige or the desire to adopt what is regarded as a more advanced solution to similar problems, membership of either a regional organization or a regulatory regime may be a demonstrable cause of similarity between legal systems.

Some caveats are called for at this stage. The first is that providing causal explanations for differences in the development of administrative laws is no easy task. This explains why writers who show an interest in them do not hesitate to clarify that they only make 'suggestive associations' in this regard.[554] The second caveat is that distinguishing the various causes does not avoid scientific controversies. For example, giving much weight to material causes can be criticized on the grounds that it is essentialist (an objection from which Aristotle himself was not immune)[555] or mechanistic. Likewise, an exclusive focus on efficient causes can be rejected as functional (a frequent accusation against the once widespread approach in comparative law) or mechanistic.[556] However, an adequate understanding of the respective weight of each type of explanation can shed light on whether a controversy is about a certain phenomenon or how it is explained. Lastly, an analysis of a causal relationship does not dispense from empirical knowledge; rather, it helps to understand why, for example, an ancient judicial institution is shaped the way it is, as well as why it is either modified or abolished at a given time. A correct use of one of those causal constructs within an appropriate empirical domain may thus not resolve all disputes, but will serve to clarify the issue.

552 Gorla (n 69) 630; G Gorla and L Moccia, 'A Revisiting of the Comparison between Continental Law and English Law (16th–19th Century)' (1981) 2 J Leg Hist 143.

553 Schlesinger, 'The Common Core of Legal Systems: An Emerging Object of Comparative Study' (n 548) 65.

554 Craig, 'Comparative Administrative Law and Political Structure' (n 1) 948.

555 Thayer (n 549) 726 (defining essentialism as an 'unwarranted hypostatizing of concepts').

556 C Curren, 'On the Shoulders of Schlesinger: The Trento Common Core of Private Law Project' (2002) 2 Global Jurist 5 (discussing functionalism in Schlesinger's approach).

2 Context Matters: History

Although attention is traditionally directed in legal discourse to the rules that characterize a certain system, the weight of history cannot be neglected. Indeed, history shapes the way we think about the law. The argument that national traditions are not composed exclusively of rules has two limbs. It is not always the case that the basic normative elements of a certain legal system are to be found in a set of written rules. Nor is it infrequent that very similar legal, if not identical, provisions adopted by two legal systems produce differing consequences. These limbs will be addressed in turn. The first will be analyzed in reference to the United Kingdom in two respects: the English Constitution and natural justice. The other will be discussed with an eye to the different effects of the judicial reforms made in Belgium and Italy during the nineteenth century. This discussion will also serve to introduce another argument, namely the claim that different routes are interdependent.

The possibility of finding a written text including the fundamental norms of the legal system is notoriously doomed to failure in the UK. Although its constitution is often described as being 'unwritten', this term is misleading for two reasons. It is true that, unlike – for example – Germany and the US, no single document in which the UK Constitution is defined exists. Nor is there any 'official collection of constitutional rules'.[557] There are, however, other aspects of the Constitution that are written down, either in primary legislation (electoral law is a good example) or in parliamentary internal rules. However, the English case is important because it shows that giving much weight to the existence of a set of rules of law about the conduct of the business of government is misplaced for a more fundamental reason: parts of the constitution are made up of customary practices and conventions, whose precise form and content are not laid down in any official document but which are regarded as legally binding.[558] Such conventions, which date from the Magna Carta (1215) and the Bill of Rights (1689), can thus be regarded as custom, in conformity with the established conception of custom confirmed in Article 38 of the Statute of the International Court of Justice; ie, 'a practice accepted as law'.[559]

---

557 G Marshall and GC Moodie, *Some problems of the Constitution* (Hutchinson 1959) 14.

558 G Marshall, *Constitutional Conventions. The Rules and Forms of Political Accountability* (OUP 1987).

559 See Article 38 (1) (b) of the Statute of the International Court of Justice (1948) and, for further remarks, A Roberts, 'Traditional and Modern Approaches to Customary International Law: A Reconciliation' (2001) 95 Am J Int L 757 (recalling the two elements of international custom; that is, state practice and *opinio juris*).

The role of custom is important also for a proper understanding of the basis of procedural constraints on the exercise of power by public authorities, which in English law is the concept of natural justice. As indicated earlier, despite its name, natural justice is not a natural law concept (though for a long period of time the law of nature was a source of law to be applied by the courts) but, rather, a term of art.[560] It includes the two fundamental maxims of the unbiased adjudicator (*nemo judex in re sua*) and of the right to be heard (*audi alteram partem*). Their historical evolution is well illustrated elsewhere.[561] What matters, for our purposes here, is that both these principles do not derive from any positive law. Moreover, precisely because they are principles, as distinct from rules, their interpretation and application have varied throughout time. Thus, for example, in the years that preceded *Ridge v Baldwin*, a case concerning the dismissal of a policeman that is similar in more than one respect to our hypothetical case discussed in Chapter 8, Wade lamented the 'defiance of natural justice'.[562]

The French legal regime for holding public authorities liable in tort, discussed in Chapter 3, is equally instructive. We have accurate accounts of the process by which the divergence between the French legal regime and others occurred. We know that, even though the decision taken by the *Tribunal des Conflits* in *Blanco* (1872) was not considered by French judges as disruptive of the accepted order of events, it implied that the rules on liability codified by the Napoleonic Code of 1804 were not applicable to public authorities. Only two aspects in this narrative need be remarked here. Formally, under the traditional understanding of equality before the law, citizens must be treated alike, but government officers were not subjected to the same rules of law. The result of this has been a reinforced separation between public law and private law. However, substantially, in the long run, the *Conseil d'État* defined standards of government liability that largely coincide with those applied by the ordinary courts.[563]

---

560 Above, Chapter 3, § 4. For a critique of the claim of legal positivism that natural law is deprived of any concrete relevance, see S Cotta, 'Positive Law and Natural Law' (1983) 37 Rev of Metaphysics 265 and JAC Grant, 'The Natural Law Background of Due Process' (1931) 31 Colum L Rev 56.

561 See P Craig, 'Natural Justice in English Law: Continuity and Change from the 17th Century', in *Liber Amicorum per Marco D'Alberti* (Giappichelli 2022), 3.

562 HWR Wade, 'Comment on Byrne v. Kinematograph Renters Society (1958)' (1959) 17 Cambridge L J 32.

563 See R Chapus, *Responsabilité publique et responsabilité privée. Les influences réciproques des jurisprudences administrative et judiciaire* (LGDJ 1954).

The argument derived from history may, as we have seen above, be reinforced by the contention that history exerts a strong influence on the application of legal provisions. This important point can be demonstrated by referring to the birth of the Italian system of administrative justice. We have seen that the Belgian Constitution was literally reproduced by the Italian legislator in 1865. Like in Belgium, the idea was that the ordinary law had to be applied by the ordinary courts. Existing administrative bodies discharging judicial functions were thus abolished. However, the Italian Council of State retained some judicial functions, such as those in disputes concerning public debt, on the grounds that this was a manifestation of sovereignty.[564] It also kept its traditional role as adjudicator with regard to the claims brought by citizens to the Crown. Twenty-five years later, it was entrusted with judicial functions over public law disputes. The main argument supporting this reversal was that the ordinary courts had shown a reluctance to ensure the protection of the substantive interests that emerged from a rapidly changing society. But tradition, too, played a role. The more general point of interest here is the necessity to go beyond the mere claim that 'history matters'. Earlier stages of administrative law exert a profound influence on the development of institutions and norms.[565]

Some problems, however, are inevitable. What, then, of the argument outlined initially in dissent from the thesis of Savigny and Dicey that administrative law is a sort of national enclave? Do not the results of our analysis forcefully indicate that the weight of history is decisive in shaping legal institutions and norms? Do they not reinforce Edmund Burke's argument that the longstanding patterns of behavior, or 'customs' (whose origin is 'dark and inscrutable'), are more important than laws because they are the main source of traditions, which reflect the views of several generations, instead of the one that supports the passing of new legislation?[566] A superficial understanding of the relationship between history and public law might, in fact, suggest this conclusion.

---

564 F Merusi, 'Il debito pubblico e la giustizia amministrativa' (2012), in id, *La legalità amministrativa fra passato e futuro. Vicende italiane* (Editoriale scientifica 2016) 163.

565 See Fromont (n 4) 2 (emphasizing the importance of traditions).

566 See E Burke, *Reflections on the Revolution in France* (1790) 139 (for the arguments that by 'a slow but well-sustained process the effect of each step is watched' is preferable to a fast one and that the accumulated wisdom of several generations is greater than that of only one). The quotation concerning customs is borrowed from R Paden, 'Reason and Tradition in Burke's Political Philosophy' (1988) 5 History of Philosophy Quart 63, at 65. For a reappraisal of Burkean ideas, see RM Weaver, *Ideas Have Consequences* (1948; 2nd edn, Un Chicago Press 2013) 28.

However, a more considered appreciation of the results of our diachronic and synchronic comparison reveals the inadequacies of this argument from two angles. Firstly, history is often considered too narrowly. In particular, most lawyers' retrospectives focus on modern law, while little attention – or none at all – is devoted to less recent periods, during which some of our administrative and judicial institutions were forged, and some central concepts of public law were elaborated, such as the 'public interest', for example. Thus, for example, Craig has observed that the predominantly modern focus precludes a more articulated analysis of the rationales for change.[567] Secondly, there is a serious risk of overrating path-dependence; that is, the idea that events, in our case legal realities, are causally determined by preceding events and their consolidated accounts. This point can be demonstrated both generally and specifically by way of a further reference to the Belgian system of administrative justice.

In general terms, Posner's remark that 'law venerates tradition ... and custom' and is 'past-dependent'[568] fits well with traditional accounts of public law. Whether the development of our institutions should be regarded in a path-dependent manner however is a much debated issue, a source of reflection for recent scholars. Three aspects of this debate deserve mention here. Firstly, economics and political science literature shows that there are costs associated with switching from one option to another, which explains the importance of issues of timing. However, the performance of institutions is the outcome of several factors, some of which promote innovative activities. This is the main reason why deterministic models do not work.[569] Organizational studies, too, have often shown that path dependency does not wholly determine behavior, as agents may perceive and interpret previous paths differently and to some

567 Craig, 'Comparative Administrative Law and Political Structure' (n 1) 953; id, 'English Foundations of US Administrative Law: Four Central Errors' (2016) Oxford Legal Studies Research Paper 3/2016 (criticizing lawyers who tend to base 'far-reaching conclusions on ... scant evidence').

568 RA Posner, 'Past-Dependancy, Pragmatism, and Critique of History in Adjudication and Legal History' (2000) 67 Univ Chicago L Rev 573–579 (criticizing the conception of history as something of intrinsic value).

569 For this remark, see D North, C Mantzavinos and S Shariq, 'Learning, Institutions, and Economic Performance' (2004) 2 Perspectives on Politics 75, at 80. See also, from the perspective of political science, P Pierson, 'Increasing Returns, Path Dependence, and the Study of Politics', (2000) 94 Am Pol Sc Rev 251 (arguing that politics differs from economics in many ways, an argument that, incidentally, also applies to law) and, for that of legal analysis, O Hathaway, 'Path Dependence in the Law: the Course and Pattern of Legal Change in a Common Law System' (2000) 86 Iowa L Rev 61 (distinguishing variants drawing on biological theory based on gradual evolution from those according to which evolution is sometimes characterized by rapid periods of change).

extent act differently from what others might expect or suggest.[570] Secondly, historians of law have pointed out that, while the nineteenth-century idea that law changes following certain determinate stages or patterns have not survived the end of that century, it is important to concentrate on the factors that make certain societies and their legal institutions 'change in one way and others in different ways'.[571] Lastly, one thing emerges clearly in the literature on due process of law: traditions are not static, they evolve.[572]

The findings of our research confirm that the shaping of legal institutions is not necessarily driven by history, as evidenced by the Belgian case. It was with the birth of the new legal system in 1831 that the Constitution laid down that all powers exercised by public authorities had to be subject to the ordinary courts. It did so because it was assumed that this was a better system than those in France and the Netherlands, where special administrative courts operated. The Belgian monistic system of judicial review of administration was thus the product of choice, rather than history. A variant of this problem regards the countries that have made different choices through time, autonomously or otherwise. Thus, for example, since Italy made opposite choices in 1865 and 1890, initially in favor of ordinary judges and eventually creating administrative courts, when the new Constitution was drawn up, on the basis of what criteria could the supporters of either solution decide which tradition should have the greatest claims of relevance? The situation is even more complex when there is an external factor. Thus, for example, in countries – such as Hungary – that had been subjected to Soviet rule between 1945 and 1989, adherence to tradition could imply re-discovering institutions suppressed during that period of time.

3 Context Matters: *Mentalités* in Public Law

While the preceding sections have confirmed that history exerts a considerable influence on the shape of legal institutions, this one will argue that culture, too, matters more than is often thought. However, it does so differently from what is believed by some comparative lawyers, whose claim is, in essence, that legal traditions are incommensurable. The structure of the argument in this section should be clarified from the outset. First, we will examine the concept of incommensurability, in itself a complex enquiry; however, it is possible to

570 J Sydow, G Schreyhogg and J Koch, 'Organizational Path Dependence: Opening the Black Box' (2009) 34 Academy of Management Rev 689.

571 P Stein, *Legal Evolution. The Story of an Idea* (Cambridge University Press 1980) 124.

572 Mashaw (n 52) 44.

refer to scientific studies showing the fallacies of the argument of incommensurability. Secondly, some examples examined in previous chapters will corroborate this view, showing the importance of culture from a different angle.

It ought to be said from the start that the incommensurability argument does not discuss facts or legal realities but concerns, rather, epistemology, because it is concerned with the human mind's relationship with reality.[573] At the heart of this argument there is the 'crucial notion of incommensurability', which has not just a critical, but a polemic thrust, as – in Legrand's words – it 'wants to fight against the received view that there exists a law-text that would present itself in its ontological self-sameness both to those operating locally and to those operating elsewhere'.[574] The underlying assumption is, however, not epistemological but prescriptive, because it is asserted that 'comparative thought must become the endless exploration of *differends*', that is, it 'must address legal cultures as radically different'.[575]

There are three problems with this argument. The first concerns its epistemological foundation. A concealed premise underlying the argument is that facts just do not matter. There is little basis for this assumption. One may agree that facts do not speak for themselves but must be interpreted in the light of other facts. However, they exist apart from perceptions. Eliding this fundamental distinction is, epistemologically, untenable.[576] In brief, we cannot prescind from what has been a set of facts – in our case of legal realities. The argument based on incommensurability is, moreover, weakened in a more specific manner, as Glenn has shown in various ways: distinguishing between incomparability and incompatibility, the latter not preventing the former; evidencing that what underlies incommensurability is, ultimately, a normative preference for singularity and diversity;[577] and observing that since legal traditions 'are constituted by information', which cannot be rigidly controlled and confined, they have not existed in isolation from one another in the past; still less can they be said

573 P Legrand, 'Comparative Legal Studies and the Matter of Authenticity' (2006) 1 J Comp L 365, at 429 (pointing out the 'absence of epistemological commensurability'); id, *Le droit comparé* (Presses Universitaires de France 1999) 15 (for the remark that comparative law must be based on epistemological reflexion).

574 Legrand, 'Comparative Legal Studies' (n 573) 427.

575 id, 453.

576 For this observation, see R Searle, *Seeing Things as They Are. A Theory of Perception* (Oxford University Press 2015) (arguing, on the basis of experiments, that perception must be kept distinct from its object, which has an autonomous existence). But see also H Putnam, *The Many Faces of Realism* (Open Court 1987) 26 (distinguishing between loose and strict causal relationship between facts) and Weaver (n 566) 4 (for a critique of relativism).

577 HP Glenn, 'Are Legal Traditions Incommensurable?' (2001) 49 AJCL 133, at 138.

to exist in isolation today, thanks to more widespread and systematic channels of communication of information.[578] The argument from incommensurability is, in the end, problematic from the viewpoint of policy choice. This problem has already been considered in the previous chapter. Suffice it to add that similar choices about instruments are not precluded by diversified views regarding the ends or final goals. The similarity among instruments might be appreciated on a temporary basis or as a second best, if the optimal solution is unavailable for some reason.

As a variation on the line of reasoning followed by Glenn, the simplistic argument that there cannot be borrowings and transplants because legal traditions are incommensurable does not withstand scrutiny in the field of administrative law. As will be argued more extensively in the following chapter, there is empirical evidence of a rich history of transplants. This history includes the early diffusion of judicial monism, based on the English experience, in Belgium (1831) and, through it, in Italy (1865), as well as the later diffusion of the French dualist model in Austria, Germany, and Italy between 1863 and 1890. This story also includes the diffusion in new States such as Czechoslovakia, Poland, and Yugoslavia of the Austrian legislation on administrative procedure only a few years after the dissolution of the Habsburg Empire. Last but not least, it includes the diffusion of Spanish administrative procedure legislation in Latin America. Narratives of administrative law divorced from these empirical findings do not meet the standard of scientific scrutiny. Nor is the oft-asserted exceptionalism of English law confirmed as far as procedural constraints on public authorities are concerned. On the contrary, our factual analysis has confirmed the finding of a Canadian writer, according to whom the fundamental maxims of natural justice in England and the requirements defined by the French *Conseil d'État* are 'strikingly similar'.[579]

After explaining why the radical view of *mentalités* must be rejected, both in its generality and more specifically from the viewpoint of public law, it remains to be seen whether it can be relevant not in an attenuated, but in a different, version. It is in this respect that Dicey's attack against the French system of *droit administratif*, for all its weaknesses, can be helpful for a better understanding of national traditions. As indicated previously, his attack was threefold. He argued that if administrative law was intended as a special body of institutions and norms concerning the powers and immunities of public authorities,

578 id, 140–1.

579 A Lefas, 'A Comparison of the Concept of Natural Justice in English Administrative Law with the Corresponding General Principles of Law and Rules of Procedure in French Administrative Law' (1978) 4 Queen's L J 197.

this was incompatible with the rule of law. He added that the establishment of special administrative courts aggravated the problem. The problem was further exacerbated by the establishment of a special regime governing the liability of public officials in their dealings with private individuals. These weaknesses, Dicey argued, inevitably led to despotism. In order to emphasize this further, he used a powerful rhetorical argument. He asserted that the French *Conseil d'État* was an institution akin to the Star Chamber.[580] This requires a slight historical digression. The Court of the Star Chamber (also called *Sterred Chambre* or *Camera stellata*, because of the golden stars that decorated the roof of the place where the court worked), was a court that sat in London from the 15th century to 1641, when it was abolished. While its members sat in the Court for judicial purposes on some days, on the other days of the week, they were engaged in the business of government.[581] Together with its procedures and the harsh sanctions imposed in various cases, this explains why the Star Chamber became a sort of negative model of a judicial body characterized by opaque, if not secretive, proceedings and arbitrary rulings. To borrow the words of a historian of law, the Court of Star Chamber 'has left its name to later times as a synonym for secrecy, severity, and the wresting of justice'.[582] Less than fifty years ago, the US Supreme Court referred to the Star Chamber as an instrument of tyranny.[583]

We have already seen in Chapter 1 that both the descriptive and normative foundation underlying the rejection of administrative law was questionable. In a similar vein, when reviewing Bonnard's comparative study on judicial review of administration, Jennings not only observed that Dicey 'quite misunderstood the nature of French administrative institutions', but he added that, unlike other continental writers, Bonnard knew 'too much about English administrative law to be led to assume that Dicey's statements about it are either adequate or correct'.[584] Nowadays, in the UK

580 Dicey, *Introduction to the Study of the Law of the Constitution* (n 22) 371 and 379 ('odious as its name has remained'). For further remarks, see above, Chapter 1, § 2.

581 M Shapiro, 'From Public Law to Public Policy, or the "Public" in Public Law' (1972) 5 Political Studies 410.

582 EP Cheyney, 'The Court of Star Chamber' (1913) 18 American Historical Review 723 at 727.

583 US Supreme Court, *Faretta v California*, 422 U.S. 806, at 821 (1975) (asserting that the 'Star Chamber has, for centuries, symbolized disregard of basic individual rights'). On the Framers' intent to lay down different institutions, see IR Kaufman, 'The Essence of Judicial Independence' (1980) 80 Columbia L Rev 671.

584 I Jennings, *Review of* R. Bonnard, 'Le contrôle juridictionnel de l'administration en droit comparé' (1936) 2 University of Toronto LJ 397.

things have changed, as there is a 'sophisticated system of administrative law'.[585]

However, as is often observed, ideas matter. Jennings himself was well aware of the fundamental importance of Dicey's ideas. The issues he discussed assumed a shape quite unlike the form they had before him. It was only in his exposition that the salient features of the English Constitution received the form that they have conserved for the cohorts of lawyers who studied his treatise of constitutional law and were taught that not only there existed, but there had to be, public administration without administrative law.[586] In brief, this has become the commonly held view. Even in the mid-twentieth century, that *mentalité* still held centre stage.[587] Borrowing Kuhn's terminology, it can be said that, as that paradigm has used to account for the legal world, 'normal science' has elaborated knowledge within such paradigm.[588] This makes it difficult to understand concepts elaborated within other paradigms. Thus, for example, lawyers trained in common law countries often note the difference between methods based on testing definitions and distinction against reality, and those based on a high level of abstraction and conceptualism, typical of Continental legal cultures.[589] Thus, certain ideas about the law, such as the cardinal distinction between public and private law, are not universally shared.[590]

This confirms the point outlined above that traditions are not based simply on facts but also on ideas and beliefs about the law that are shared and persist through time.[591] It would be a mistake, therefore, to assume that the canons of administrative conduct that exist in a group of nations will be shared by their neighbors. However, it would equally be a mistake to assume that traditions are inevitably static and immutable, a point of general importance that requires further analysis.

---

585 J Jowell, 'The Universality of Administrative Justice' in Ruffert, 'The Transformation of Administrative Law as a Transnational Methodological Project' (n 58) 61.

586 Jennings, 'Administrative Law and Administrative Jurisdiction' (n 110) 99; Loughlin (n 23) 17.

587 F Lawson, 'Le droit administrative anglais' (1951) 3 RIDC 412.

588 T Kuhn, *The Structure of Scientific Revolutions* (Un Chicago Press 1962).

589 Stein, *Legal Evolution. The Story of an Idea* (n 571) 191.

590 For this remark, see C Harlow, '"Public" and "Private" Law: Definition without Distinction' (1980) 43 Modern L Rev 241.

591 For further remarks, see JH Merryman and R Pérez Perdomo, *The Civil Law Tradition. An Introduction to the Legal Systems of Europe and Latin America* (3rd edn, Stanford UP 2007) 2.

4 Policy Considerations and Change

Montesquieu's idea of legal evolution provides an interesting starting point. His acknowledgement of the infinite diversity of human laws[592] is often cited as authority supporting a contractive or contrastive approach to comparative law, ie, one that emphasizes diversity. However, he did not rule out the possibility that some invariable laws (*lois invariables*) existed and could be found. Methodologically, his approach implied a deviation from the traditional deduction from first principles that characterized theories of natural law. Moreover, he stressed the fact that legal precepts change from one country to another, straight after a river or a chain of mountains. The fact that he gave weight to factors such as climate or latitude reinforced his general thesis that the particularities of legal orders must be considered within the general state of each society. However, such particularities do not depend only on fundamental beliefs and values but also from other factors.

Finally, he observed that such differences are not unchangeable. This emerges, in particular, from his analysis of safeguards against arbitrariness. Montesquieu addressed the *audi alteram partem* maxim in the judicial process. He began by saying that this maxim had been codified in the French legal order for more than a thousand years. He added that the principle was much older and provided two plausible reasons for its codification, namely that a different practice had existed in some particular cases or within non-civilized nations ('*chez quelque peuple barbare*').[593] For him it was axiomatic that different nations can, and most frequently do, follow different rules, but this does not prevent them from adjusting their rules, either gradually or all of a sudden, in this case through codification. In other words, whether institutions are driven by history is the issue that Montesquieu considered, and his answer was that they are not immutable. He thus adopted a dynamic perspective against determinism.[594] Moreover, he drew attention to the factors that may require change. Given his concern for the preservation of freedom, it is not surprising that he sought to ensure that justice was done for the individual. Recognizing and protecting the right to be heard in a code was thus a requirement to achieve the ends of justice. By contrast, the practice to the contrary

---

592 Montesquieu (n 16) 123.

593 id, 328.

594 For further remarks on this point, see R Howse, 'Montesquieu on Commerce, Conquest, War and Peace' (2006) 31 Brooklyn Journal of International Law 693, at 708. See also G Radbruch, *Der Geist des englishen Rechts* (Vanderbroeck & Ruprecht 1958) (arguing that Montesquieu assigned only to legislation the task of achieving social change).

was unacceptable in a civilized nation. In so saying, Montesquieu referred to the intent to distance one's own country from another that is regarded as less civilized. The same could be done with regard to a country that is a neighbor, but which is regarded as distant for purely political reasons such as the nature of government. We have already touched upon this argument when it was observed that Belgian reformers in 1831 decided not to adopt the dualist system of administrative justice that characterized both the Netherlands and France.

The origin of the French tradition of administrative justice is itself of interest to our line of reasoning. Before the Revolution, administrative activities were controlled by the courts of law called '*parlements*', the most important of which were those of Paris and Toulouse. Their action was often criticized for opposite reasons: by the Crown, on the grounds that the courts were unduly enmeshed in the exercise of administrative powers, and by citizens, because sometimes those courts refrained from rendering justice on grounds that the law either did not exist or was obscure.[595] The Crown's reaction against the *parlements* emerged in the edict of Saint-Germain of February 1641, which prohibited the *parlements* from judging and cases concerning the State, its government and the administration, reserving them to the King.[596] The edict was re-affirmed in 1661, a fact that shows the resistance of *parlements*. In the revolutionary period, a transformation occurred. It was initially the National Convention that decreed in 1790 the annulment of all proceedings and judgments that had taken place in the ordinary courts against the members of the administrative corps and committee, based on claims for property seized, or arising out of revolutionary burdens imposed on individuals and families, or any other acts of administration, and imposed upon those courts repeated prohibition against taking cognizance of any acts of administration of whatever character. This prohibition was followed by the creation of the *conseils de préfecture* and subsequently by the establishment of the *Conseil d'État* in 1799,[597] within which a judicial section was established in 1806, though the Council's advisory and judicial functional were separated between 1831 and 1839.

595 See G Gorla, 'Civilian Judicial Decisions – An Historical Account of Italian Style' (1969–1970) 44 Tulane L Rev 740, at 748 (for the observation that among other things, French courts did not give reasons for their decisions); Perelman, *Logique juridique* (n 16) § 15 (same remark).

596 For further details, see Lochak (n 15) 12; Neville Brown, Bell and Galabert (n 26) 45–46 and B Schwartz, *French Administrative Law and the Common Law World* (New York University Press 1954) 11.

597 See J Chevallier, *L'élaboration historique du principe de séparation de la juridiction administrative et de l'administration active* (LGDJ 1970) (remarking that local administrators were initially entrusted with the power to decide disputes).

Two strands of thought interpret these facts differently. The first argues that the Revolution brought a radical change, a mutation. According to this line of thinking, in brief, modern France was born with the Revolution. More specifically, although the *Conseil d'État* had 'certain resemblances' with its predecessor, the *Conseil du Roi* of the *ancien régime*, it was a Napoleonic creature.[598] According to the other strand of thought, the edicts adopted since the 17th century, together with the existence of the *Cour des Comptes* and other special courts, show a pre-existing tradition. Rivero, among others, has observed that the underlying idea owed much to Montesquieu's doctrine of separation of powers and that the Convention and Bonaparte added something important to the prohibition; that is the creation of administrative courts. Referring to Montesquieu, however, poses more problems than it solves, because he was in search of a system that could ensure a better safeguard against abuses of power. He found that the English system achieved this goal thanks to the separation between the executive and judicial branches of government. He then theorized the necessary distinction between these and the legislative branch.[599] Some decades later, faithful to Montesquieu, Article 16 of the *Declaration of the rights of men and the citizen* (1789) affirmed that 'a society in which the observance of the law is not assured, nor the separation of powers defined, has no constitution at all'. This was perhaps the clearest and strongest assertion of the virtues of the separation of powers. But only one year later, the Convention interpreted it differently when it was confronted with the issue of judicial review of administration. This debate corroborates the argument set out above, ie, that a tradition is characterized not only by a succession of events but also by the existence of a certain set of ideas and beliefs about public law, which also implies giving more weight to some events than to others. In this sense, a tradition may imply a limitation to law reform,[600] but it does not necessarily do so, either if there are good reasons for rectifying some aspect of it or if a more sweeping change occurs.

598 Rivero, *Droit administratif* (n 10) 13.

599 Montesquieu (n 16) livre XI, chapitre VI. In secondary literature, see HE Yntema, 'Book Review, La pensée politique et constitutionnelle de Montesquieu' (1953) 2 AJCL 85, 87 (for whom the essay published therein by Charles Eisenmann had the merit of rescuing Montesquieu's doctrine from the dogmatic view of the three powers, showing that the concern for despotism was 'the central point in his doctrine').

600 For further discussion of this aspect, see EM Wise, 'Legal Tradition as a Limitation on Law Reform' (1977–1978) 26 AJCL 1.

5 Diverging Traditions: Rules and Legal Formants

The preceding arguments suggest that a strong dose of caution is required in order not to give excessive weight to history and culture, and thus to avoid the connected risk of determinism and reductionism. They also suggest that it is preferable to focus on legal traditions. Various arguments support this choice. First, the idea that what matters more is the existence of a set of written legal rules is untenable because, as various studies in both history of law and legal sociology have shown, several other factors or formants concur in shaping the law.[601] Second, it is more appropriate to speak of legal traditions, as distinct from other organizing concepts, because this concept has the advantage of focusing on the contents characterizing each tradition.[602] As a variation of the previous argument, the term tradition is used in comparative studies concerning administrative law, pointing out its relationship with national traditions.[603] Last but not least, the term 'tradition' is no longer only one that is used only in academic studies but is increasingly referred to in legal documents such as the treaties upon which the EU is founded and its Charter of Fundamental Rights. The last two arguments will now be addressed more in detail.

The results of our comparative enquiry confirm the existence and importance of distinct administrative traditions in Europe. Fully understanding them is a large project. Here I will only discuss three elements that can be helpful for such an understanding: operational rules, legal formants, and values. Even the rich case law of the ECJ concerning the general principles of law common to national legal orders and the vast legal literature that discusses such principles are dotted with the remark that they coexist with different operational rules. Two brief but apposite examples will serve to demonstrate this. Even one of the closest things to an invariant, the individual's right to be heard before a decision adversely affecting his rights or interests is taken, is differently shaped depending on whether there is a hearing, as is the case with the majority of European laws, or only the possibility to have access to the documents held by the public authority and to submit other documents and

---

601 A Barak, *The Judge in a Democracy* (Princeton UP 2008); P Selznick, '"Law in Context" Revisited' (2003) 30 J of L & Soc 177, at 179 (for the remark that, especially when harder cases must be solved, general principles and moral considerations are relevant).

602 HP Glenn, 'The State as Legal Tradition' (2013) 2 Cambridge J Int & Comp L 704, 705; id, *Legal Traditions of the World. Sustainable Diversity in Law* (5th edn, Oxford University Press 2014) 1 (on the 'presence of the past' as an element defining traditions).

603 Cassese, 'New paths for administrative law: a manifesto' (n 4) 603; Fromont (n 4) 13; E Schmidt-Aßmann, 'Les fondements comparés des systèmes de droit administratif français et allemand' (2008) 127 Revue française d'administration publique 525.

evidence, as in Italy, for instance. Another example will serve to demonstrate the same point in a related context, that of the duty to give reasons. As for citizens, this is a means of obtaining justice in individual cases, as well as ensuring the accountability of administrators. In the settled case law of the ECJ, reasons 'give an opportunity to the parties of defending their rights, to the Court of exercising its supervisory function'.[604] This reflects a widely held conception of reasons. Some national courts argue that the requirement to give reasons is part of the common legal patrimony. Other courts will most probably agree with this proposition, but at a very abstract level. However, operational rules differ – and sometimes remarkably. For example, in the UK there is no general duty to give reasons in common law. Nor does statutory law establish it. This does not imply that the existing limits to legal rights cannot be challenged. Even a positivist lawyer might wish to reflect on whether such limits are justified in the light of the obligations stemming from membership of European organizations, such as those of Article 6 ECHR. He may deem that the guarantees of due process it establishes can be relevant for interpreting national rules. Indeed, he might go further and wonder whether such rules should even be assessed against such a backdrop.

This remark about the role of judge-made and statutory law also serves to shed light on legal formants. Sacco introduced the phrase 'legal formants' in legal discourses, drawing from phonetics. His claim is that 'living law contains many different elements, such as statutory rules, the formulations of scholars, and the decisions of judges'.[605] He calls these elements legal formants. Although these elements are the fundamental components of any given legal system, they may vary in type from one country to another. Their respective importance varies, too. This becomes evident when considering, for example, the diverse relevance of constitutional conventions in the UK and elsewhere. It is equally evident when considering the increasing importance of general legislation on administrative procedure, as distinct from sector-specific rules. Interestingly, in this respect there is no divide between common law and civil law systems: rather, we can speak of a fragmented situation, because the US has adopted general legislation since 1946 and, in one form or another, it has become common in Europe and the Americas. In addition to these more obvious components of a legal order, there are other legal formants that may be partly or wholly hidden to outsiders. Among these formants, which are less evident but important, there are both practices and uses, on the one hand, and

604 ECJ, Case 24/62, *Germany v Commission*; for further analysis, see C Harlow, 'Law and public administration: convergence and symbiosis' (2005) 71 Int Rev Adm Sc 287.

605 Sacco (n 62) 22.

styles of legal reasoning, on the other. The former encompass, among other things, the ways different institutions perform their controlling functions. The latter is characterized by the 'high level of abstraction and conceptualism' typical of continental academic works.[606] Another example concerns the background theories of the State that underlie certain judicial decisions, for example as far as the liability of public authorities in tort is concerned in Hungary. Whether there is an even more striking diversity in the Russian legal system is an interesting question, which deserves further analysis. A study of this kind would also be important from the perspective of values now that the Russian Federation has ceased to be part of the Council of Europe.[607] This clearly marks a striking diversity *vis-à-vis* the other legal systems, which remain subject to the principles of the rule of law and the universal enjoyment of human rights and fundamental freedoms.

6 The Legal Relevance of National Traditions

The differences between European legal systems just outlined are not relevant only from an empirical or factual perspective, but also from the deontological or normative point of view. This can be appreciated with regard to both the CoE and the EU.

Within the wider Europe, bound by the ECHR, various provisions of the Convention recognize that it is a prerogative of national institutions to decide how best to balance the various interests expressed by society. The basic assumption is that the majority can decide what is considered to be the public interest. On this basis, the European Court of Human Rights has often (even too often, according to some critics)[608] applied the 'margin of appreciation'. This doctrine is not unknown, though differently formulated from other supranational judges such as the CJEU. It implies a degree of deference to the limitations to the fundamental rights that States deem it necessary to impose. This makes it possible to balance legal and political necessities, an exercise common to several higher courts.

606 P Stein, 'Book Review of JH Merryman, The Civil Law Tradition' [1973] South African LJ 491.

607 CoE, Council of Ministers, Resolution (2002)2 on the cessation of the membership of the Russian Federation to the Council of Europe, adopted on 16 March 2022. The ECHR has ceased to be binding in Russia on 16 September 2022.

608 See JA Brauch, 'The Margin of Appreciation and the Jurisprudence of the European Court of Human Rights: Threats to the Rule of Law' (2005) 11 Columbia J Eur L 113.

Within the EU, there is an increasingly widespread but often unclear debate concerning the meaning of the reference made by the treaties to the respect of 'national identities', which is said to be inherent in national 'fundamental structures, political and constitutional' (Article 4 TEU). A more secure foundation for national traditions is provided by other provisions of the treaties. First, the phrase that best encapsulates the political project on which European integration is based, that is, 'determined to lay the foundations of an ever closer union among the peoples of Europe' is legally relevant and significant. It shows that pluralism, from a social perspective, is an element that characterizes the EU not just from a factual perspective but also from a deontological or prescriptive one. Secondly, although Article 6 TEU refers only to 'common constitutional traditions', there are obviously other traditions that are not common, belonging to each nation. Third, the preamble of the Charter of Fundamental Rights, which makes a clear reference to the existence of both common 'constitutional traditions and international obligations', recognizes 'the diversity of the cultures and traditions of the peoples of Europe'.[609] Since the Charter has the same legal value of the treaties, it can be said that there are various provisions supporting a pluralist vision of the legal order of the EU.[610] Fourthly, a specific but important provision laid down by the other Treaty upon which the EU is founded, that concerning the area of freedom, security and justice, affirms that it is based on respect for fundamental rights and 'the different legal systems and traditions of the member States'.[611]

Two brief conclusions follow on from this. On the one hand, the differences previously noticed with regards to operational rules and legal formants must be not only understood, but also respected, in their essence. On the other hand, this is not without consequences for legal theories. An approach that emphasizes only commonality would be, prescriptively, particularly weak in the European context.[612] An approach that emphasizes only diversity would be equally weak, as will be argued in the next chapter.

609 Charter of Fundamental Rights, Preamble, third indent. For further analysis, see A von Bogdandy and S Schill, 'Overcoming Absolute Primacy: Respect for National Identity in the Lisbon Treaty' (2011) 48 Common Market L Rev 1 (arguing that the revised identity clause supports a doctrine of relative primacy, like that developed by various national constitutional courts).

610 C Harlow, 'Voices of Difference in a Plural Community' (2002) 50 AJCL 339 (arguing that diversity and legal pluralism are to be preferred).

611 TFEU, Article 67 (1). Similarly, Article 82 (2), concerning judicial cooperation in criminal matters, requires EU institutions, when defining norms, to 'take into account the differences between the legal traditions and systems of the Member States'.

612 C Harlow, 'Law and public administration: convergence and symbiosis' (2005) 71 Int Rev Adm Sc 287.

CHAPTER 11

Explaining Commonality

This chapter discusses the causes of commonality. The discussion addresses the roles played by various factors. As in the previous chapter, the discussion begins with a cautionary note, which concerns the legal relevance and significance of what is commonly regarded as the legacy of 'European common law'. The discussion continues with a distinction between two types of causes of commonality. Some concern the spontaneous developments of national legal systems, either in adhesion to the 'nature of the things' or following a foreign model. Others are induced by European integration, including the definition of general principles, legal harmonization, and institutional isomorphism.

1 The Legacy of *ius commune*: A Qualified View

As observed earlier,[613] previous studies concerning the common core took history into account. At the beginning of his innovative research, Schlesinger affirmed that his hypothesis – that is, between legal systems there were not only differences but also 'shared and connecting elements' that could be formulated 'in normative terms' – gained plausibility from historical studies.[614] There were two sides to the same coin. During the seven centuries that elapsed between the emergence of the first scholarly works and the codification of private law in most civil law countries, there had been various waves of migration and the reception of legal ideas and institutions. Accordingly, legal comparison had been characterized by what Schlesinger called an 'integrative' approach; that is, one 'placing the main accents on similarities', as opposed to the following period characterized by contractive comparison, during which the emphasis was on differences.

Subsequently, as European integration has advanced, a distinction has emerged between two possible uses of historical studies. The first is to look at history as confirming the plausibility of the working hypothesis. So long as there has been a long period in which the differentiation of numerous legal orders coexisted with the existence of some shared legal formants, in particular

613 Above, Chapter 10, § 1.

614 Schlesinger, 'The Common Core of Legal Systems: An Emerging Object of Comparative Study' (n 548) 65.

judicial decisions and the works of learned jurists, then it is not unreasonable to conjecture that similar circumstances could occur again, though under a different guise. The second way is to argue that a new *ius commune* is emerging, similarly to that which existed for many centuries. While the first statement is by no means unreasonable, the second one must at least be qualified in more than one way.

Firstly, and obviously, there are some analogies between the current time and the long period of *ius commune*, especially from the viewpoint of the relationships between legal orders, which affected not only continental Europe, but England too.[615] The phrase 'European common law' has an appeal for many lawyers. However, historians of law have repeatedly and convincingly pointed out the institutional diversity between the two historical periods. Three distinctive traits, in particular, have been highlighted: the existence of the States, with their panoply of legal sources,[616] the incomparably greater role of legislation, and their persistent monopoly on the legitimate use of force, though what is 'legitimate' now also reflects common principles. Our factual analysis has confirmed this, with regard to police powers, which belongs only to national authorities, though they must exercise such powers in conformity with the obligations stemming from membership of regional organizations.[617]

Secondly, a specification is needed with regard to a recurring theme: whether and to what extent national legal systems share a common basis or substratum in Roman law. The language in which this opinion is expressed differs. Some writers have spoken of the direct influence of Roman law on modern public law. Others have held that Roman law has been no more than a source of inspiration for administrative law. Both opinions will be briefly addressed here.

Lawyers who have evinced an interest in Roman law have not been motivated by purely historical interest. They have sought to draw upon this great tradition to determine the direction which modern public law should pursue. The objective has been both descriptive and prescriptive. In descriptive terms, many have observed that Roman law provides a vast arsenal of both legal concepts, such as *imperium* and right, as well as the distinction between public law and private law. In prescriptive terms, it has been argued that Roman law developed a concept of respect for the human person, which is preferable to others. Interestingly, different writers such as American historian of law

---

615 Gorla and Moccia (n 595) 144. See also HE Yntema, 'Roman Law and its Influence on Western Civilization' (1949) 835 Cornell L Rev 77 (for the remark that even in the area of Anglo-American common law 'the Roman conceptions had had pervasive … influence').

616 AM Hespanha, *Cultura juridical européia: sintese de un Milénio* (Almedina 2012).

617 Above, Chapter 8, § 5.

McIlwain and German lawyer and political scientist Schmitt have been two of the principal advocates of this prescriptive view. McIlwain criticized the long-standing strand in Anglo-American legal thinking whereby Roman law, from the political perspective, was an instrument of absolutism. He observed that Bracton and other writers had approved of the Roman law doctrine according to which all law 'is the common engagement of the republic'.[618] He added that it was not fortuitous that Roman law was repudiated by Nazi Germany.[619] After WWII, Schmitt argued that it was from Roman law that sprang ideas of justice and due process, a minimum requirement of legal procedure without which there is no law at all.[620] Similar themes were said to be identifiable in modern public law.[621]

Hauriou reached a different conclusion. He acknowledged the importance of the Roman conception of public power, which could not simply be based on force but also had to be legitimate.[622] However, he argued that Roman political authorities developed a vast administrative regime without being subject to justice themselves. It was only with the development of modern public law that the executive had become subject to justice. This was, for Hauriou, the most salient manifestation of the '*soumission de l'Etat au droit*', a concept akin to the rule of law.[623] Writing in the same years, Cammeo, an Italian administrative lawyer, acknowledged the importance of Roman law in laying the foundations of 'juridical thought' but circumscribed it because 'many influences besides that of Roman law' had acted during the previous centuries.[624] On the one hand, the growth of administrative law has owed so much to recent technological developments, such as the postal service and railways, that it could hardly have any connection with Roman law. On the other hand, he argued that the connection of Roman law with those of several countries had been 'broken at many points by the French Revolution'. On a more overtly prescriptive tone, he

618 CH McIlwain, 'Our Heritage from the Law of Rome' (1941) 19 Foreign Affairs 605.

619 id, 597.

620 C Schmitt, *Die Lage der europäischen Rechtswissenschaft* (1950), English transl 'The Plight of European Jurisprudence' (1990) 83 Télos 35. For a retrospective, see C Tomuschat, 'Carl Schmitt's Diagnosis of the Situation of European Jurisprudence Reconsidered. Autonomy of Basic Elements of the Legal Order?' (2020) 80 Heidelberg J Int L 709.

621 See also F Wieacker, 'Foundations of European Legal Culture' (1990) 1 AJCL 1 (same remark).

622 M Hauriou, *Principes de droit public* (Dalloz 1910; 2010) 331.

623 id, 333. See, however, N Cornu-Thénard, 'Le modèle romain du "corps du droit administrative" dans la pensée de Maurice Hauriou' (2015) 41, 209, at 222 (arguing that drew on Roman law to build his theory of administrative decisions' executory nature).

624 F Cammeo, 'The Present Value of Comparative Jurisprudence' (1918) 4 Am Bar Ass J 645, at 649.

asserted that administrative law entails an attachment to three central commitments, namely the 'new ideas of liberty, equality, and free competition'.[625] Several decades later, drawing extensively on Tocqueville, Spanish public lawyer Garcia de Enterria took this further. He argued that the French Revolution had ushered in a new language of rights based on equality.[626] It was the same driving force that Tocqueville had noticed in the US in the early 1830's.[627] Such a change had a profound influence on public law. Not only had the whole of society been redefined in terms of 'nation', but the relationship between the State and individuals had changed as well.

In a society that is often sharply divided between different visions of the good, and in a legal landscape characterized by a growing variety of individual and collective interests, national laws have recourse to administrative procedure in order to reach decisions and define rules that are both sound and acceptable. The fact that this is increasingly regarded as an instrument of modern government within European laws and that it is subject to principles that are largely similar, if not the same, can hardly be explained by emphasizing the legacy of the past. In fact, it largely depends on other causes, including the individual choices made by national policymakers and the consequences that follow from membership of regional legal orders.

2 The 'Nature of Things'

In the previous chapters, the 'nature of things' has been mentioned more than once. The thematic structure of the argument based on this must now be explained. Two interconnected claims can be delineated. The primary theme is consonant with an old and prestigious school of thought that goes back to the science of legislation, associated with thinkers such as Montesquieu and Smith. The secondary theme is that, with the growth of government caused, among other things, by technological progress, the laws and institutions of modern societies are increasingly similar. Both will be addressed in this section.

As observed earlier, Montesquieu's approach was innovative because it deviated not only from blind respect for tradition but also from the ancient school of natural law. The fundamental criterion he set out for his enterprise was that

625 id, 650.

626 Garcia de Enterria, *La formación del Derecho Público europeo tràs la Revolución Francesa* (n 41) 58 and 80.

627 Tocqueville, *De la démocratie en Amérique* (n 13) 57 (pointing out that equality was the most striking feature of the US).

of the 'nature of things'.[628] In his thought this concept had a twofold dimension, descriptive and prescriptive.[629] When applied to a certain legal institution or norm, the concept of the nature of things considered its essence. But there was also a prescriptive dimension, when a certain institution or norm was said to correspond to the nature of things, especially in civilized nations, as Montesquieu observed of the right to be heard in criminal proceedings.[630] Subsequently, when the idea of progress was increasingly emphasized, laws, customs and institutions were seen in a sequential manner, in the sense that they passed through various stages before reaching civilization, as Smith and others argued. When this way of thinking was extended, it led to the assumption that, because a certain institution or norm was in the nature of things, it could be expected to be shaped similarly in all similar circumstances. Not surprisingly, Smith sought to define an account of the general principles of law and government, though he did not complete this project.[631]

This kind of reasoning became controversial in the following century when the majoritarian view was that the laws reflected, or had to reflect, the spirit of each society. However, it was not abandoned. Writing at the end of the century, Laferrière identified the main issue of administrative law in terms of an appropriate balance between two necessities: achieving the goals set by legislation, and the protection of individual rights. For him, it was axiomatic that the best way to balance such interests was to place jurisdiction over disputes between individuals and the State in the hands of an institution that possessed the technical expertise and experience necessary to ascertain whether discretion had been fairly and appropriately used. Thus, for example, he thought that the creation of an administrative court within the Italian Council of State in 1890 confirmed that, at some stage, public law disputes require a specialized review body.[632]

During the first half of the last century, this way of thinking about public law has become increasingly widespread. With the greater involvement of the State in society and in the economy, and the expansion of its capacity to impinge upon the interests of both individuals and social groups (or to

628 Montesquieu (n 16) 115.

629 For this distinction, see W Maihofer, 'Droit naturel et nature des choses' (1965) 51 Archives for Philosophy of Law and Social Philosophy 233.

630 Montesquieu (n 16) 328. This shows that between Montesquieu and Smith there was a difference of emphasis on progress, but not the diversity asserted by Loughlin (n 23) 5.

631 See the last section of A Smith, *The Theory of Moral Sentiments* (1759), ed by EG West (Liberty Fund 1969) 535.

632 Laferrière (n 100) 15.

interfere with them, according to critics), for instance through licensing and the disbursal of public funds, a growing demand for the applicability of the rule of law and principles of good governance has emerged. As a result, public lawyers have held that the similarity of the problems facing modern administrations implies that the solutions, too, will probably be very similar, if not the same. In the 1950s, Lawson, a British professor of comparative law argued that 'in the field of administrative law all civilized countries have much the same problems and much the same desire for their proper solution'.[633] Few years later, Rivero called this 'parallelism of solutions'.[634]

A further stimulus for the development of functionalist thinking about public administration and administrative law came from European integration. The impact of both EU law and that of the Council of Europe will be discussed at a later stage in this chapter; meanwhile, it can be observed that the gradual transfer of functions and powers from national to common institutions stimulated new thinking about how the various legal systems dealt with the problems that emerged. From the observation that all the six founding States had administrative bodies that exercised authoritative powers under the control of the courts, one could reasonably conclude that administrative powers and judicial remedies were the 'natural' features of modern government. Thus, the Schuman Plan envisaged that both had to be reproduced at Community level.[635]

There are, however, some difficulties with this way of thinking about the fundamental unity of public law. They can be briefly summarized as follows. There is a risk of assuming that the process of refinement of legal institutions can be regarded as necessarily leading in one direction, while history is replete with differences and failures.[636] There is a risk of taking for granted that certain principles can be regarded as optimal for every legal system, regardless of history and institutional context. For example, the gist of Laferrière's argument – ie, that judicial specialization has several advantages – is confirmed

---

633 FH Lawson, 'Review of C.H. Hamson, Executive Discretion and Judicial Control and B. Schwartz, French Administrative Law in the Common-Law World' (1955) 7 Stanford L Rev 159. See also Schlesinger, 'The Common Core of Legal Systems: An Emerging Object of Comparative Study' (n 548) 65 (for the remark that decision-makers, though 'widely separated by time or space, more often than not would respond in a similar way').

634 Rivero, *Cours de droit administratif comparé* (n 71) 15 (noting the '*similitude des problèmes administratifs modernes, largement commandée par des facteurs techniques identiques de pays à pays*').

635 Supra, Chapter 3, § 7.

636 See G Frankenberg, 'Critical Comparisons: Re-thinking Comparative Law' (1985) 26 Harv Int'l L J 411.

by the developments of national systems of administrative justice. However, specialization can, and does, take more than one form, including the establishment of special panels within courts endowed with general jurisdiction and the creation of administrative courts. Moreover, the latter may be granted advisory functions, as in the case of France, Italy, and other nations, but not in others, such as Austria and Germany. Similarly, administrative procedure legislation has been adopted within most European legal orders, but not in all. The nature of things can therefore be a concurring cause of commonality, but neither the only nor the main one. Another kind of relationship between administrative systems will be discussed in the next section; here, one of them can be regarded not only as an ideal-type in the Weberian sense but also as a prototype due to the influence it exerts over others.

3 Legal Transplants: Authority, Prestige, and Quality

This theme will be addressed in two ways, one of which is general because it concerns legal transplants, while the other focuses on the borrowings and exchanges examined in the previous parts of this essay.

Rivero can be said to have been a forerunner. After noting in previous studies that public law had been replete with exchanges across national boundaries during the nineteenth century,[637] in the early 1970s he examined these phenomena more systematically in the field of administrative and constitutional law.[638] He observed that a State, especially in a period of rapid political or social transformation, essentially has two options. The first is to create its legal structures and processes from nothing. The second is to copy, and if necessary to adjust, those of another State. He argued that the latter option was empirically prevalent. He brought this argument to a further point by asserting that the entire history of constitutions, apart from a few prototypes, was studded with borrowings and transpositions.[639] He made more than a mere hint at the metaphor of the transplant, drawn from surgery. Both the phenomena and the terminology (prototypes and transplants) were thus well identified, though not all subsequent academic works have shown adequate knowledge

637 J Rivero, 'Maurice Hauriou et le droit administratif' (1968) in *Pages de doctrine* (LGDJ 1980) 34.

638 J Rivero, 'Les phénomenènes d'imitation des modèles étrangers en droit administratif' (1972) in *Pages de doctrine* (LGDJ 1980) 459.

639 id, 459.

of this fundamental contribution to the understanding of the real forces that lead to commonality.

Few years later, Watson published his seminal work on legal transplants, reaching the same conclusion from the viewpoint of private law.[640] He argued that if we pay attention to the development of law over a long period of time and in several societies, it becomes evident that 'the transplanting of individual rules or of a large part of a legal system is extremely common',[641] the reception of Roman law in Germany and the spread of civil codes based on the *Code civil des Français* being only some of the most notable examples. Turning from description to explanation, he argued that 'transplanting is in fact the most fertile source of development' of legal systems.[642] There is more than one reason why this is so. Transplants provide reformers with solutions that have the advantage of being 'socially easy'.[643] This is the case, in particular, when the receiving society is less advanced than the exporting one.[644] It is also the case when two societies are equally developed, but in one of them, many are dissatisfied with the ambiguities and gaps that beset the legal system, and reformers can point out that a certain legal mechanism has the further advantage of having been successfully tested elsewhere. From these two reflections, it follows that legal transplants rest on a variety of rationales, including authority (in the transplants that are said to have a divine origin),[645] prestige, and intrinsic quality.[646]

Legal transplants can be better understood thanks to these studies. They can be either voluntary or coerced. Both private and constitutional law provide examples of the use of external coercion, such as the imposition of the French Civil Code on Italy after 1805[647] and the US imposition of the Japanese

640 Watson (n 19). There has been much discussion about Watson's theory, with a distinction depending on whether the transferability of legal institutions and norms is either accepted albeit in a relative manner, or excluded in general terms: for the first position, see O Kahn-Freund, 'On Uses and Misuses of Comparative Law' (1974) 37 Modern L Rev 1 and E Stein, 'Uses, Misuses – and Nonuses of Comparative Law' (1977) 72 Northwestern Univ School of L 198; for the other, see P Legrand, 'The Impossibility of Legal Transplants' (1997) 4 Maastricht J Eur & Comp L 111.

641 Watson (n 19) 95.

642 id, 96.

643 id, 97.

644 id, 88.

645 id, 89 and 100.

646 id, 99.

647 See A Kocourek, 'Factors in the Reception of Law' (1935) 10 Tul L Rev 209 (distinguishing accord from conflict and assimilation from imposition).

Constitution of 1946, respectively.[648] Administrative law does not lack cases of external forces exerting coercion, though not necessarily with a view to imposing foreign institutions and norms but to weakening existing institutions or even suppressing them. Thus, for example, administrative courts were abolished in Hungary when it fell under Soviet rule after 1945. Conversely, two main events that have characterized administrative law in the last couple of centuries are characterized by both prestige and quality: the spread of the French model of administrative justice during the second half of the nineteenth century and that of the Austrian model of administrative procedure legislation after 1925.[649]

Though there is variety of opinion about the remote origins of national systems of administrative justice, our analysis has traced the diffusion of the English model in both Belgium in 1831 and Italy in 1865. Subsequently, the French prototype was borrowed and adapted to different institutional frameworks such as those of the German states, the Habsburg Empire, and Italy in 1980. Laferrière observed that new Italian legislation followed the French model and quoted the parliamentary report according to which the reform served 'to give a judge to matters which did not have one'.[650] He also noted that Spain, which had abolished administrative courts in 1868, reversed the decision in 1875. His analysis then turned from describing legal change to explaining it. Laferrière thus quoted the opinion of a foreign observer, Goodnow, for whom the jurisdiction of French administrative courts ensured broader protection for citizens than the system in the US.[651] When Goodnow reviewed Laferrière's treatise, he noted the 'great influence' exerted by the French model and found two reasons for this: the 'wider knowledge of the real needs of the administration' and the 'most effective remedy against illegal administrative action'. He thus emphasized the quality of the French system of

648 For further analysis, see HS Quigley, 'Revising the Japanese Constitution' (1959) 38 Foreign Affairs 140 (for a critical assessment of the 'foreign imposition not wholly suited to a people of very different legal and social tradition', such as that of Japan). But see also J Williams, 'Making the Japanese Constitution: a Further Look' (1965) 59 Am Pol Sc Rev 665 (for whom more recent studies have brought additional information showing that the Japanese side supported innovations).

649 On the concept of diffusion, see Twining (n 257) 203; S Farran and C Rautenbach, 'Introduction' in S Farran, J Gallen, J Hendry and C Rautenbach (eds), *The Diffusion of Law. The Movement of Laws and Norms Around the World* (Routledge 2016) 2.

650 Laferrière (n 100) v.

651 id, ix. The citation was taken from Goodnow, 'The Executive and the Courts' (n 134) 557. See, however, F Melleray, 'Les trois ages du droit administratif comparé o comment l'argument de droit comparé a changé de sens en droit administratif français' in F Melleray (ed), *L'argument de droit comparé en droit administratif français* (Bruylant 2007) 17 (for the remark that Laferrière recognized the importance of context).

judicial review.[652] Other external observers have also pointed out the prestige and authority that the *Conseil d'État* has acquired over the years, as the 'bulwark of liberty and tradition'.[653] It is precisely for this reason that it is traditionally regarded as the maker of a model of administrative justice from which all other legal systems of Continental Europe have drawn.[654] In this sense and within these limits some writers have suggested that French law is the common source of European public law.[655] In a similar vein, Croce, a philosopher well versed in legal institutions wrote that:

> When the Napoleonic adventure was at an end … among all the peoples hopes were flaming up and demands were being made for independence and liberty … In Germany, in Italy, in Poland, in Belgium … and among other peoples, there were longings for many things: for juridical guarantees; for participation in administration and government, by means of new or revised representative systems. Since the historical antecedents and existing conditions, the spirits and customs of the various nations were diverse, these demands differed in the several countries in question, as to order of appearance, as to magnitude, as to details and as to their general tone.[656]

French writers have not disdained the view that emphasizes the prestige of their institutions.[657] However, they have shown awareness of the fact that it is precisely the success of the French model of administrative justice that, among other things, has long prevented any serious step in the direction of adopting administrative procedure legislation. In other words, there has been an all too evident bias in favor of the judicial process rather than the regulation of administrative procedure.[658] This partly explains why the leadership in innovation was taken by Austria and Spain. These cases

652 FJ Goodnow, 'Review of Laferrière, Traité de la jurisdiction administrative et des recours contentieux' (1896) 1 Pol Sc Quart 352.

653 HG Crossland, 'Right of the Individual to Challenge Administrative Action before Administrative Courts in France and Germany' (1975) 4 Int & Comp L Q 707, at 745.

654 E Garcia de Enterria, 'Le contrôle de l'administration: techniques, étendue, effectivité des contrôles, contentieux administrative objectif et subjectif à la fine du XXe siècle: analyse historique et comparative' (2000) 53 Rev admin 125, at 131.

655 A Salandra, *La giustizia amministrativa nei governi liberi* (*con speciale riguardo al vigente diritto italiano*) (Unione Tipografico-Editrice 1904) 146.

656 B Croce, *Storia d'Europa nel secolo decimono* (1932), English translation, *History of Europe in the Nineteenth Century* (Harcourt, Brace and Company 1965) 3–4.

657 R Alibert, 'The French Conseil d'Etat' (1940) 3 Modern L Rev 257, at 265; Galabert (n 136) 700.

658 JB Auby, 'Introduction' in Melleray (n 651) 9.

of diffusion must be distinguished, because the former has one single exporter and several receivers while the latter is characterized by the existence of both direct and indirect transplants. However, they also have two shared elements concerning the rationale of transplants and the conditions of transferability. The rationale of both transplants has been the prevalent opinion among the receiving legal systems, that the general legislation on administrative procedure was a high-quality product, able to bring significant advancement. From the viewpoint of transferability, the factors that seem to have played a role are cultural affinity and the traditional links between the legal systems involved, rather than geographical or social factors. The continuity of such legislation, notwithstanding the changes in the political systems, confirms the adaptation of the receiving legal systems. As other clusters emerged, including the Scandinavian legal systems, several countries have set a process of approximation of national laws in motion which has greatly reduced the environmental obstacles to legal transplants in other countries, such as Italy, Greece, and the Netherlands and, after 1989, the Baltic countries. In brief, shared beliefs and ideas about administrative procedure have paved the way for legal assimilation,[659] as distinct from harmonization within the EU.

4 General Principles

Parallel developments and legal transplants are driving forces that affect commonality and diversity among national legal systems without any stimulus from regional organizations. However, they are affected by the principles defined by such organizations. These principles are important in themselves because they characterize the legal landscape, especially after 1945. Moreover, only in very limited areas (for example, public procurement, the recognition of professional qualifications, and procedural requirements for the protection of the environment) does the harmonization of laws replace national law and become the new legal framework, usually based on a comparative study of the systems to be harmonized and the choice of a standard. In the great majority of cases, national laws will remain unmodified, but will be subject to common general principles.

Our focus on general principles of law deserves further discussion. While less recent doctrines either ruled out that general principles could

---

659 See Stein, *Legal Evolution. The Story of an Idea* (n 571) 199 (for the remark that, of the various factors indicated by Montesquieu, those of a political nature, such as the nature of government, seem to prevail over other factors).

be included among legal norms or ascribed them a limited function, namely filling gaps when the law was obscure or absent, there is an increasing awareness that they are foundational norms. Unlike their international predecessor, the International Court of Justice, neither the European Court of Justice nor the European Court of Human Rights have an express legal basis referring to the use of general principles in the treaties. However, they have found grounds to define general principles. The former has referred to its mission to ensure that the law is respected in the interpretation and implementation of the treaties, as well as its duty to ensure the observance of any rule of law. The latter has systematically interpreted the ECHR, in particular, in order to refine the principle of proportionality. Both European courts have thus expressed their intent to apply general principles when relevant to a dispute. However, there is no codified statement of the content of the general principles, and no authoritative prescribed method for identifying and applying them.

Historically, as indicated earlier, the most important principles materialized in national judicial decisions. In some cases, principles had a meagre legislative basis. In other cases, they filled gaps existing in legislation, the emblematic case being the development of the general principles by the French *Conseil d'État*. In still other cases, judges applied general principles as inherent elements of their legal systems. Thus, for example, the individual's right to be heard before an administrative authority takes a decision adversely affecting his interest has been regarded by both the Austrian and Italian administrative courts as a requirement imposed by the nature of things. It is precisely this judicial work that explains why most general principles are unwritten constructs, gradually institutionalized as case law, even though subsequently they have been referred to either by constitutions or by legislation. It is no exaggeration to say that much European public law has been constituted by the construction of general principles.

Taken as a whole, these general principles show what Rivero called parallel development. When judges identify and apply a new general principle to resolve a dispute, the law they make, it is asserted, already exists as a matter of law, to the extent that other judges in neighboring legal systems have developed the same principle in ways that have made it both normal and legitimate for use by all judges. Thus, for example, an Italian administrative court has held that the necessity to annul or withdraw unlawful acts or measures taken by public authorities must be regarded in the light of the settled jurisprudence of German administrative courts.[660] Not surprisingly, those who worry about the destabilizing effects of judicial lawmaking, and who believe that judges can

660 Tribunale amministrativo regionale of Trento, decision No 305 of 2009.

effectively resolve disputes without becoming lawmakers, will find no comfort in jurisprudence that justifies the emergence of new law with reference to prior episodes of judicial lawmaking undertaken elsewhere.

The existence of general principles shared by a plurality of legal orders is not only significant from a factual perspective. It also entails normative consequences. In this respect, a distinction must be made between two ways in which general principles are individuated. First, legal assimilation is enhanced by the standards defined by the Council of Europe. Although it has no legislative authority, the recommendations adopted by its Committee of Ministers draw inspiration from the laws of the member States and are often regarded as indicative of best practices. Among these recommendations, three should at least be mentioned. The first is the recommendation of 1980 concerning the exercise of discretionary powers by administrative authorities, which, among other things, requires them to respect the right to be heard in adjudicative procedures.[661] The second is the Recommendation of 1987 regarding administrative procedures affecting a large number of persons, which defines principles which all member States are required to respect, including the participation of persons claiming to have either an individual or collective interest that is potentially affected by administrative action.[662] A more recent recommendation on good administration includes the principles according to which public authorities must act within a reasonable time limit and must provide individuals with an appropriate opportunity to participate in the procedures affecting them.[663] These standards of good administrative conduct promote the respect of procedural values in the interpretation and application of the principles that legislators developed prior to the ECHR, or subsequently. They can be, and increasingly are, considered by the courts, which read legislation as far as possible to be compliant with them.[664]

Secondly, when the courts regard a certain norm as a general principle of law, important consequences stem from it. On the one hand, general principles express values essential to modern legal orders. In this respect, they are relevant from an axiological perspective. It is in this sense that Rivero, among others, argued that the founders of the EC shared a set of fundamental values, which provided the repository of principles against which legal control of

661 Recommendation No R (80) of 11 March 1980.

662 Recommendation No R (87) 16 of 17 September 1987.

663 Recommendation No R (2007) 7 of 20 June 2007.

664 P Birkinshaw, *European Public Law* (Wolters Kluwer 2014) 289 (noting the influence of the Council of Europe on the substantive and procedural laws of its members); Stirn, (n 81), 45.

government should be measured, as far as the protection of the human person is concerned.[665] On the other hand, general principles serve to render justice, especially in hard cases. Thus, failure to respect procedural guarantees in the exercise of administrative powers is regarded by the European Court of Human Rights as incompatible with Article 6 ECHR.[666] Moreover, the proportionality principle provides an analytical procedure for reconciling opposed values and interests or to resolve conflict between two sets of norms. And virtually all general principles can be deployed to adjust the law dynamically in the face of changing circumstances, as well as to ensure coherence.[667]

General principles bind national authorities when they act within the scope of the treaties, regardless of whether such principles exist within the domestic legal order. This is a consequence of the existence of a duty for all the organs of each State to obey the law. It follows that they must apply precepts of, for example, legal certainty, protection of legitimate expectations, and due process. National courts and other institutions, including those with advisory functions and higher audit institutions, ensure this duty is respected. The other consequence is that legal assimilation is greater than before regional legal orders were established.

5 Legal Harmonization

While general principles, defined either judicially or in recommendations, have a broad scope of application, legal harmonization is a product of EU law in particular areas. It differs from unification of the law, as it serves to coordinate national laws in order to remove obstacles to the Common Market.[668] It is the product of a twofold political choice. There is, first, the choice agreed by the drafters of the treaties to entrust common institutions with the power to adopt norms aiming at harmonizing national legal systems. Then, there is

665 Rivero, 'Vers un droit commun européen: nouvelles perspectives en droit administratif' (n 81) 389.

666 ECtHR, Judgment of 20 October 2009, *Lombardi Vallauri v Italy*. For further remarks from a UK perspective, see P Craig, 'The Human Rights Act, Article 6 and Procedural Rights' (2003) 47 Public L 753.

667 For further discussion about the ECHR, see A Stone Sweet and C Ryan, *A Cosmopolitan Legal Order* (Oxford UP) 155 (arguing that the Convention goes well 'beyond rights minimalism').

668 See E Stein, 'Harmonization of European Company Laws' (1972) 37 Law & Contemp Probl 318, at 324 (distinguishing harmonization from the unification pursued by the Nordic Council).

the decision to adopt such norms. Both aspects deserve attention and can be examined in the light of the Treaty of Rome.

The aim of integration was obviously of far wider scope than harmonization,[669] but the latter, too, had a broad scope of application, as it concerned the Common Market. It was precisely for this reason that different strategies were available to obtain economic integration. In abstract terms, more than one option was available. One option was to keep national regulatory autonomy, but to exercise it in respect of the principle of non-discrimination. As a result, producers would have had to adapt their goods to the requirements set by each State. Another option was the multilateral enactment of identically structured and worded statutes by the member States. There was still another option: the adoption of a regulation or directive by the institutions of the EC, with the purpose of overcoming national diversity. A choice had, therefore, to be made.

The drafters of the Treaty made their choice, identifying both a problem and the solution. The problem was the existence of 'such legislative and administrative provisions of the Member States as have a direct incidence on the establishment or functioning of the Common Market'.[670] The problem was not, therefore, national diversity in itself, but its negative impact on the Common Market. Harmonization was the solution, with a slight differentiation between the title of the third chapter of Title I of the Treaty and the text of Article 100. The rubric of Chapter 3, in the French text, referred to the '*rapprochement des législations*' (similarly, the Italian text used the phrase '*ravvicinamento delle legislazioni*' and the German one the phrase '*Angleichung der Rechtsvorschriften*'): the approximation of laws. The text of Article 100, however, had a wider reach, because it included both legislative and administrative provisions. Article 100 expressly equated legislative and administrative

669 For further analysis, see G della Cananea, 'Differentiated Integration in Europe After Brexit: A Legal Analysis' in I Pernice and AM Guerra Martins (eds), *Brexit and the Future of EU Politics. A Constitutional Law Perspective* (Nomos 2019) 45 (distinguishing two visions of European integration, one aiming at achieving 'ever closer union' and the other favorable to a wider and looser union); A von Bogdandy, 'European Law Beyond Ever Closer Union Repositioning the Concept, its Thrust and the ECJ's Comparative Methodology' (2016) 22 European L J 519 (suggesting that a new idea, the European legal space, should be explored, rather than the 'ever closer union', which is characterized by the goal of further integration).

670 Article 100 (1) of the Treaty provided that: 'The Council, acting by means of a unanimous vote on a proposal of the Commission, shall issue directives for the approximation of such legislative and administrative provisions of the Member States as have a direct incidence on the establishment or functioning of the Common Market'. For further analysis of the various national texts, see JG Polach, 'Harmonization of Laws in Western Europe' (1959) 8 AJCL 153.

provisions. For both, what mattered was whether they prevented the good functioning of the Common Market, in which case, national diversity had to be overcome.

The implementation of this norm has, however, proved to be difficult. Before 1978, some harmonizing directives were adopted, but they entailed significant negotiation costs, as it implied the transfer of sovereignty from the national to the supranational level and met the opposition by special national interest groups.[671] The difficulties that emerged in reaching political agreements within the Council of ministers explain why the Commission readily endorsed the alternative solution envisaged by the ECJ in its *Cassis de Dijon* ruling; that is, mutual recognition of national legal rules.[672] Many commentators have agreed that the new strategy was preferable to the old ones, on the grounds that regulatory powers remained in the hands of national authorities, especially with regard to the marketization of goods. Others, however, have observed that there is another, horizontal, type of transfer of sovereignty, distinct from the vertical type associated with harmonization.[673] Moreover, with regard to services, the EU has adopted several directives. Some of them, eg, the directives that liberalize the telecommunications, electricity, and gas markets, define the general principles which national regulatory authorities must apply. Included among these principles are those of non-discrimination, transparency and public consultation.[674] Since the early 1970s, other directives, especially those concerning public procurements, lay down the general principles of open competition and transparency. Throughout the years, these directives have also included increasingly detailed provisions requiring contracting authorities to respect certain publicity requirements, as well as to abide by certain procedures in the choice of private contractors.[675] The shared legal framework has thus become increasingly similar to a sort of code, thus reducing room for national regulatory autonomy.[676]

---

671 W Feld, 'Legal Dimensions of British Entry into the European Community' (1972) 37 Law & Cont Probl 247, at 257 (referring to the directive aiming at creating an EC company law).

672 ECJ, Case 120/78, *Rewe-Zentral AG v Bundesmonopolverwaltung für Branntwein*.

673 P Craig and G de Burça, *EU Law: Text, Cases, and Materials* (5th edn, OUP 2011) 596.

674 See, for example, the EU directive n. 2002/21 on a shared regulatory framework for electronic communications networks and services, in particular Articles 6 and 12 (regulating consultation and transparency mechanisms and establishing that during consultation 'all interested parties must be given an opportunity to express their views').

675 EC Directive n. 2004/18 (Public Sector Directive) for the coordination of procedures for the award of public works contracts, public supply contracts and public service contracts.

676 S Arrowsmith, 'The Past and Future Evolution of EC Procurement Law: from Framework to Common Code?' (2006) 35 Public Contract L J 337; id, 'The Purpose of the EU

The distinctive trait of harmonization consists, therefore, in the fact that national laws retain their distinctiveness, but the main differences are either attenuated or eliminated so that the effects that such laws produce are roughly the same.[677] Moreover, there are various instances where EU law has a 'spill-over' effect for the efficacious resolution of similar problems of a domestic character,[678] an effect that is coherent with the principle of equality, which is established either by national constitutions or by the courts.

It can thus be noted by way of conclusion that the relationship between national laws and the law of the two regional organizations has a twofold dimension. On the one hand, Rivero's remark that the most frequent way to shape new institutions is to borrow from others is confirmed, in the sense that both European courts have drawn inspiration from national administrative laws. On the other hand, the last seven decades have 'had the effect of bringing the public law systems of the differing European countries closer together' and has increased the awareness of the mutual dependence of its various component parts.[679] It is for this reason that a further aspect deserves adequate attention, namely, the adjustment of those components to the perceived necessities, which will be examined in the next section.

6 Institutional Isomorphism

There is still another factor of commonality which bears some analogies with others; that is, institutional isomorphism. As a first step, we clarify the meaning of this expression. Some of its manifestations in the field of administrative law will then be considered.

The term 'isomorphism' is used both in mathematics and in social sciences. In mathematics it designates two or more structures of the same type and having the same properties (isomorphism is, in effect, derived from the Greek concepts of equal form or shape). As a consequence, they cannot be distinguished from the viewpoint of the structure alone, while there may be additional elements. The social sciences have built on the concept of isomorphism, especially in the world of organizations, in order to seek to explain

---

Procurement Directives: Ends, Means and the Implications for National Regulatory Space for Commercial and Horizontal Procurement Policies' Cambridge Ybk European Legal Studies 14/2012, 1.

677 D Thompson, 'Harmonization of Laws' (1965) 3 J Common Market St 302, at 304.

678 Leyland and Anthony (n 27) 59.

679 Craig, *Administrative Law* (n 23) 324. Fromont (n 4) 3 (same remark).

homogeneity among organizational structures and practices.[680] The starting point is the observation that in their initial stages, various social environments 'display considerable diversity in approach and form', but subsequently, 'once the field becomes well established, … there is an inexorable push towards homogenization'.[681] Three more specific features of institutional isomorphism are then identified. The first is the temporal dimension, which makes it possible to consider structuring an organizational field as a result of the activities of a set of institutions. The second is that, especially in well-organized networks, there is a set of requirements or threshold, the respect of which provides legitimacy. The fact that such requirements are normatively established and that there are controls to ensure that commitments are taken seriously (coercive isomorphism) 'increases the likelihood of their adoption'.[682] However, adjustment is often spontaneous because the various components learn appropriate responses and adjust their conduct accordingly (mimetic isomorphism). As a result, organizations are 'increasingly homogeneous within given domains'.[683] The third feature, the 'connectedness' which ties organizations to one another may be established both horizontally, among such organizations, and vertically, between one placed at the top and all the rest. Thus, for example, there are records of meetings between members of national administrative courts since the first stage of European integration,[684] and more recently these courts have created a network for managing regular exchanges of views and experience.[685] Vertical networks exist, instead, between regulatory agencies.

This theory can provide a better understanding of some of the phenomena we identified earlier. It explains why certain changes are necessary to honor legal commitments, such as the due process of law, for instance. Institutional isomorphism also explains the adoption of general legislation on administrative procedure by new entrants to the EU. Whereas in the founding States and

680 I am grateful to Alec Stone Sweet for drawing my attention to this body of literature.

681 PJ Dimaggio and WW Powell, 'The Iron Cage Revisited: Institutional Isomorphism and Collective Rationality in Organizational Field' (1983) 28 Am Sociol Rev 147, at 148. See also JW Meyer and B Rowan, 'Institutionalized Organizations: Formal Structure as Myth and Ceremony' (1977) 83 Am J Sociol 340.

682 Dimaggio and Powell (n 681) 148–9.

683 id, 150.

684 For example, 1964 saw a meeting of Dutch and Italian administrative judges. Regular meetings are organized in the framework of ACA-Europe, the association of councils of State and supreme administrative courts.

685 Thirty-four jurisdictions are represented within the network, as the judges of EU member States are joined by those of Albania, Montenegro, Serbia, and Turkey, which have observer status, while those of Norway, Switzerland and the United Kingdom are invited as guests.

those that had joined the EC few decades later, the general principles of administrative procedure had been defined and refined by the courts, for those that sought to join the EU at the turn of the century it was easier to define those principles by way of primary legislation. Lastly, institutional isomorphism explains why even the most consolidated and prestigious organizations must adjust their rules and practices from time to time. This is the case of the general rapporteur before the French *Conseil d'Etat*, when the Strasbourg Court found that the absence of a duty to give reasons for reports was in contrast with the guarantees imposed by Article 6 ECHR.[686]

7 The Growing Impact of Common Standards

At the end of the preceding chapter, it was observed that a comparative approach that emphasizes only commonality would be, prescriptively, particularly weak in the European context and that an approach emphasizing only diversity would be equally weak. Two arguments support the latter remark.

First, there are not only standards of administrative conduct that are shared by all national legal systems, or by most of them. There are also the standards established by supranational laws. For example, national authorities are required to respect the Charter of Fundamental Rights, of the same legal value as EU treaties. Among the protected rights is the right to good administration, which is recognized and protected by Article 41. This states that 'every person has the right to have his or her affairs handled impartially, fairly and within a reasonable time', and goes on to specify that this right includes the right to be heard, access to files, and the duty to give reasons. Even if this is considered a closed list, it can nevertheless be argued that the meaning, for instance, of the right to be heard should be considered in the light of the standards shared by European legal orders, including the right to prior notification and legal assistance. If, on the other hand, the right to good administration is regarded as an open repository of shared standards, it can be interpreted against the background of these standards, thus ensuring procedural safeguards against arbitrariness, unfairness, and favoritism, as well as providing the opportunity for judicial review.

---

686 ECtHR judgment of 7 June 2001, *Kress v France* (Application No 39594/98). For further analysis, see J Bell, 'From 'Government Commissioner' to 'Public Reporter': A Transformation in French Administrative Court Procedure?' (2010) 16 Eur Public L 533. See also Fromont (n 4) 4 (for other examples of national rules revised in order to ensure compliance with EU law).

Moreover, there remains the question of the applicability of shared standards in the interpretation of Treaty provisions applicable to national authorities in the discharge of their own functions and powers. Administrative officers and judges are often requested to enforce vague, open-textured provisions. These standards are merely stated, with no further definition. The most obvious example is the due process clause laid down in Article 6 ECHR. As the Court considers Article 6 as a repository of standards of administrative conduct, such as the right to be heard and the duty to give reasons, it can be argued that – logically – it should take into account existing shared standards, for example, when it considers whether the right to be heard implies entitlement to receive legal assistance. Similar remarks can be made concerning the standards of impartiality, openness, and participation as defined in some EU directives.

CHAPTER 12

The 'Common Core' of Administrative Laws: Concept, Nature, and Extent

After examining the causes of both commonality and diversity, that is so say the etiology of the common core, this final chapter will be concerned with the two topics indicated initially; that is the 'minor' theme, concerning the methodology of legal comparison, and the 'major' theme, which regards the nature and extent of the common core.[687] The latter can be approached from several directions. The phrase 'common core' may appear self-evident to some, convinced that between legal systems there must be 'some kind' of common core or common ground, yet appear enigmatic to others. As a first step, therefore, there will be discussion about the methodology employed in this essay. Next, the structure of the ensuing argument will be outlined, followed by a discussion of the main features of the common core.

1 Factual Analysis and Theory Development

As indicated in Chapter 1, it is part of the thesis of this book that the nature and extent of the common core of European administrative laws can be better understood through a change in methodology. The argument presented initially, already illustrated more extensively in a previous article,[688] is that there appears to be an increasing awareness that the traditional approach to legal comparison adopted is inadequate. First, it has a preeminent, if not exclusive, focus either on commonality or on diversity. This is questionable because both commonality and diversity are important, particularly in the European context, where the recognition of common principles and constitutional traditions coexists with the duty to respect national laws and traditions, as shown in the previous two chapters. Second, all too often the traditional approach has been limited to the juxtaposition of the solutions to certain problems which can be found within each legal system, without moving to comparison, properly intended. This implies considering not just matters of style, but the

687 Above, Chapter 1, § 1.

688 See della Cananea and Bussani (n 61).

similarities and dissimilarities between legal systems concerning *le fond du droit*.[689] Thirdly, moving from the critical to the constructive side, our analysis must be an analysis of law not only as it is established by legislation, but also as it is applied.

Arguably, a factual analysis is all the more helpful in the field of administrative law for the two reasons illustrated in Part 1. Historically, the consolidation of administrative law during the 19th century was not the product of legislation, but of judges and jurists. Even when legislation has become more pervasive, during the 20th century, it rarely has had a general scope of application. An exception is the adoption of administrative procedure legislation, which is increasingly a common trait of European systems of administrative law, especially within the EU. However, there are significant exceptions concerning not only the UK and Ireland, but also legal systems where private law is codified since more than two centuries, such as Belgium, or one and a half centuries, such as Romania. A factual analysis has, therefore, been utilized in a series of workshops where hypothetical cases have been discussed to ensure they were fit for all the legal systems selected for comparison. Hypotheticals have revealed both similarities and differences, concerning the deep structures of European administrative laws.

One of the most interesting hypothetical cases is that which concerns the revocation of a license *inaudita altera parte*.[690] A public authority decides to withdraw the license for selling a certain type of product, such as newspapers or pharmaceuticals on the grounds that certain conditions specified by the license have not been respected. The licensee claims that the withdrawal of the license without a hearing to ascertain the facts alleged by the public authority constitutes a deprivation of benefits incompatible with procedural due process of law, in terms of a fair hearing. What matters is not simply whether the licensee's claim is likely to be successful before a court. It is also which arguments would be relevant, including constitutional provisions and those of general and particular statutes, and how they would be interpreted by the courts; for instance, whether what is required is a hearing before the withdrawal is

689 Schlesinger, 'Introduction' (n 2) 3–6. For an early exposition of the difference between the law and its application, see R Pound, 'Law in Books and Law in Action' (1910) 44 Am L Rev 12. For a reappraisal, see JL Halperin, 'Law in Books and Law in Action: the Problem of Legal Change' (2011) 64 Maine L Rev 46. On the importance of empirical research in the field of administrative law, see N Abrams, 'Some Observations on Basic research on Administrative Procedure and the Idea of a Procedural Continuum', (1980) 32 Admin L Rev 99.

690 Above, Chapter 7, § 4.

formally decided or at some stage after the decision. The issue is whether there are similarities that could be expressed in terms of principles and standards of administrative action. Factually, a common procedural standard exists and can be formulated in terms of a requirement that the licensee be given a reasonable opportunity to be heard before the final decision is taken. Failure to comply with such requirement makes the administrative decision invalid. Operational rules differ, though, as to whether a hearing must be held. The consequence of invalidity differ, too, because in some legal systems the licensee may only obtain its annulment and a limited amount of damages, while in others these would be granted more widely.

This case confirms the general points made earlier and raises two further ones. It confirms, first, that the areas of agreement and disagreement are interlaced, often in complex ways. Accordingly, the area of agreement cannot be formulated without taking its limits into account. Second, it shows the difference between a mere juxtaposition of national solutions and a comparison, precisely because the purpose of the factual analysis is to shed light on similarities and dissimilarities. A factual analysis also differs from a compilation of judicial decisions. It concentrates on specific cases or situations, but it implies a diverse type of intellectual exercise; that is, consideration of a variety of legal formants, including governmental practice and background theories of public law. Consequently, we must guard ourselves from creating a sort of unreal courtroom atmosphere as if the courts were the only key actors in the field of administrative law. This is the implicit assumption underlying the traditional approach to judicial control of the executive. However, administrative law has a much wider ambit and is characterized by the existence of political and administrative institutions. Accordingly, it is always important to consider both political guidance, for example through circulars and guidelines. It can be helpful, moreover, to take a serious interest in the reports of non-judicial bodies, such as external audit institutions and ombudsman, especially when considering the management side of administrative law, for example in cases concerning the delivery of benefits for unemployed persons.

The further points which arise concern the limitations of factual analysis and its relationship with theory development. One thing is to say that there are good reasons to be skeptical of a legal analysis restricted to rules, because there are problems that are not covered clearly by existing rules or new problems. Moreover, rules are often not self-operative, in the sense that their application is influenced by the facts that are found, as well as the doctrines of law that are deemed to be best applicable to a given case. Another thing is to say that attention should not be directed to rules, especially those made by legislatures. This would be questionable in the field of administrative law and for the law *tout court*, because both officers and judges do not enjoy unlimited discretion. Moreover, parliamentary legislation, including that governing administrative procedure, plays an important part in recognizing the ideals and values that are shared within a certain society. Thus, for example, the fact that several codes of administrative procedure define general principles such as legality, due process, proportionality and transparency may be viewed as a symptom of the willingness to show adhesion to the values upon which regional organizations are based, if not as a rhetorical exercise. Concretely, a factual analysis has to be seen in proper perspective and this implies devoting adequate attention to rules.

It also implies that factual analysis and theory development should not be seen as being methodologically independent and static. On the one hand, legal theories, particularly those concerning general principles such as those just mentioned, are important for the attempts to fashion a generally acceptable framework within which facts can be evaluated. On the other hand, if we consider the standards of administrative conduct that may be inferred from general principles as testable hypotheses, a factual analysis provides us with a valuable test of both legal relevance and generality. The above indicates that a better understanding of both the common core and the limits of its extent is unlikely unless we simultaneously focus on the order of the events that are legally relevant and on the order of representations of those events; that is, legal theories.[691] Hopefully, this will become clearer when discussing the terms in which the common core may be delineated.

In the meantime, we shall discuss another issue, which concerns constructivism, a two-faceted topic involving related but distinct aspects. To begin with, while some deem that legal theory should simply explain how to identify the laws and customs that relate to a specific legal question, others contend that it should be acknowledged that those who construct theories also build knowledge, rather than passively ascertaining legally relevant facts. There is nothing necessarily wrong with any of these assumptions. A theoretical bias underpins each assumption, and each perspective has implications for research. That said, for the sake of intellectual clarity, assumptions should be made explicit,

691 See E Schmidt-Aßmann, 'Administrative Law within the Legal System and in Relation to Practice' in Ruffert, 'The Transformation of Administrative Law as a Transnational Methodological Project' (n 58) 276 (emphasizing the 'essential role of legal research', viewed as a fourth source of legal development, in addition to judge-made law, legislation, and governmental practice); G Davies, 'The Relationship between Empirical Legal Studies and Doctrinal Legal Research' (2020) 13 Erasmus L Rev 3 (observing that such relationship can be of mutual support).

and their consequences must be considered.[692] In the previous chapters, this task has been accomplished, first, by observing that not only judicial doctrines but also background theories of public law are crucial to determining the solutions to both old and new problems and, second, by showing the relationship between the standards of administrative conduct and the values upon which regional legal orders are based. In brief, the argument here is that such values have implications for administrative procedure and that a theory of administrative procedure that takes into account how these standards are shaped in the real world has added value in terms of understanding the meaning and importance of values.

The other facet requires a slight digression into the literature concerning the common core. When discussing the fundamental experience gathered over more than twenty years in the field of private law, Shapiro observed that, despite every good intention, a legal comparison that was meant to be a purely scientific endeavor could turn out to be something different, i.e., that it could be used for prescriptive ends and, as a result, become involved in law 'reform', even without formally being a lawmaking activity.[693] It cannot be said that there is little possibility of this happening, or none at all. However, the crucial empirical question that this essay has examined is whether there exist shared standards of administrative conduct and which are their limits, while the crucial theoretical question concerns the nature of the common core. Whether judges and other public institutions should use those standards is, of course, another important question, but a different one, because it concerns the normative sphere. In other words, a distinction must be made between the discovery that, in concrete terms, there is agreement among the majority of European legal systems concerning a certain standard of administrative conduct – lacking in only a few – and the observation that it would be desirable for either functional or equitable reasons to adopt it within the latter.[694]

692 For further discussion, see GS Alexander, 'Interpreting Legal Constructivism' (1985) 71 Cornell L Rev 249 (discussing Ackerman's opinion about 'legal constructivism'). The concept of 'constructivism', in the way in which it is employed here, has not the negative sense Hayek gave to it in *The Road to Serfdom* (Routledge 1944) and in later essays.

693 M Shapiro, 'The Common Core: Some Outside Comments' in M Bussani and U Mattei (eds), *Making European Law. Essays on the 'Common Core' Project* (Università di Trento 2000) 221. See also JH Merryman, 'On the Convergence (and Divergence) of the Civil Law and the Common Law' (1983) 17 Stanford J Int'l L 379 (noting that even a search for general principles of law may have the effect, if not the aim, of facilitating a *rapprochement*).

694 On this aspect, see RB Schlesinger and P Bonassies, 'Le fonds commun des systèmes juridiques. Observations sur un nouveau projet de recherche' (1961) 15 RIDC 501 (n 694) 538 (suggesting that the solution that exists within a certain legal system may be less suitable than others).

2 The Common Core: An Overview of the Argument to Come

What are the consequences of our diachronic and synchronic comparison for the hypothesis set out at the beginning of this essay, namely that there are not only numerous differences, both old and new, between European administrative laws but also some shared and connecting elements, or a common core? Obviously, it is not sufficient to intone the expression 'common core', as if it provided a self-evident answer. For some, the existence of the common core should be taken for granted,[695] while others are skeptical about it. There may be agreement that there is indeed a legacy from the past, from *ius commune*, yet this does not necessarily imply that there is anything more than a set of shared general, if not generic, ideas, such as 'justice'. There may be agreement that, after seven decades during which 'regional' organizations have defined standards of administrative conduct, the common core that initially existed has changed. However, national traditions persist and must be respected. This section thus provides an overview of the argument to come.

First, the meaning and importance of the 'common core' of legal systems can be approached from several angles. The historical development of the concept is itself relevant. It is an interesting and instructive story. Contrary to the popular belief that in England there was no such thing as administrative law, and there could not be because it was incompatible with constitutional principles and values, England developed administrative law well before the Victorian age (1837–1901). Moreover, in the absence of extended and systematic legislation such as the laws established by the civil codes of many civil law countries, everywhere the courts developed standards of administrative conduct, with striking similarities. It may be tempting, therefore, to follow the functionally oriented literature that focuses on the 'convergence of European administrative laws'. However, the idea of convergence is itself questionable. And so is the use of broad concepts such as the 'common legal heritage'.

Second, it is precisely because one of the distinctive traits of the comparative enquiry, whose results are discussed in this essay, is a strong awareness of history that an evolutionary view of the common core is necessary. If there is one thing that emerges from the literature on due process, it is that 'tradition evolves'.[696] However, an adequate understanding that history does not follow a linear and progressive path is equally necessary. Recent developments

695 Kahn-Freund (n 3) 429.

696 Mashaw (n 367) 44. For a similar remark, from a historical perspective, see J Le Goff, *L'Europe est-elle née au Moyen Age?* (Seuil 2003) 3 (arguing that the past does not dispose).

concerning the relationships between civil law and common law systems must also be considered and assessed.

Third, even if a common core exists, its contours must be fixed. Schlesinger observed that while the existence of 'some kind of 'common core' [was] hardly challenged', there arose questions 'as to its *nature* and *extent*'.[697] Others added, 'the extent to which the common core can be used as a working tool'.[698] Our comparative inquiry suggests some answers to those questions. As regards the nature of the common core, it does not consist merely in ideals, such as justice, which can be said to exist in every legal system, but in a set of canons of administrative conduct.[699] The extent of the common core is another important aspect for which the factual analysis has proven to be helpful because it has shown that the area of disagreement between legal systems is less significant than could be expected on the basis of the comparative study of administrative procedure legislation. There remains, lastly, the question of the use of the common core as a 'working tool'. This is apparently a simple question in the light of the research's intent to contribute to the advancement of knowledge. But some of its practical implications deserve further attention.

The structure of the ensuing argument is, therefore, as follows. The discussion begins with the concept of 'common core'. The focus then shifts to its development. This is followed by discussion of the nature, extent, and uses of the common core.

3 The Common Core: Concept and Issues

There is a wealth of literature exploring the common core, but considerably less dealing with the concept itself. It is necessary, therefore, to press further and to inquire more specifically as to the nature and relevance of the common core of administrative laws in the European legal area. The argument proceeds in three stages. It is reiterated that the incommensurability issue is less problematic than had been thought by some, and that a proper appreciation of the reasons why it is not also has implications for the debate concerning the

697 Schlesinger, 'The Common Core of Legal Systems: An Emerging Object of Comparative Study' (n 548) 65 (emphasis in the original).

698 Kahn-Freund (n 3) 429.

699 While Schlesinger and Bonassies, (n 694) 501 characterized these elements as '*règles juridiques*' (that is, rules), in the following sections they will be characterized as legal standards.

common core in our case. The second step will be a discussion of why the concept of common core is to be preferred to other analytical tools. Thirdly, it will become apparent that the concept under consideration here is not a substitute for 'common ground' and similar phrases; it is a concept that must have a precise definition for various reasons.

It might be contended that the hypothesis that a common core exists is implausible. Two complementary arguments might be brought to this end. The first is grounded on epistemology as it does not discuss facts or legal realities but concerns their interpretation. It is central to this argument that legal cultures are incommensurable. The other argument does not rule out that there may be commonality among certain legal systems; it is in fact admitted in relation to Continental Europe. However, it rules out that this commonality can affect common law systems. Thus, it was central to Dicey's argument, in the last years of the Victorian age,[700] that while some States had a distinct system of administrative law, others had even complex administrative machinery, but there was no administrative law as a distinct body of law governing public authorities.

These arguments will be briefly addressed in turn. To begin with, it can be observed that both are mixed arguments. Although at the heart of the first argument lies the notion of incommensurability, a closer look reveals that it is used prescriptively. As a matter of fact, the underlying assumption is that 'comparative thought must [...] address legal cultures as radically different'.[701] As indicated earlier,[702] there are three problems with this argument: first, the elision of the distinction between facts and perceptions; second, the juxtaposition between incomparability and incompatibility, as well as disregard for the existence of channels of communication between legal cultures; third, the fact that similar choices about legal instruments or institutions are not precluded by diversity of views about the final ends. The weaknesses of this argument are further demonstrated by the existence of similar normative preferences in the sense that it is important to preserve legal pluralism and the diversity that it permits,[703] that do not preclude the recognition of the existence of some areas of agreement between legal systems, which are increasingly significant.[704]

700 Above, ch 1, sec 2.
701 id, 453.
702 Above, ch 10, sec 3.
703 Harlow (n 610), 199.
704 C Harlow and R Rawlings, 'National Administrative Procedures in a European Perspective: Path to a Slow Convergence' (2010) 2 IJPL 259.

As regards the other argument, reasoning which derives its authority from that of the author should be viewed with much caution. It is one thing is to acknowledge – as was the case previously[705] – the importance of Dicey's thought in forming a distinct *mentalité*. Another is to say that his account of public law was correct. Indeed, the idea that there was an extensive administration without administrative law was misconceived descriptively, and its prescriptive foundation was unconvincing. Moreover, Dicey's harsh attack on French *droit administratif* did not prevent him from admitting that a comparative enquiry between England and France could, and did, reveal not only diversity but also similarity. Factually, our comparative inquiry has shown that similarities grew over the last century.

After explaining why the possibility that a common core exists and can be identified cannot be excluded *a priori*, it is time to trace its contours. This is more difficult than the previous analysis since the term 'common core' is used in various ways, sometimes as equivalent to 'common legal heritage', while others talk of 'convergence'. It is important, for the purpose of conceptual clarity, to distinguish them.

Two decades ago, there was much talk of the convergence of administrative laws, as well as the convergence of European laws *tout court*. Both Cassese and Schwarze, among others, contributed to this body of literature. Cassese observed that, in contrast with the less recent theories about judicial review, there is a convergence of dualist and monist systems in a common pattern: judicial specialization in the supervision of administrative decisions.[706] Turning from observation to prediction, he has also conjectured that a more or less unitary model of administrative might emerge.[707] This change can be facilitated by European integration, according to Schwarze and others.[708] But, while both parallel developments and the influence exerted by European integration are important for a better understanding of commonality, it is doubtful whether the same can be said of convergence. It can be perceived in three distinctive,

705 Above, Chapter 11, § 3.

706 Cassese, 'New paths for administrative law: a manifesto' (n 4) 603. See also T Heukels and J Tib, 'Towards Homogeneity in the Field of Legal Remedies: Convergence and Divergence' in Beaumont, Lyons and Walker (n 545) 111 (same remark).

707 S Cassese, 'Le problème de la convergence des droits administratifs: vers un modèle administratif européen' in *L'État de droit – Mélanges en l'honneur de Guy Braibant* (Dalloz 1996) 47.

708 J Schwarze, 'The Convergence of the Administrative Laws of the EU Member States' in FG Snyder (ed), *The Europeanization of Law: the Legal Effects of European Integration* (Hart 2000) 164.

albeit related, ways. First, the concept of convergence is problematic in itself because it indicates both the process of converging or moving toward uniformity, and the property of being convergent. Accordingly, clarification is required. Second, as observed earlier, the convergence of two or more systems of administrative law can be either spontaneous or favored (or, from a critical standpoint, imposed) by a third one, such as that of the EU.[709] The third difficulty regarding the idea of convergence is that, symmetrically to the contrastive approach, it sheds light only on only some parts of the real, that is, those that allegedly converge. Conversely, it neglects the parts that diverge, although the reasons for divergence are important and must, therefore, be explained.

A word or two can also be said to explain why the concept of common core looks more appropriate than others to convey the meaning of the existence of an area of agreement between legal systems. There has been some discussion, before the ECJ and in legal scholarship, about the existence of a common legal heritage. Thus, for example, in a pioneer case raised by a German administrative court about the proportionality of restrictive measures on economic rights, AG Dutheillet de Lamothe outlined a new perspective. He argued that the Community order included a 'philosophical, political and legal sub-stratum common to the Member States from which through the case law an unwritten Community law emerges' and added that 'fundamental rights form[ed] the common heritage of the Member State'.[710] The Court followed his advice and famously ruled that respect for fundamental rights was inspired by the 'constitutional traditions common to the member States'.[711] A decade later, AG Warner referred to the existence of a 'shared patrimony'.[712] There is, of course, nothing wrong with this expression, nor with that focusing on 'common heritage'. However, it is clear that they place emphasis primarily on respect for the past, as does the Preamble to the TEU, which refers to the 'inheritance of Europe'. Conversely, they pay less attention to the dimension of change and, consequently, to the innovative features of some standards of administrative conduct, such as openness, participation and transparency, which belong to a more recent generation of process rights.[713]

---

709 RJ Widdershoven, 'Developing Administrative Law in Europe: Natural Convergence or Imposed Uniformity?' (2014) 7 Rev Eur Adm L 5.

710 Opinion of AG Dutheillet de Lamothe in Case 11/70, *Internationale Handelsgesellschaft*, § 11 ('*le patrimoine commun des Etats membres*' in the original French text).

711 ECJ, Judgment of 17 December 1970, Case 11/70, *Internationale Handelsgesellschaft*, § 4.

712 Opinion issued by AG Warner in Case 63/79, *Boizard v Commission*.

713 For a similar remark, see E Hobsbawm, 'Introduction: Inventing Traditions' in E Hobsbawm and T Ranger (eds), *The Invention of Traditions* (Cambridge UP 1983) 2 (contrasting traditions, viewed as immutable, and custom, which does not preclude innovation).

A second, more important, distinction that must be made is between the common core and 'common constitutional traditions'. Unlike the 'common legal heritage', the phrase 'common constitutional traditions' has a normative basis, as Article 6 TEU makes a reference to it, as well as to the ECHR.[714] The limitation just mentioned – the focus on the past – also concerns this concept, to a certain extent. The object and purpose of 'common constitutional traditions' bear, additionally, a clear and exclusive relationship with the protection of fundamental rights,[715] while the standards of administrative conduct examined in this essay may, and often do, have other purposes. This can be exemplified by a fair hearing, a fundamental requirement that is characterized by a balancing of the needs of effective government against the necessity to protect individuals and groups from oppressive or mistaken governmental action. Balancing is a task of greater complexity for another procedural requirement; that is, the duty to give reasons, for which administrative efficiency must be weighed against the individual's right to know the reasons upon which an adverse decision is based, also in view of an effective judicial review, as well as on parliamentary oversight on executive action.

The distance is even greater with another concept that has sometimes been regarded as equivalent to that of the common core; namely, the 'common law of mankind'.[716] Even leaving aside the problematic nature of the concept itself, it is easy to observe that those who elaborated it sought to give a sense of the evolution of international law, or the organized world community, while our focus is on Europe.[717] Moreover, as Friedmann observed, this concept fails

714 S Cassese, 'The «Constitutional Traditions Common to the Member States» of the European Union' (2017) 66 Riv trim dir pubb 943 (for whom this clause is not '*bonne à tout faire*'). The Court's elaboration of this phrase is illustrated by M Graziadei and R De Caria, 'The «Constitutional Traditions Common to the Member States of the European Union» in the Case-Law of the European Court of Justice: Judicial Dialogue at its Finest' (2017) 66 Riv trim dir pubb 949.

715 For further remarks, see F Bignami, 'Three Generations of Participation Rights Before the European Court of Justice' (2004) 68 L & Cont Probl 61.

716 Schlesinger, 'The Common Core of Legal Systems: An Emerging Object of Comparative Study' (n 548) 64. On the other concept, see CW Jenks, *The Common Law of Mankind* (Praeger 1958) XI (arguing that international law could no longer be regarded as the law governing the relation between States, but had to be 'regarded as the common law of mankind in an early stage of its development').

717 For further discussion, see F Feliciano, 'Book review of CW Jenks, The Common Law of Mankind (1958)' (1959) 68 Yale L J 1037, at 1040 (observing that it was difficult to discover the 'comprehensive unifying structure, the organizing principles and criteria' of the concept).

to acknowledge the different values upon which various legal systems are based.[718]

That having been said, criticism of a concept is all well and good, but it must be replaced with something else. An attempt must thus be made to move from a critical perspective to a constructive one. Concepts such as common core, common ground and others all rest on the same underlying assumption; namely that between legal systems there are not only the differences on which comparative studies shed light, but also some shared and connecting elements.[719] However, the expression 'common core' is the one that best clarifies two basic features. On the one hand, it points out that between the various legal systems included in our comparison there is not simply a common ground, or an area of agreement, because what they share is their central part, as distinct from the remaining parts, and it is their foundational part, as it is related to the values, principles and standards shared by those legal systems. On the other hand, what they share is only their core because, as has been seen at the close of Chapter 10, regional legal orders are required by their founders – that is, the States – to respect national traditions and norms. The question that thus arises is how it is possible to reconcile these aspects. This question will be examined in the discussion of the nature of the common core. In the meantime we shall discuss its dynamics.

4 A Dynamic View of the Common Core

The discussion in the previous chapter about the legacy of *ius commune* has two ramifications. It shows that the desire to affirm that the common core of our era is grounded on that of the past should not cloud the diversity of modern legal systems and the innovative challenges our societies have to face. The other ramification of the preceding discussion concerns the development of administrative law. This does not simply mean that an understanding of the antecedents of our present set of administrative institutions is necessary. It has a more profound implication for the common core, which is not fixed

718 W Friedmann, 'Book review of CW Jenks, The Common Law of Mankind (1958)' (1959) 59 Columbia L Rev 533, at 536 (referring, for example, to socialist legal systems, while Friedmann pointed out that within the EC there was 'homogeneity of values and interests').

719 Schlesinger, 'The Common Core of Legal Systems: An Emerging Object of Comparative Study' (n 548) 64. In a similar vein, Fromont (n 4) 8 focuses on the most important rules of administrative law.

and immutable but has evolved over the last two centuries. This point, one of more general importance, can be illustrated in two ways. The first is to look at the change that occurred in the last part of the *Belle Époque*. The second way is to point out the discontinuity that occurred after 1945, with the advent of regional legal orders, and at the same time to illustrate the reasons that advise against considering such legal orders in a linear and progressive perspective.

There is a strand in the history of institutions that highlights not simply the succession of different periods but also their differences. Demarking eras in this way can be useful in making headings for a narrative, but there is a fundamental problem with it. A period seems self-contained, characterized by 'unique' features, and these features obscure all the others. This problem emerges in the contraposition between the nineteenth century and twentieth centuries; the former viewed as the age of liberalism and the latter as the age of collectivism. In reality, Bismarck and other rulers took unprecedented measures to deliver certain goods and services to the citizenry, often with the aim of reducing the threat posed by socialism.[720] The problem is equally evident in the contrast outlined by some, including Schlesinger, between a nineteenth-century characterized by a contrastive approach, as opposed to the previous period of *ius commune*, when the integrative approach prevailed.[721] Our diachronic comparison has shown that during the nineteenth century there was passionate parliamentary debate about administrative justice, in the same way that there were vibrant debates as to the foundational values underpinning other wide-ranging subjects, such as property and social security. It would be impossible in this section to convey the differences in focus and tone within the literature; nor is this the purpose of the present inquiry. It is the nature of these debates that interests us here as they were characterized by a polarity between legal nationalism and the idea of a common core. We have seen, in particular, that there were exchanges and transplants between England, Belgium, and Italy, as well as, at a later stage, between France, the Habsburg and German empires, and Italy. We have seen, moreover, the emergence of shared standards. These results of our research are confirmed by recent scholarship in the history of law.[722] Notwithstanding the rise of legal nationalism, throughout the century, the Code Napoléon spread across many European

720 For further remarks, see G della Cananea, 'Commonality and Diversity in Administrative Justice: Fin de siècle' in della Cananea and Mannoni (n 111) 6.

721 RB Schlesinger, 'The Past and Future of Comparative Law' (1995) 43 AJCL 477, 479.

722 T Le Yoncourt, A Mergey and S Soleil (eds), *L'idée du fonds juridique commun dans l'Europe du XIX siècle. Les modèles, les réformateurs, les réseaux* (Presses Universitaires de Rennes 2014).

and Latin American countries. In the same period, whilst rejecting the hegemony of France, Spain, too, adopted a centralized administrative model.[723] These processes of borrowings and transplants were favored by transnational intellectual circles, including the network that was built around the *Société de legislation comparée*, founded in 1867 and the network of international lawyers, promoted by the first sessions of the Hague conference held between 1893 and 1904. Those lawyers deemed that the legal landscape was characterized by a strong sense of belonging to a shared civilization.[724]

The other way to point out that an adequate understanding of the common core must be firmly grounded in the awareness of its development is to recall the twofold discontinuity over the years following 1945. When the first European Community – the ECSC – was founded in 1950, the bases of administrative authority had changed in all its members as a consequence of the new constitutional settlements. The common denominator was not only constitutional democracy but also that of recognizing and protecting human dignity. It was axiomatic that there had to be limits that served to keep public authorities within their assigned sphere of power, as well as controls to check whether those limits had been infringed. It is in this sense, and within these limits, that the constitutions adopted in Western Europe after 1945 could be said to express a 'common ideology', expressing the 'common beliefs of the populations about the way they should be governed'.[725] It is important to recognize that all the constitutions possessed these features to a greater or lesser degree. It is equally important to note that this ideology and rights-based guarantees are common to the countries that joined the EU after the transition from one-party States to constitutional democracies in the 1990s.[726] Membership of regional organizations has reinforced these features. European integration after 1950 cannot be viewed solely as the business of sovereign States not dissimilar to other international treaties in the light of the transfer of functions and powers to shared

723 MA Chamocho Cantudo, 'La circulation du modèle administrative français en Espagne: entre nationalism juridique et fonds juridique commun' in Le Yoncourt, Mergey and Soleils (n 722) 127.

724 B Benneteau, 'L'Europe au-delà des nationalismes' in Le Yoncourt, Mergey and Soleils (n 722) 302.

725 Fromont (n 4) 11. For similar remarks about England, France and Germany, see J Raz, 'On the Authority and Interpretation of Constitutions: Some Preliminaries' in L Alexander (ed), *Constitutionalism* (Cambridge University Press 1998) 152–153; G Vedel, 'Les bases constitutionnelles du droit administratif' in *Etudes et documents du Conseil d'Etat* (*Conseil d'Etat* 1965) 21; EW Böckenförde, *Staat, Verfassung und Demokratie* (Surhkamp 1991).

726 For a comparative analysis, see Elster (279) 447.

institutions. Indeed, treaties granting rights to individuals, who can enforce them in their own name before domestic courts, and creating supranational courts acting as guardians of those rights, have entailed a new form of social ordering.[727] Additionally, supranational legal systems have adopted norms aiming at ensuring coherence, such as Article 52 (4) of the EU Charter of Fundamental Rights, according to which "the meaning and scope" of the rights it contains shall be the same as those laid down by the ECHR. In conclusion, there is, other things being equal, a greater commonality between national systems of administrative law than there was prior to the establishment of the CoE and the EU, since, as mentioned previously, their general principles of law are binding on national authorities.

A word of qualification is, however, necessary. The growth of regional organizations has generated the expectation that the developments they have either caused or facilitated are 'here to stay',[728] but it is not necessarily so. The UK case is instructive. Even before the accession took place, some argued that it would constitute an encounter between the common law tradition and the civil law tradition.[729] The following decades saw the partial fulfilment of that expectation. The courts gradually revised old principles or their conceptions (for example, unreasonableness) and have embraced new ones, such as proportionality. There was even speculation about the retreat of the main pillar of English public law, parliamentary sovereignty,[730] and in the same vein many studies indicating the emergence of new doctrines of rights. However, after almost five decades, Britain left the EU.[731] There has been a return of the principle of parliamentary sovereignty. The courts have not hesitated to redefine at least certain tenets of proportionality. This does not imply that it will be possible to return to the pre-accession State. Rather, it can be argued that membership of regional organizations should be regarded as a continuing process of adaptation, not without stasis and regress, as opposed to a legal bargain sealed once and for all time. The upshot of all this is that the concept of the common core provides us with a helpful vector for thinking about various issues

727 See A Stone Sweet, *The Judicial Construction of Europe* (OUP 2004) (showing the dynamics of change through both quantitative analysis of aggregate data and qualitative analysis).

728 Loughlin (n 23) 261.

729 V Grementieri and CJ Golden, 'The United Kingdom and the European Court of Justice: an Encounter between Common and Civil Law Tradition' (1973) 21 AJCL 664.

730 Early commentators, including Feld, 'Legal Dimensions of British Entry into the European Community' (n 671) 253, raised doubts as to whether parliamentary sovereignty was limited by the accession treaty. On the impact of the ECJ's ruling in *Factortame*, see W Wade, 'What happened to the Sovereignty of Parliament?' (1996) 112 L Q Rev 568.

731 P Craig, 'Brexit: A Drama in Six Acts' (2017) 41 Eur L Rev 447.

concerning administrative law. But its contours are not fixed and immutable. Quite the contrary, they have altered over time and will most probably continue to change.

5 The Nature of the Common Core

At the beginning of this essay, we stated that the hypothesis to be tested was that there are not only differences between European administrative laws, highlighted by previous studies, but there are also some shared and connecting elements, or a 'common core', and that such elements relate not only to general ideals, such as justice, but can be formulated in 'normative terms'. It is now possible to delineate the contours of the common core. There are various ways to organize the material that constitutes public law in the broad sense. This task will be accomplished in three ways, including the types of standards and the consequences that ensue from them, as well as the tools of legal thinking.[732]

As a first step, it is necessary to briefly clarify how the shared and connecting elements that form the common core are legally relevant and significant. It is not our intent here to give even a tentative summary of the general principles of administrative law in the current epoch. What may be usefully attempted, rather, is to outline three different *types* of legal requirements as they can be applied to various *aspects* of administrative procedure. These requirements fall into these different categories: a) requirements concerning the respect of the purposes for which public authorities are granted administrative powers and the limits cast on their exercise; b) minimum standards of procedural fairness and propriety; c) substantive principles of law which more or less directly influence the discharge of administrative powers.

In the first category is the legality of administrative action, which is beyond doubt an essential principle in modern systems of public law. It is manifest – among other things – in requiring the normative basis of each authoritative power, as well as in imposing the respect of the objectives set out in legislation; this is the source, for example, of abuse of power, or *détournement de pouvoir*. There is also a duty to respect any previously established procedure, in the sense that no alternative course of action may be followed; otherwise, an *error in procedendo* or a procedural error will arise (a *détournement de procedure* in the French terminology). Quite apart from their concrete manifestations,

732 See Kahn-Freund (n 3) 430 (for the remark that both legal techniques and tools of legal thinking are important and must, therefore, be considered).

these requirements provide a yardstick, a way of measuring the discharge of administrative functions and powers, though the consequences of disregarding them may vary, as will be observed later.

Secondly, it may be said that there is another part of the common core of European administrative laws, including minimum standards of fairness and propriety, below which there is, at least, a strong presumption that administrative action does not fulfil the requisites to be regarded as valid. Among these standards are the fundamental maxims of natural justice; that is, *nemo iudex in re propria* and *audi alteram partem*. In particular, the latter implies, in addition to the right to be heard, other related rights, including to receive notification of the commencement of a procedure, to receive legal assistance, to gain access to documents held by the administration, and to submit documents and evidence. Increasing weight is given to the accuracy of the fact-finding activity that must precede any decision.[733] Such minimum requirements of fair administrative procedure shape not only action that interferes with the individual's rights, but also the positive State, including the disbursement of public money. They are completed by two other requirements. There is, on the one hand, a duty to give reasons. This duty is particularly appropriate to give a sense of the distinction between not so much a minimum requirement, but a procedural one, that is, to state the reasons for a given decision and the duty to provide adequate or sound ones, which implies converting the procedural requirement into a substantive one. On the other hand, there are duties to make the consultation and participation of both individuals and social groups not only possible but also meaningful, as has been observed with regard to the involvement of users and the reformulation of policy statements. It should, however, be noted that these standards are less clear cut than those concerning adjudication. It is one thing to hold that a procedure is unfair if the addressee of the final decision has not had any meaningful opportunity to be heard; it is another to determine how to provide equal opportunities for all those who seek to influence the adoption of new policy or rules because the procedure may become 'terribly cumbersome'.[734]

Thirdly, it is with regard to the substantive principles of administrative law that a greater degree of uncertainty exists and, therefore the greatest amount of work remains to be done. It is in this field that further use of a factual analysis can render a valuable service to the advancement of knowledge. That being said, the use of established general principles to govern administrative conduct

733 Wiener (n 277) 20.

734 Mashaw (n 52) 23.

has been illustrated in some cases, of variable frequency in the daily management of public policies. Included among these principles, there is, first and foremost, proportionality, especially when administrative authorities exercise powers that impinge on fundamental rights, as in the case of disciplinary and sanctioning procedures. There is also a principle of transparency, which bears a strong connection with both the giving of reasons and the publication of rules. In this latter respect, there is also a connection with another principle, that of legal certainty, as we have seen with regard to partially unpublished rules.

In the light of these findings, the initial hypothesis – that is, that the common and shared elements that constitute the common core can be defined normatively, as distinct from mere ideals – can be examined at various levels of abstraction. As for values, within the CoE all legal systems can be said to respect background moral or political principles such as fairness and justice or respect for the rule of law and fundamental rights.[735] At this abstract level, many courses of action, though not all, may appear to be justified. When we move away from values to general but still mid-level principles that serve to promote good governance, as well as the respect for rule of law and fundamental rights, such as judicial independence, due process of law and effective judicial protection, action taken by certain national authorities finds little justification or none at all. The ongoing debate, in political and judicial discourses, as well as in public law scholarship, concerning threats to judicial independence can be important in this respect. It remains to be seen whether public authorities must respect standards that have a different level of general application, though operational rules may vary.

The use of the term 'standard' is not without issues, both practically and theoretically. Practically, standards of broad applicability may not prove very helpful in deciding concrete cases. In legal theory, standards can be – as Hart puts it – both variable and invariable.[736] The former translate general principles into mid-level but still general standards that decisionmakers must apply to particular cases and facts, for example by providing some type of hearing. The latter constrain exercises of power more rigidly. Thus, for example, the requirement to give reasons whenever the final decision adversely affects someone represents a minimum one, distinct from a requirement to give reasons that are adequate or even sound. What characterizes the common core of European administrative laws is precisely this: in addition to the commonality that exists at the level of values and principles, there is a set of common

735 For this remark, see SA De Smith, 'The Right to a Hearing in English Administrative Law' (1955) 68 Harvard L Rev 570.

736 For this distinction, see LA Hart, *The Concept of Law* (Clarendon 1964) 133.

standards of administrative action. Their legal relevance and significance can be appreciated from three points of view.

First, general principles, standing alone, often fail to indicate the preferred course of action. They fail to specify sufficient constraints on public authorities, with the exception of 'egregious' cases, such as manifest and intolerable executive interference in the duration of judicial appointments.[737] Conversely, the mid-level but still general standards of administrative conduct previously illustrated differentiate more clearly legal from illegal conduct. They do not stop government bodies from acting but require decisions to be made or actions to be taken in specific ways. Thus, for example, there is a right to be heard before a decision having unfavorable effects is taken, but the hearing can take more than one form. Likewise, there is a requirement to publish administrative rules, but the operational norms can and do differ. On the other side of the typology of legal precepts, these standards differ from precise rules. There are two reasons for this: they serve to guide administrative action as a whole, including the exercise of discretionary powers,[738] and they reflect ideas and beliefs about the law shared by legal systems which differ in many important respects. The concept of 'common core' thus conveys the idea that what is common is the most basic or important part of national legal systems, in our case the mid-level standards of good administration which go beyond what is normally expressed by constitutional provisions, including the procedural constraints and requirements that serve to limit and structure the exercise of power and make it accountable.[739]

Secondly, as government action is subject to these standards, the rule of law requires public authorities to comply with these standards. As a consequence, any deviation from these standards may imply that an administrative action may not achieve the aim that it would otherwise fulfil. Corrective mechanisms are therefore available and interested parties can insist on government compliance. There are a number of options in this respect, one of which takes the form of the decision by a national court that a certain act or conduct disregarding one or more standards is either annullable or null. Another option, in the EU, is that after an infringement procedure commenced by the Commission, the ECJ reaches the conclusion that a State has failed to comply with its obligations

---

737 This was declared unconstitutional by the Hungarian Constitutional Court in its judgment of 16 July 2012 and was regarded by the ECJ as incompatible with the rule of law in its judgment of 6 November 2012, Case C-286/12, *Commission v Hungary*.

738 On this aspect, see Davis, *Discretionary Justice* (n 457) 15 (distinguishing rules from 'meaningful standards').

739 On this way of understanding the principles of good governance, see P Craig, 'Constitutions, Constitutionalism and the European Union' (2001) 7 Eur L J 125, at 128.

stemming from EU law. If the infringement persists, an economic sanction can be inflicted. There is yet another option in the case of conditional funding as compliance with certain standards constitutes the condition for the disbursement of Union funds.[740] Lastly, within the CoE, the European Court of Human Rights has often found that national laws and practices breached the ECHR regarding, among other things, the impartiality of adjudicators, the right to be heard, the duty to give reasons, and the right to effective judicial protection.[741] There are two consequences when the Court finds that a State has failed to respect the Convention: it must revise its laws and practices and provide pecuniary compensation for unjust damage suffered by physical or legal persons.

A word of qualification is necessary, however. The consequences of disregarding these standards of administrative conduct differ. As we have just seen, more often than not, failure to respect them impinges on the validity of administrative action, on the basis of the fundamental precept that when a public body makes an invalid decision, in principle, this should be annulled, with a retrospective effect.[742] However, it is precisely because these standards of administrative conduct are procedural rather than substantive, any action that deviates from them is not necessarily invalid. Thus, for example, there are circumstances when the interested party either may not be informed of all the grounds supporting a potentially adverse decision or may be heard only after a public authority has taken certain measures to protect a collective interest.[743] Likewise, full access to the documents held by a public authority may be postponed if an overriding public interest so requires. In this sense, and within these limits, the relevant standards of administrative conduct from the common core perspective are 'flexible'.[744] In other words, they differ from rules, although a part of administrative law scholarship holds that this may generate uncertainty and raise concern in terms of the rule of law.[745]

Finally, an important dimension of the common core concerns the tools of legal thinking. On the one hand, there are some basic concepts that are

---

740 ECJ, Judgments of 16 February 2022, in Cases C-156/21, *Hungary v Parliament and Council* and C-157/21, *Poland v Parliament and Council.*

741 Fromont (n 4) 4.

742 For this precept, see Craig (n 197) 20.

743 ECJ, Judgment of 3 September 2008, Joined cases C-402/05 P and C-415/05 P, *Kadi and Al Barakaat v Council and Commission*, § 338 (for the argument that communicating those grounds would 'jeopardise the effectiveness' of the measures adopted).

744 See Harlow and Rawlings, *Law and Administration* (n 393) 611 (for the characterization of procedural justice as a 'flexible friend').

745 For this view, see A Scalia, 'The Rule of Law as a Law of Rules' (1989) 56 Un Chicago L Rev 1175, but see also Davis, *Discretionary Justice* (n 457) 31, for the contrary opinion.

increasingly being shared within the European legal area. Although not all legal systems have adopted one type of administrative procedure legislation or another, as observed by Schmidt-Aßmann, the 'idea of procedure constitutes [the] basic expression of a common European administrative law'.[746] On the other hand, as national legal systems have been brought closer within the European legal area, jurists and judges have shown an increasing interest in the ways certain principles of administrative law are shaped elsewhere. Thus, for example, there has been widespread interest in the German conception of the principle of proportionality though similar precepts existed within other legal cultures. It is important to be clear, however, that this proposition does not mean that the content of particular administrative law principles is the same everywhere.

6 The Extent of the Common Core

It is equally important to be clear about the extent or scope of the common core of European administrative laws. What are important in this respect are the extent and limits of the common core.[747] In other words, we are not only interested in discovering the areas of agreement between legal systems but also in examining the areas of disagreement. The areas of agreement and disagreement can be assessed both subjectively and objectively, ie, in terms of the legal systems affected and the functions and powers discharged by public authorities.

Subjectively, the findings of our comparative inquiry suggest three remarks. Firstly, the areas of agreement and disagreement between legal systems – to borrow Schlesinger's words once more – 'cannot be drawn in the simple terms of the traditional dichotomy between civil law and common law'.[748] In fact, as we mentioned in Chapter 3, at the close of the nineteenth century there was widespread awareness that legal formants in the field of administrative law differed from private law in that principles and standards were defined, and refined, by the courts, often in conjunction with the work of rationalization and systematization being carried out by academics. Moreover, the findings of

746 E Schmidt-Aßmann, 'Structures and Functions of Administrative Procedures in German, European and International Law' in J Barnes (ed), *Transforming Administrative Procedure* (Global Law Press 2008) 66.

747 Schlesinger (n 2) 24.

748 id, 62.

our research confirm the impression of some commentators that judicial standards were similar as early as the *Belle époque*. This is even more evident today with regard to the factors examined in the previous chapter: general principles, legal harmonization, and institutional isomorphism.

Secondly, and as a variation of the preceding argument, the dichotomy between civil and common law systems is untenable from the administrative procedure perspective. On the one hand, whereas in the nineteenth century the concept of the administrative act took centre stage in Continental Europe, the twentieth century has been marked by the emerging notion of administrative procedure, viewed as a central tool for limiting and structuring the exercise of power by public authorities. Interestingly, this notion has emerged in US public law, too. On the other hand, and consequently, after the codification of administrative procedure in Austria and its diffusion in some neighboring countries, the other great codification is the US APA of 1946. This suggests that the UK can no longer be regarded as exemplary of common law systems. The absence of general legislation on administrative procedure is, rather, a trait shared with other Westminster-like democracies, such as Australia and Canada.[749] Incidentally, it can be observed that some of these democracies, such as Canada and Ireland, have adopted a written constitution and a Charter of rights, respectively, allowing the emergence of various judicial techniques for limiting the impact of primary legislation on rights. This seems to suggest that if there is an exceptional legal discipline in matters of public law, it is not so much that of France or Austria, but the UK.

Thirdly, the findings of our research, while confirming the initial choice to focus on the common core of European administrative laws, raise new issues. They confirm the existence of shared and connecting elements among European legal systems, although the effectiveness of the standards of administrative conduct previously outlined is weaker in some of those legal systems. The question that thus arises is whether the initial hypothesis should be subjected to further tests. Countries such as Russia and Turkey might be targeted for further testing,[750] although there some problems may surround the choice of national experts. On the other hand, the research findings have shown that, if the focus of legal comparison is on administrative procedure, there is, at first sight, an important area of agreement with the legal systems of Latin America, thanks to the spread of Spanish ideas and norms. This conclusion will have

749 On the 'Westminster tradition' common to those jurisdictions, see Daly (n 478) 17.

750 For the opinion that Russia should not be regarded as part of the West, see A Toynbee, *The World and the West* (Oxford UP 1953) 15.

to be corroborated in the course of the ongoing line of research. But another question that arises is whether a similar test should be conducted on legal systems that are geographically and culturally close to Europe, such as Egypt.

We may make similar observations when the common core is considered objectively; that is, with regard to the functions and powers discharged by public authorities. In this respect, the decision to combine history and legal comparison, in addition to including a factual analysis in the latter, has proven to be fruitful. The inquiry has shown that, although most, but not all, European legal systems have adopted some kind of administrative procedure legislation, there is a vast area of agreement between legal systems as far as the standards of administrative adjudication are concerned. It has shown, furthermore, that, although administrative procedure legislation governs rulemaking only in a few cases, there is increasing agreement on consultation, participation, and transparency. In a similar vein to what we have just said regarding the subjective dimension of the common core, the question that arises is whether the degree to which it extends into other areas should be further tested. If so, coercion by public authorities, which touches on the less recent understanding of administrative law in relation to powers, and the management of welfare benefits (eg, unemployment subsidies), which instead emphasizes the bureaucratic or managerial character of administration,[751] could be targeted for further testing.

7 The Variety of Uses of the Common Core

Our initial hypothesis was that a multinational 'common core' exists in administrative procedure, a relatively wide area of public law, noting, however, the many differences. The hypothesis was tested in several ways, including a comparison of national laws and a factual analysis. We will now add a few remarks with regard to the uses of the common core.

First and foremost, we must consider the production of knowledge about the law. This essay has argued that only a combination of history and legal comparison captures the causes and patterns of both commonality and diversity. It has shown that, for a proper understanding of the standards of administrative conduct, it is necessary to go beyond the commonly stipulated alternatives of 'convergence' or 'persistence', in order to explain their interplay. Interestingly, legal systems have adopted very similar – if not identical – invariable or

751 See J Mashaw, *Bureaucratic Justice. Managing Social Disability Claims* (Yale UP 1983).

variable standards, while differences in operational rules prevail, and there are even greater differences in the underlying institutional framework. With reference to the terminology employed earlier, isomorphism is more significant at the procedural level than in terms of the institutions themselves. In sum, what emerges is a pattern of 'diversity within commonality'. Within the European legal area, if diversity is sometimes surprising, it is so because we look at it in the light of shared values, principles, and standards. As a result, it is an 'enabled' diversity, though it should not be forgotten that, as previously indicated, what is held in common is only the core, beyond which diversity does not merely remain, but flourishes.

There is a second possible use of the common core, as presented in this essay. It concerns legal education, namely the courses to be taught, the materials to be used, and the textbooks to be read by law students interested in the comparative study of administrative law,[752] transnational public law, and EU law, given that public law issues have an increasingly transnational dimension, and law students should be fully aware of them. Interestingly, even those who have vehemently argued against any attempt to enact a single body of rules applicable to the Member States of the EU have acknowledged that this does not exclude the possibility that a body of law common to those countries may arise through legal education.[753] This is not to be regarded as a call for a focus on similarities rather than differences but for a better knowledge of both. Whether this can stimulate the awareness that the distinct legal systems of Europe provide legal scholars with a *reservoir* of solutions that are often based on the same general principles is not in contrast with the purpose of our research.

There are, third, some implications from the viewpoint of professional education in the field of public administrations, for which there is an increasing need of better knowledge about standards of conduct. The experiences of the various European countries are often considered by supranational institutions, so that the lessons of experience can be learned and, if possible, used by others. There is nothing wrong in this. However, some observers think that looking for 'best practices' is a questionable and often vain exercise. It is perhaps preferable, to borrow the expression used by economists, to focus on the conditions that, other things being equal, may make certain desired outcomes

752 Increasing interest was noticed in the late 1950s by Rivero, *Cours de droit administratif comparé* (n 71) 2.

753 P Legrand, 'European Legal Systems are not Converging' (1996) 45 Int'l & Comp L Q 52, at 53.

possible or easier. These are but possible and indirect uses of a 'basic' research, to use the word that is common in the natural sciences, but, as explained earlier, they have different purposes, such as legislative change, and thus require autonomous treatment.

Index

Printed in the United States
by Baker & Taylor Publisher Services